Latin America in Colonial Times

Few milestones in human history are as dramatic and momentous as the meeting of three great civilizations on American soil in the sixteenth century. *Latin America in Colonial Times* presents that story in an engaging but scholarly new package, revealing how a new civilization – Latin America – emerged from the encounter. The authors give equal attention to the Spanish and Portuguese conquerors and settlers, to the African slaves they brought across the Atlantic, and to the indigenous peoples whose lands were invaded. From the dawn of empires in the fifteenth century, through the Conquest age of the sixteenth, to the end of empire in the nineteenth, *Latin America in Colonial Times* combines broad brushstrokes with the anecdotal details that bring the era to life.

Matthew Restall is Edwin Erle Sparks Professor of Latin American History at Pennsylvania State University. His areas of specialization include colonial Yucatán and Mexico, Maya history, the Spanish Conquest, and Africans in Spanish America. Since 1995 he has published some forty articles and essays and a dozen books, including *2012 and the End of the World: The Western Roots to the Maya Apocalypse* (2011), *The Black Middle: Africans, Mayas, and Spaniards in Colonial Yucatan* (2009); *Mesoamerican Voices* (Cambridge, 2005); and *Seven Myths of the Spanish Conquest* (2003). Professor Restall also serves as coeditor of the journal *Ethnohistory*.

Kris Lane is France V. Scholes Chair of Colonial Latin American History at Tulane University. He has published widely on slavery, witchcraft, mining, and piracy in the Andes region of South America and is the author or editor of multiple books, including *Defense of the Western Conquests* (2010), *Colour of Paradise: Emeralds in the Age of Gunpowder Empires* (2010), and *Quito 1599: City and Colony in Transition* (2002). Professor Lane has served as Visiting Professor at the National University of Colombia, Bogotá, and the University of Leiden, Netherlands, and currently edits the interdisciplinary journal *Colonial Latin American Review*.

LATIN AMERICA IN COLONIAL TIMES

Matthew Restall

Pennsylvania State University

Kris Lane

Tulane University

CAMBRIDGE
UNIVERSITY PRESS

CAMBRIDGE UNIVERSITY PRESS
Cambridge, New York, Melbourne, Madrid, Cape Town,
Singapore, São Paulo, Delhi, Tokyo, Mexico City

Cambridge University Press
32 Avenue of the Americas, New York, NY 10013-2473, USA

www.cambridge.org
Information on this title: www.cambridge.org/9780521132602

First published 2011

Printed in the United States of America

A catalog record for this publication is available from the British Library.

Library of Congress Cataloging in Publication Data

Restall, Matthew, 1964-
Latin America in colonial times / Matthew Restall, Kris Lane.
    p. cm.
Includes bibliographical references and index.
ISBN 978-0-521-76118-5 (hardback) – ISBN 978-0-521-13260-2 (pbk.)
1. Latin America – Civilization.   2. Latin America – Colonization.   3. Latin America – History –
To 1830.   4. Acculturation – Latin America – History.   5. Latin America – Ethnic relations.
I. Lane, Kris E., 1967-   II. Title.

F1411.R485   2011
980'.01 – dc22   2011002210

ISBN 978-0-521-76118-5 Hardback
ISBN 978-0-521-13260-2 Paperback

CONTENTS

LIST OF MAPS AND IN FOCUS BOXES

Maps

In Focus Boxes

ACKNOWLEDGMENTS

We are grateful to the many colleagues and scholars who have contributed to the development of this book. Although we used primary archival sources for many of our examples and case studies, we have inevitably drawn on the works of dozens of other historians for most of our information. Because the textbook format does not allow for individual citations, please accept this as a general acknowledgment (you know who you are: thank you!).

We have greatly enjoyed and appreciated working with Eric Crahan and his colleagues at Cambridge University Press; thank you for your patience and hard work.

We also thank Rob Schwaller and his Penn State students in History 178 (spring 2006) and Mark Christensen and his Penn State students in History 178 (fall 2008) for their feedback on earlier drafts of the book.

Finally, we raise our glasses to James Lockhart and Stuart Schwartz, in whose footsteps we have sought to tread in numerous ways (this book being but one), and to whom the book is a humble tribute.

La V. M. Maria de Iesus de Agreda, Predicando
à los Chichimecas del Nuebo-mexico. Antt. del Cerro f.

The Colonial Crucible

C HRISTOPHER COLUMBUS "SAILED FROM SPAIN," wrote one Spaniard in the sixteenth century, "to mix the world together and give to those strange lands the form of our own." That mixing of the world together, or "the discovery of the new world," as Europeans of the day put it, was characterized by the Paduan philosopher Buonamico in 1539 as the greatest achievement of human history, comparable "not only to Antiquity, but to immortality." In various forms that sentiment has been repeated many times during the past five centuries; one historian recently called the European discovery and conquest of America and its native peoples "the most astonishing encounter of our history."

With as many motivations as there were individuals, men and women sailed across the Atlantic Ocean seeking power, wealth, social status, religious mission, scientific knowledge, and personal adventure. At the same time, they often failed to recognize that the lands they claimed as their own were already occupied. Tens of millions of Native Americans had over thousands of years developed sophisticated societies from which the newcomers could learn a great deal. Yet despite European attempts to reshape the Americas into known forms, Native Americans – and the millions of Africans brought against their will by Europeans – contributed as much as willing newcomers did to the formation of colonial societies. Native American foods, meanwhile, such as maize, potatoes, chocolate, and chili peppers, quickly revolutionized world cuisine and spurred population growth.

This book tells the story of that astonishing encounter among Iberians, Africans, and Native Americans – and then examines the many regional stories and general social and economic patterns that developed in its aftermath. But the book does more than simply tell stories about colonial Latin America. Our concern is also with the question that has been raised as often as the "discovery" has been called history's greatest event – the question of how. How had Europeans come to think that they could simply "give to those strange lands the form of their own"? How were so few Spaniards able to conquer the great and powerful empires of the Aztecs and the Incas? How were small numbers of Spanish and Portuguese settlers able to build, maintain, and defend such vast colonies across three hundred years?

The answer is simple: they didn't; or at least, they didn't do it alone. Europeans neither embarked on conquests nor created colonies without substantial contributions from non-Europeans. In both endeavors, they were accompanied and assisted by much more numerous Native Americans and sub-Saharan Africans. Such peoples were usually – but not always – subject to Spanish and Portuguese rule and exploitation. But European settlers were very much dependent on the Native Americans and Africans who consistently outnumbered them. Colonial Latin American societies were not segregated; they were crucibles in which many peoples and cultures mixed and changed one another. It was therefore not only Spaniards and Portuguese who gave form to colonial Latin America but also the Mexica and the Maya, Quechua and Tupi speakers, Yorubas and Congolese, and many others.

Our narrative journey through the great encounter and into the mixed-together world – the crucible – of colonial Latin America takes the form of fifteen chapters. In Chapters 1–3, we look at what historians now call the Atlantic world, as it was when the ocean divided, rather than bridged, the Eastern and Western hemispheres. The civilizations of native America; the Iberian Peninsula (Spain and Portugal); and western, or "Atlantic," Africa, are each introduced in turn.

In Chapters 4–7, the peoples of the Atlantic continents are brought together, beginning with the birth of Spain and its imperial ambitions, Portuguese expansion into the Atlantic and toward Asia, and the 1492 voyage of Columbus that grew from those Portuguese and Spanish roots. The story continues with the experience of Spaniards, Native Americans, and Africans in the Caribbean in the decades after 1492. We then cross to the American mainland to explore the nature of native empires on the eve of the Spanish invasion, the events and patterns of that invasion, the roles played by Native Americans and Africans, and the birth of a Portuguese colony in Brazil. The sum of these transformative events is here called the Long Conquest.

The book is less chronological and more thematic in Chapters 8–12. These chapters paint a social portrait of colonial Spanish America and Brazil from the time when colonial rule began in the sixteenth century through to the early eighteenth century, when change began to gather pace. We have dubbed this period the "colonial middle." These chapters give support to the assertion that Native Americans and Africans played indispensable and central roles in the formation and florescence of Spanish and Portuguese colonial societies, as these roles are examined in detail alongside the efforts and endeavors of Iberian settlers.

The final part of the book, "The Age of Change," shifts back to chronology, as the period treated – roughly 1750 to 1825 – was marked by momentous events, culminating in independence. Chapters 13–15 trace the growing pressures of war and administrative reform in an era when colonial society was increasingly complex, growing in size and wealth, and otherwise changing. Imperial administrators struggled to reorder colonial power structures and to generally raise taxes, all against the wishes of colonial subjects. Dissenters included Iberians descended from early settler and conquistador families, along with some Native Americans and mixed people of color. A spate of regional revolts laid bare the fault lines of colonial society. Despite widespread dissatisfaction with late-colonial reforms, the Latin American colonies remained faithful to Spain and Portugal into the early nineteenth century, when they were overtaken by a combination of events in Europe and local discontent. Led by able commanders such as Simón Bolívar, the colonies at last became independent nations.

At the book's close, we revisit our argument as to how Latin America's fabled conquests – followed by some three centuries of largely unchallenged, transoceanic colonial rule – were possible. We summarize and conclude by reiterating the importance of the complementary roles played by Iberians, Africans, and Native Americans in both processes. It is our firm belief that conquest and colonialism succeeded despite what seem in retrospect to have been very long odds, because both were perceived – most important by indigenous, black, and mixed-race participants – as shared ventures. On the flip side, understanding how this widespread acquiescence to Iberian invasion and long-term rule came about and functioned in the Americas is fundamental before attempting to interpret rebellions and other forms of resistance, including the final push to independence.

In 1566, St. Francis Borja sent a present of a globe to his son (who was himself the father of a future viceroy of Peru); the son wrote back, "Before seeing it, I had not realized how small is the world." The world had indeed become small and, as another observer had said, "mixed," within a few generations of Columbus's famous transatlantic voyage, shrinking the distance among European, African, Asian, and American peoples while expanding both the threat of conflict and the potential for human growth. Colonists did not succeed in giving European form to American lands, but nor did America remain the same. Conquest and colonization made America near in the European consciousness but very far from its people in practice.

Our subject, the history of colonial Latin America, may seem as vast as the world once did to Borja. Our hope is that this book will render it, like Borja's globe did the world, manageably small but still wondrous.

BEFORE THE GREAT ENCOUNTER

Before turning directly to the great question of how Iberians were able to conquer and colonize Native Americans, we need to know something about the three civilizations that were brought together in the wake of Christopher Columbus's first Atlantic crossing of 1492. Such is the purpose of Part One of this book.

Chapter 1 ("Native America") examines the development of human societies in the Americas from first settlement to the fifteenth century. We look in comparative detail at the two most notable cradles of civilization, Mesoamerica and the Andes. Not all native peoples lived in these two areas, however, and the entire range of native societies present a vast and varied picture; we therefore offer four categories of native societies – concentrated, segmented, semisedentary, and nonsedentary.

The pre-1492 background of Spain and Portugal is the subject of Chapter 2 ("Castile and Portugal"). We emphasize the nature of social organization in the Iberian Peninsula, the importance of urban life, and the central role played by Castile in Spain's formation in the fifteenth century. Above all, our concern is to identify some of the key historical patterns that help explain what Iberians later did in the Americas.

The societies of sub-Saharan Africa – especially West and West Central Africa – made up the third civilization brought into contact with others as a result of Iberians crossing the Atlantic. Past historians have tended to begin discussion of African roles in the colonial Americas with the Atlantic slave trade. But because people of African descent made major contributions to colonial Latin American societies, we have devoted a full chapter to the African background. Chapter 3 ("Atlantic Africa") traces the development of civilization in the region, focusing on a cultural description of peoples in the two regions from where most African slaves in the Americas would have originated (West Africa and West Central Africa).

By the end of Chapter 3, the stage is set for the triumphs and tragedies of the dramatic encounter of Iberians, Western Africans, and Native Americans in the sixteenth century.

1

Native America

TIMELINE

20,000–12,000 b.c.:
People cross the land
bridge from Asia into the
Americas

6000–3000 b.c.: People
make the transition from
hunting and gathering to
sedentary lifestyles in many
regions

200 b.c.–1300 a.d.: Great
civilizations develop in
Mesoamerica and the
Andes

1420s–1520s: The
Mexica (Aztec) Empire in
Mesoamerica and the Inca
Empire in the Andes rise
and expand

On the mainland the Indians eat human flesh. They are more given to sodomy than any other people. There is no justice among them. They go naked. They have no respect either for love or for virginity. They are stupid and silly. They have no respect for truth, save when it is to their advantage.

ARLY IN THE SPANISH INVASION OF THE AMERICAS, a Dominican friar wrote those words to the Council of the Indies, the royal council responsible for colonial matters. Few Spaniards derided native peoples in such hostile terms, especially in official correspondence. Yet although the European discovery of the Americas generated a wide variety of opinion on the nature of Native Americans, including a great official debate on the topic in the mid-sixteenth century, the overwhelming European tendency was to view natives as a single, inferior people. Europeans called them Indians because the Americas were "the Indies," a name originally given to East Asia but applied to the Americas after Columbus discovered the New World while looking for a sea route to East Asia.

The name *Indian* is thus a confusing product of the twists of fifteenth-century European history. But it is more than that. It also symbolizes the homogeneous and pejorative identity assigned to Native Americans. To understand the extraordinary encounter that gave rise to colonial Latin America, we must understand the nature of native societies before the European invasion; and to do that, we must see through that "Indian" identity and into the rich and diverse world of precolonial cultures and civilizations. This chapter is an introduction to those cultures and civilizations, placing them briefly in their historical and geographical contexts, and offering some analytical tools to help grasp something of their complexity and diversity.

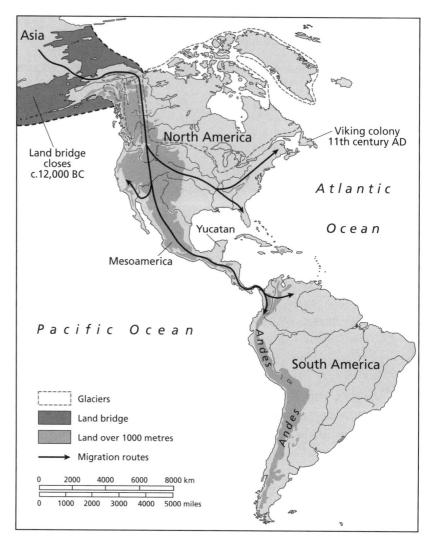

Map 1.1
Early Migrations into
the Americas

"Aztecs" and "Amazons": Categorizing Native Americans

Human beings did not evolve independently in the Americas, but human civilizations did. That simple sentence encapsulates much that is important about the Native American past.

Homo sapiens evolved in Africa and began to migrate to Europe and Asia at least one hundred thousand years ago. Human beings entered North America by walking across a land bridge from Asia more than twenty thousand years ago. By at least twelve thousand years ago, bands of hunters lived throughout the Americas, from Canada's Northwest Territories to Tierra del Fuego, at the tip of South America. Around that time, rising sea levels at the end of the last Ice Age caused the land bridge from Asia to disappear, leaving the peoples whom we will call Native Americans cut off from the rest of the globe until the European invasion that began in 1492.

There were some exceptions to this isolation; around A.D. 1000, the Vikings who had shortly before set up outposts in Greenland planted a settlement in Newfoundland, on Canada's East Coast, that survived for several decades. Others may have visited the Americas from Asia, Africa, and Europe prior to 1492, but clear evidence of such voyages, much less their consequences, is sorely lacking. Even the Viking colony in Newfoundland, the only one for which there is firm archaeological and written evidence, seems not to have had any impact on the development of Native American societies. Attempts by scholars and others to show that Native Americans were influenced by other human civilizations have failed to persuade most people.

Still, the notion that Native Americans could not have developed sophisticated civilizations on their own goes all the way back to Columbus and constitutes an important part of the perceptions and misconceptions of native peoples by nonnatives (see In Focus 1.1). Early European travelers to the Americas, from Columbus to Sir Walter Raleigh a century later, brought with them preconceived notions of what natives would look like. As a result, Columbus reported to the Spanish monarchy that one Caribbean island was inhabited by cannibals, another by people with tails, and a third by Amazons – women warriors who lived in communities entirely without men. Raleigh looked in vain for acephali, or headless people, described to him by Spaniards and natives in the Americas as having "their eyes in their shoulders, and their mouths in the middle of their breasts."

Such human monsters are no longer pursued, yet Native Americans continue to be viewed primarily through the prism of the nonnative imagination; the Mexica, for example, have repeatedly been invented and reinvented as the "Aztecs," alternately derided as cannibalistic savages and celebrated as symbols of Mexican national glory. Despite the immense amount of knowledge that archaeologists, ethnohistorians, and other scholars have compiled on the native peoples of central Mexico, the popular and common image of them still centers on so-called Aztec human sacrifices – as did the prejudiced first impression by conquistadors such as Bernal Díaz.

The reluctance of sixteenth-century Spaniards to believe that Native Americans built their own civilizations is thus part of a thread of Western thought that survives to this day. In the decades after Columbus, it was argued that American natives were descended from one of the lost tribes of Israel or refugees from Atlantis, or they were "taught" civilization by Egyptians and Carthaginians. We may chuckle at such theories, but they were as popular in their day as were late-twentieth-century notions of alien assistance or a lost ten-thousand-year-old global civilization.

Some sixteenth-century Europeans were willing to credit America's natives with the civilizational developments that were very much still visible after the Spanish Conquest. One of these was the Franciscan friar Diego de Landa, who asserted that the pyramids and other buildings he saw in the

Figure 1.1. From Jan van der Straet, Nova reperta. Speculum diuersarum imaginum specuatiuarum, 1638. ID: SIL28-198-06. Couresy of Smithsonian Institution Libraries, Washington, DC.

NOBLE SAVAGERY: EUROPEAN VIEWS OF "INDIANS"

A Dutch artist, Jan van der Straet, engraved the image above around 1575. Titled *America*, it has been published in numerous books about the New World ever since that date. The man standing, dressed elaborately and holding an astrolabe and a bannered cross, is Amerigo Vespucci – the Italian navigator after whom the Americas became named. The astrolabe was an instrument used to determine the position and altitude of the sun or of those planets or stars visible to the naked eye. Along with the impressive ocean-going ship in the background, the astrolabe is intended to represent European civilization and the achievement of crossing the Atlantic. Vespucci is thus Western Europe. The naked woman is native America, a representation that is blatantly gendered. The woman and her surroundings convey three related European views of Native Americans: they were innocent (arguably shown in the woman's pose), they lacked civilization and even culture (reflected in the paucity of material goods, with people depicted as living like the animals among them), and they were barbarous in a highly negative sense (symbolized by cannibalism).

Yucatán "have not been built by any people other than these Indians." Landa was right. He was referring to the Mayas, but he would have been equally correct making the same observation anywhere in the Americas.

Beginning as early as 8,000 years ago, Native American populations began to abandon nomadic hunting in favor of a more settled and permanent existence. The earliest evidence of this transition is found in the Andes region of South America and in Mesoamerica. Beginning about 3000 B.C., native peoples in these two regions developed more sophisticated societies and distinctive styles of art and architecture. In this period Andeans developed the great Chavín civilization in the northern Andes while Mesoamericans produced the great Olmec civilization of Mexico's Gulf Coast. Between 200 B.C. and A.D. 1300 a number of distinct civilizations rose and fell in the Andes and Mesoamerica, some of them reaching imperial status and all of them building on and borrowing from their predecessors. Before the period of the Incas, the Moche and the Sicán civilizations stand out in northern Peru, while to the south there rose the Nazca, Huari, and Tiahuanaco. The two greatest civilizations to develop in Mesoamerica before the famous Aztec-Mexica, meanwhile, were Teotihuacán in central Mexico and the Classic Maya. All of these civilizations centered on large, ceremonial cities with substantial stone temple complexes.

Many cultures flourished in Mesoamerica and the Andes in the centuries before Europeans arrived, but it was only in the last hundred years or so before Columbus's first voyage in 1492 that the vast Mexica and Inca empires rose to dominate central Mexico and the Andes, respectively. Their millions of subjects, though diverse, shared many cultural traits as a result of long-standing interregional contacts.

We will return to look at these empires in more detail in Chapter 5. For now, let us get a firmer grasp of the nature of one of the great Native American regional traditions, that of Mesoamerican civilization, by viewing it through ten characteristics or defining features. Those ten features will then be used as a framework for a comparison of Mesoamerican and Andean civilizations (see In Focus 1.2).

Many Mesoamericans lived in cities that featured (1) monumental architecture, in particular pyramids and other massive structures facing large, open plazas. The cities also tended to contain (2) ball courts (see In Focus 1.3) and (3) specialized markets, which operated both at local and regional levels. Such markets featured numerous items, but (4) several items had particular cultural and economic importance – jade (used decoratively), obsidian (used decoratively and to create blades for tools and weapons), and cacao (the chocolate seed used both as money, in bean form, and as a highly prized beverage, in liquid form). Equally significant were the everyday items that formed the basis of the Mesoamerican diet: (5) maize (corn), squash, and beans. Of these, maize was the most important; over millennia, Meso-americans had not only domesticated maize but also developed a method of preparing it that released niacin, a crucial vitamin.

The Mesoamerican worldview (6) was oriented toward two principles, that of the cardinal directions and that of duality (whereby everything in the universe formed part of a pair, such as day and night, life and death, super-natural and natural, and male and female). These principles were also part

IN FOCUS 1.2

A COMPARISON OF THE TEN MAIN FEATURES OF MESOAMERICAN AND ANDEAN CIVILIZATIONS

Cultural Practice	Mesoamerica	Andes
(1) Monumental architecture	pyramids with plazas	U-shaped temples
(2) Ball game	widespread and important	nonexistent
(3) Public markets	highly specialized	specialized; some suppressed
(4) Precious market goods	jade, obsidian, cacao	shells, textiles, metal goods
(5) Diet base	maize, squash, beans	potatoes, maize, squash
(6) Landscape seen in	terms of cardinal directions	radial terms
(7) Religion	pantheistic, tied to politics	pantheistic, tied to politics
(8) Sacrificial rituals	of animals; some humans	animals, rarely humans
(9) Planetary knowledge	considerable	considerable
(10) Writing system	complex hieroglyphic writing	quipus, but no writing

Figure 1.2. **a.** Tikal (Guatemala), Temple 1. Photograph by Raymond Ostertag (August 2006). **b.** Small detail of a reproduction of a mural at the Tepantitla complex of Teotihuacán. Photograph by Daquella Manera. **c.** Machu Picchu. Photograph by Amanda J. Smith. **d.** Mayan vase depicting a costumed noble; burial offering. Late classical period (**a.d.** 600–900). Copán, Honduras. Photograph by Durova.

of (7) Mesoamerica's complex pantheistic religion (a religion of many gods), which included such features as nature deities, deified royal ancestors, and a multitiered heaven and underworld. At times, human communication with the gods involved (8) sacrificial rituals, ranging from the offering of animals to self-sacrificial bloodletting and the ritualized execution of human captives through decapitation or heart removal.

Related to religious beliefs, but also to Mesoamerican understandings of agricultural cycles, was (9) a sophisticated knowledge of the celestial bodies and their movements. This formed the basis of a complex permutation calendar that featured a long count (rather like our years, centuries, and millennia), a 365-day solar year (like our year), and an additional cycle of 260 days. Calendrical knowledge, religious beliefs, and – above all – political and historical records were all written down on materials ranging from fig-bark paper to bone and stone; for Mesoamericans had developed (10) a complex hieroglyphic writing system – more accurately, a set of three related

Figure 1.3. a. Four ballgame players in elaborate costumes in front of steps; text mentions the Hix Witz (jaguar mountain) place. Rollout Photograph K2803 © Justin Kerr. b. Copán ball court. Photograph by Amara Solari.

PLAYING BALL

When Spaniards invaded in the sixteenth century, Mesoamericans had been playing rubber ball games for almost three millennia. Ball games were played across a vast region – from Puerto Rico to Honduras, across Mexico to Arizona. Almost 1,600 ancient ball courts have been discovered so far. Called *ullamaliztli* (the ball game) or *tlachtli* (the ball court) by the Mexica and other Nahuas, contests were presided over by Xochipilli, god of the ball game. The game is still played today in northern Mexico, where it is called *ulama*. Hernando Cortés was so impressed by the Mexica game that he took a team of ballplayers back to Spain, where they played for Charles V.

The ball game had profound ritual significance in Mesoamerica; it was as important as ball-playing sports are to modern societies. It was also a cosmic ceremony, with the two teams representing life's great dualities. Players struck rubber balls with their hips and buttocks (and, less commonly, arms and elbows), wearing leather hip guards; elite players wore more elaborate gear (as in the illustration here from a Classical Maya pot). Courts varied in shape but typically had two stone sides with a vertical hoop on each side (seen here, from the court at Copán).

systems, named after the Mexica (Aztecs), Mixtecs, and Mayas. These systems were partly pictographic and partly phonetic. The most complete system was that of the Mayas, meaning that the literate Maya minority could express anything they wanted in writing. The sophistication and cultural significance of writing also meant that, in the sixteenth century, Nahuas, Mixtecs, Mayas, and some other Mesoamerican groups would easily make the transition to alphabetic writing.

For their part, Andean cities were also carefully planned and oriented, and they contained similarly oriented (1) stone or adobe temples of great size, some of them pyramidal but more often U shaped. As in Mesoamerica (and unlike ancient Egypt), the enormous monuments served as stages for religious-political drama rather than personal sepulchers for elites – though there were (2) no ball courts to compare to those in Mesoamerica.

Andean cities were also (3) places of material exchange and craft specialization. Items traded over great distances included (4) *Spondylus* and other marine shells, salt, fine textiles, and a variety of utilitarian and decorative metal items. Andean metallurgy was in fact far more advanced and widespread than that of Mesoamerica; long before the rise of the Incas one finds arsenical bronze tools, copper currency, and even platinum jewelry.

The Andean diet varied considerably but generally consisted of (5) potatoes and other high-altitude tubers, maize, beans, squash, and capsicum peppers. At lower altitudes, manioc (a tuber), seafood, and freshwater fish were equally important. Guinea pigs, or *cuyes*, and llamas, the only domesticated animal of any size in the Americas, were eaten on special occasions; curiously, llamas were never milked. Tobacco was sometimes employed in ritual healing ceremonies, but from Colombia to Chile, mildly stimulating coca leaves and maize beer were the preferred stimulants. Intensive agriculture entailed complex terraces, long aqueducts, and extensive raised fields.

These human-constructed features in the landscape, along with many natural ones, were – like the ubiquitous ancestor mummies (see In Focus 1.4) – regarded as deeply sacred. Unlike that of Mesoamerica, the Andean worldview tended to conceive of the landscape in (6) radial rather than strictly cardinal terms. Surviving temples contain sculptures of fierce, semi-human feline and reptilian creatures, suggesting (7) religious themes still evident in lowland South American shamanism. Religion and politics were not separate concerns, however, as Andean temples from the earliest to latest times were clearly the site (like their counterparts in Mesoamerica) of (8) human sacrifice. It is likely, however, that human sacrifice ("ritual execution" is perhaps a more neutral phrase) was practiced on a relatively small scale.

Like Mesoamericans, Andeans gave considerable attention – and mythic weight – to (9) astronomical phenomena. However, Andean peoples appear

Figure 1.4. **a.** Drawing 112. Burials of the Inka: Inka illapa, aya, the deceased Inka, his corpse. From The Guaman Poma manuscript (GKS 2232 4°) at the Royal Library, Copenhagen, Denmark. Credit: The Royal Library, Copenhagen, Denmark. **b.** Drawing 115. Burials of the Qullasuyus. From The Guaman Poma manuscript (GKS 2232 4°) at the Royal Library, Copenhagen, Denmark. Credit: The Royal Library, Copenhagen, Denmark.

MOUNTAIN MUMMIES

At left: "First chapter, burial of the Inca, the Inca Illapa Aya, deceased": the ruling Inca and his wife (standing on the left) make liquid offerings to the mummified corpses of a previous Inca king and queen (on the right, the dead king sitting on a stool, the queen kneeling). An open burial tower is in the background.

At right: "Burial in Collasuyu": A nobleman and his wife in Collasuyu, part of the Inca Empire, drink corn beer while he also pours some of it as an offering to the mummified sitting corpse of an ancestor. In the background are the bones of older ancestors.

One of the great mysteries of Inca history and culture surrounds the ritual burial or sacrifice of children atop some of the Andes' highest peaks, including the highest mountain in the Western Hemisphere, Aconcagua. Several of the burials were happened upon by mountaineers in the late twentieth century in Argentina, Chile, and Peru. A few intrepid archeologists soon followed, hoping to beat looters to what were clearly some unusually well-preserved sites. What the archeologists found were scattered offerings of well-dressed boys and girls – usually solitary adolescent girls – interred in simple stone tombs linked to the surface by tubes and openings. The children apparently died of hypothermia, or exposure, after consuming maize beer, and all were naturally mummified by the extremely dry and cold high-altitude environment.

IN FOCUS 1.4

MOUNTAIN MUMMIES, *continued*

Why would the Incas select children – rather than enemy warriors – for sacrifice? And why bury them in such forbidding environments? In fact, warrior sacrifices somewhat similar to those found in Mesoamerica were practiced by ancient Andean peoples such as the Moche, who also built substantial pyramids. More common, however, was mummy worship, an ancient Andean tradition found in both lowlands and highlands. Mummified ancestors, rulers, and shamans were thought to inhabit an intermediary world between the here and the hereafter, and they were thus revered for their alleged ability to act as intermediaries for the living in their communications with the spirit world. In Andean cosmology, then, mummified humans were not thought to be entirely dead but rather in a state of suspended animation.

In the case of the child mummies of the southern Andes, a few documentary fragments from just after the Spanish Conquest suggest that regional lords subject to the Incas occasionally gave up their most beloved children to serve as intermediaries between the world of the mountain spirits and the world of the Inca state. Priests from Cuzco oversaw the sequence of rituals that ended following a somber and no doubt exhausting mountain climb. The mountain burials have been linked to the Incas' highly complex radial system of spatial organization and to the older tradition of venerating mummies linked to high-status families, as in the images here.

---

not to have developed writing systems of the traditional kind, instead employing (10) knotted strings, called quipus (*khipus*), to record numbers, lineages, and perhaps historical events.

Concentrated, Segmented, Semisedentary, and Nonsedentary

Across the several millennia prior to 1492, Native Americans had developed a wide array of societies and civilizations. Despite their diversity, native societies can be divided into four categories or types. Using such a typology helps us to understand native America before the European invasion, but it also aids our understanding of diverse native reactions to the European invasion and to the demands of Spanish and Portuguese colonists (as we will see in Part Two).

We use these four categories: "concentrated sedentary," "segmented sedentary," "semisedentary," and "nonsedentary." The first two refer to permanently settled societies whose members lived in built communities, for example villages, towns, and (in some cases) cities. In the tropical Americas, where most people lived, such sedentary societies tended to occupy valleys or plateaus rather than densely forested areas. Most importantly, sedentary societies relied on permanent, intensive agriculture for their survival. Intensive farming, which often entailed irrigation and other complex and labor-intensive water control systems, allowed populations to swell. The Mexica capital of Tenochtitlán, for example, reached a population of some 250,000,

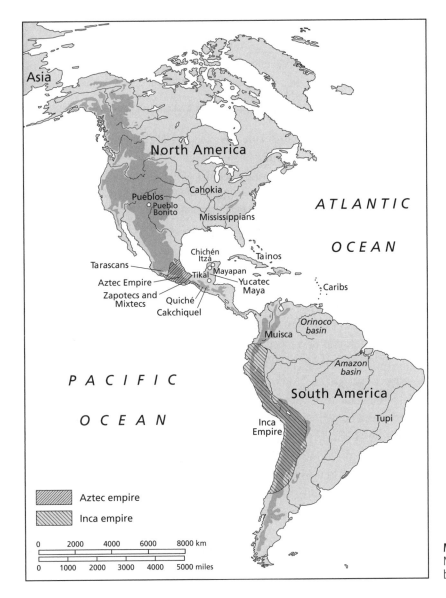

Map 1.2
Native Americans
before 1492

making it one of the largest cities in the world. Intensive agriculture also fostered social stratification. In nearly every sedentary Native American society, the majority of subjects engaged in farm labor while a minority lived and worked as merchants, artisans, warriors, nobles, and royalty – thus giving rise to many of the distinctive regional features of civilization outlined in the previous section.

It is almost a global truism that sedentary societies are built to expand, and this applies to the two most densely populated regions of the Americas, the Andes and Mesoamerica. Substantial empires rose and fell in both areas across the two centuries prior to the European invasion. During the fifteenth century, when Europeans were beginning to expand into the Atlantic, the latest in these series of empires came into being – the Incas in the Andes (greater Peru), and the Mexica (Aztecs) in Mesoamerica. There were also some smaller polities in Mesoamerica that expanded from time to time on a more limited scale and might be classified as incipient or miniempires; namely, the Tarascans in western Mexico, and the Cakchiquel Mayas and Quiché Mayas in highland Guatemala.

All of these societies constitute our category of "concentrated" – that is, permanently settled agricultural peoples organized into some kind of empire. But there were also other sedentary peoples who occupied lands where there were no empires or large polities; these societies we call segmented. Key examples of segmented sedentary societies could be found to the north of the Inca Empire – principally the Muisca of what is now northeastern Colombia – and in southern Mesoamerica. Segmented Mesoamerican societies included the Zapotecs, Mixtecs, and other smaller groups to the south of the Mexica Empire, as well as the Mayas of the Yucatán Peninsula and smaller Maya polities in Guatemala. These peoples were all fully sedentary, and many had in previous centuries been part of larger regional polities, some of which had developed into incipient empires of sorts, centered on such cities as Tikal (at the Yucatán's southern end) and Chichén Itzá (to its north). But at the time of the Spanish invasion, the Mayas were at the segmented stage of a cycle marked by periods of expansion and centralization followed by periods of political and demographic collapse. For example, as recently as the early fifteenth century, much of the Yucatán Peninsula had been organized into a miniempire centered on the city of Mayapan; had their invasion of the peninsula been delayed by a century or so, the Spaniards may have encountered a similar such polity instead of the two dozen loosely delineated city-states (i.e., segmented societies) they in fact found in the sixteenth century.

In terms of total population, the vast majority of Native Americans living at the time of European contact were sedentary agriculturalists, yet it was semisedentary peoples who occupied the most territory. Semisedentary societies relied only partially on agriculture, requiring them to hunt and forage to meet the remainder of their dietary needs. Semisedentary peoples were not nomads, but their subsistence needs and sometimes cultural or religious factors caused them to move to new areas for fresh land. Periodic movement, sometimes over great distances, prevented semisedentary peoples from developing dense populations and, since they had to carry their belongings with them, it also reduced the complexity of material culture and craft specialization. Semisedentary groups could and did expand – the Tupi, for example, were still moving north along the coast of Brazil when Europeans reached them around 1500. The Tupi planted crops as they moved, and mostly fought with each other, but many other semisedentary peoples expanded at the expense of sedentary neighbors, acting partly as parasitical raiders.

A great number of semisedentary peoples occupied two vast portions of the Americas. In the south, they inhabited the Caribbean islands plus eastern and central South America. To the north, they controlled at least half of North America, but were most densely settled around the Great Lakes, Mississippi basin, Eastern Woodlands, and Pacific Northwest. Some semisedentary peoples came close to forming fully sedentary societies. The Ancestral Pueblo of northern New Mexico built substantial stone dwellings and ritual complexes sustained by maize agriculture, and the Mississippian culture centered on the Cahokia ceremonial site boasted populations in the tens of thousands. Both the Ancestral Pueblo and Mississippian cultures traded with Mesoamericans, but for reasons that remain disputed their population densities dropped before the arrival of Europeans.

Other semisedentary peoples influenced by Mesoamerica included the Taínos, who controlled the Greater Antilles, or larger Caribbean islands. Taíno towns centered on plazas, featured large ball courts, and housed up to several thousand inhabitants. Rather than relying on maize – the Mesoamerican and greater North American staple – the Taíno diet was based on manioc and fish. This diet matched that of Brazil's Tupis and neighboring peoples of the Amazon River basin. Scholars dispute the size and permanence of precolonial settlements on the lower Amazon, but the first Europeans to penetrate the region in the 1540s described large settlements along the river's banks. Archeological evidence supports this view.

In the Amazon and neighboring Orinoco basins, semisedentary and nonsedentary, or nomadic, peoples often competed with one another for access to waterways and forests, and some groups went back and forth between the two life ways. Truly nonsedentary peoples were most prevalent in the nontropical Southern Cone of South America. The same was true in the vast deserts, plains, and arctic regions of North America. Although their numbers were small and their material goods simple and portable, the Americas' nonsedentary peoples were everywhere masters of adaptation to demanding environments. Such societies, including the Tehuelche of southern Argentina, were highly mobile, and often followed the seasonal movements of game. Compact, itinerant, hunting bands were typical, and many nonsedentary peoples preyed on sedentary neighbors in times of stress. Nomadic or nonsedentary societies had few material possessions, yet nearly all passed down elaborate oral histories and complex spiritual beliefs. Their medicinal practices, which often drew from long experience with plants, insects, and animals, were sometimes sought out by sedentary peoples as well.

Native American settlement patterns and categories might be imagined as concentric circles emanating from two great centers. The two centers constitute the two core regions of sedentary population – the Andes, with some 15 million people, most within the Inca Empire, and Mesoamerica, with about 30 million people at the time of European contact, most of them in central

Mexico. The first great circle encompasses semisedentary peoples, surrounding Mesoamerica to the north (North America), to the east (the Caribbean), and to the south (the lower half of Central America), and adjacent to the Andes, to the north and the east. The second ring encompassed nonsedentary peoples, those who dwelt mostly in interior regions of South America and at the most southern and northern edges of the Americas. All these outer circles, the semisedentary and nomadic populations of the Americas, made up roughly another 20 million people. Thus the total native American population at European contact was approximately 65 million, similar to that of western and central Europe at that time, and probably not so different from that of Atlantic Africa.

Why were Native American societies so diverse in type and structure? Why did some remain nonsedentary gatherer-hunters as others marched from temple to empire building? Were the empire builders superior peoples, as they themselves sometimes assumed, or were all simply different kinds of "barbarians," as early Europeans, appalled by different customs, claimed? The analogy of concentric circles should not be taken to suggest that civilization emanated out from the Inca and Mexica empires. Nor should the circles be thought of as some sort of judgmental scale, with the core superior and civilized and the outer limits inferior and savage.

It is instead more useful to think of differences among native groups (and between them and Europeans or Africans) in terms of geographical constraints and opportunities. Native Americans were not unique in building the kinds of societies that their environments best sustained. When challenged, as in the steep Andes and drought-prone Mexican highlands, native farmers developed ingenious systems of water control and soil protection, greatly increasing fertility and food security. Hunting and fishing peoples, likewise, developed ingenious lures and traps to bag some of the world's most elusive game. It is another myth to claim that all Native Americans lived in perfect harmony with their surroundings, but it is clear that most peoples developed practices and religious beliefs that paid much attention to such an ideal.

* * *

The diverse environmental underpinnings of native cultures are important to understanding the Americas before European contact – and to understanding the colonial period. For just as precolonial societies sought out and exploited the geographical environments that best sustained their hopes and ambitions, so did the geographical and human environment of the Americas determine where and how Spaniards and Portuguese would build colonies.

SUGGESTIONS FOR FURTHER READING

A fine article-length study is John E. Kicza, "The Peoples and Civilizations of the Americas Before Contact" (American Historical Association's Essays on

Global and Comparative History, 1998; reprinted in *Agricultural and Pastoral Societies in Ancient and Classical History*, edited by Michael Adas, pp. 183–223, 2001, and incorporated into Kicza's *Resilient Cultures: America's Native Peoples Confront European Civilization, 1500–1800*, 2003, chapters 1–2).

For book-length coverage, we recommend, for Mesoamerica, Michael D. Coe's two books, *Mexico* and *The Maya* (updated every few years with a new edition), and David Webster's *The Fall of the Ancient Maya: Solving the Mystery of the Maya Collapse* (2002); for South America, Karen Olsen Bruhns, *Ancient South America* (1994), Michael Moseley, *The Incas and Their Ancestors* (2003), and Terrence D'Altroy, *The Incas* (2002).

Among numerous additional works worth consulting by those writing class papers are Jared Diamond's *Guns, Germs, and Steel: The Fates of Human Societies* (1997) and Charles C. Mann, *1491: New Revelations of the Americas before Columbus* (2005).

GLOSSARY

Acephali [a-SEF-a-lee]: mythical headless people (some Europeans thought there were acephali among Native Americans)

Mexica [me-SHEE-ka]: popularly called Aztecs in modern times; the native group that created the city of **Mexico-Tenochtitlán** [me-SHEE-ko tenoch-teet-LAHN] and the Aztec Empire

Mesoamerica [may-zo-a-MEH-ree-ka]: civilizational area stretching from northern Mexico down to the middle of Central America

Olmec [OL-mek], **Teotihuacán** [tay-o-tee-wah-KAHN], **Chavín** [cha-VEEN], **Moche** [MOH-cheh], **Sicán** [see-KAHN], **Nazca** [NAS-cah], **Huari** [WAH-ree], **Tiahuanaco** [tee-ah-wan-AH-ko]: names of places and cultures in Mesoamerica and the Andes

Cacao [ka-KA-oh]: the cocoa seed, used by Mesoamericans as currency and to make chocolate drinks

Manioc [MAN-ee-ahk]: also called cassava; a tuber, similar to a potato, grown in lowland tropics

Pantheism: the belief in and worship of many deities or gods (all Native American religions were pantheistic)

Nahua [NAH-wah], **Mixtec** [MEESH-tek], **Maya** [MY-ah]: native groups in Mesoamerica; the Mexica were a Nahua people

Cuy [KWEE]: a guinea pig domesticated and eaten in the Andes (plural: *cuyes*)

Quipu [KEY-pooh]: also called *khipu*, knotted strings used by Andeans to record numbers, lineages, and possibly historical events

Taíno [ta-EE-no], **Quiché** [kee-CHAY], **Cakchiquel** [kak-chee-KEL], **Tikal** [tee-KAHL], **Chichén Itzá** [chee-CHEN eet-SAH], **Mayapan** [MY-a-pan], **Muisca** [MWEES-cah], **Tupi** [TOO-pee]: places and cultures in Native America

Chinampa [chee-NAM-pa]: floating fields built by the Nahuas in central Mexico

2

Castile and Portugal

My Cid's men sack the Moorish camp, taking shields and arms and riches in profusion. They gather up the horses of the Moors and find they have five hundred and ten. And how great their joy when they learn they have lost but fifteen of their men! They have so much gold and silver that they do not know what to do with it. The Christians are all rich with booty.

(The Poem of My Cid)

W HAT WERE THE JUSTIFICATIONS for the Spanish and Portuguese conquests and settlements in the Americas? In the early seventeenth century, the Spanish jurist and colonial administrator Juan de Solórzano Pereira wrote a two-volume book that remained for the rest of the colonial period one of the major texts on the topic of law in the colonies. The second volume of Solórzano's *De Indiarum Jure* discussed the legitimacy of Spanish activities in the Americas, reviewing a kind of legal top-ten list of arguments made by Spaniards over the preceding decades. Although Solórzano gave some credit to all the arguments, he concluded that only one had sufficient legal basis to justify the existence of Spanish and Portuguese America. This was the papal grant, or the fact that Pope Alexander VI had "given" the Americas to Spain and Portugal in 1493.

Solórzano's dry Latin tome may seem like an odd place to begin a chapter on the Iberian background to colonial Latin America. But his perspective on the colonies and the enduring importance of his book during colonial times point directly to the medieval origins of Iberian expansion. Solórzano was not working with radical new ideas; one scholar of the *De Indiarum Jure*, James Muldoon, has called it "the fullest expression of a *medieval* Christian conception of religious and social order" (emphasis added). Nor did the papal grant of 1493 come out of nowhere. Pope Alexander's pronouncement – like Queen Isabella's decision to extend patronage to Columbus the year before, like Pedro Álvares Cabral's voyage to the coast of Brazil seven years later, and like the

TIMELINE

218 b.c.–a.d. 470s Roman period in Iberia

711: Muslims from North Africa invade Iberia

850–1250: main Muslim-Christian wars of the Reconquista

1179: Portugal becomes an independent Christian kingdom

1391–1490s: persecution and expulsion of Jews by Castile and Portugal

15th century: Portuguese kings sponsor exploration of the Atlantic Ocean and African coast

1469: Isabella, queen of Castile, marries Ferdinand, king of Aragon

1488–1492: Castile, the largest kingdom in Iberia, conquers the last Muslim kingdom, Granada (effectively creating Spain); sponsored by Queen Isabella, Columbus discovers the Caribbean and claims its islands for Castile; major expulsion of Jews from Spain

1493: Pope Alexander VI gives the Americas to Spain and Portugal

letters of Cortés to the Spanish king two decades later – can be understood only through an appreciation of the medieval context from which they all emerged.

This chapter offers an overview of similarities and differences between the Spanish and Portuguese. The first section is intended to provide a sense of how Iberians were organized socially, and the second section explains the Spanish and Portuguese emphasis on urban life and the relationship between town and countryside. The ultimate goal of the discussion is to show how later developments in the Americas were rooted in processes that took shape in the Iberian Peninsula in the centuries before Columbus and Cabral crossed the Atlantic.

"El Cid" and the "Wicked Queen": Categorizing Iberians

The historian David Brading has remarked that "1492 was a Janus year for Spain, a year of warfare and exploration, filled with patriotic euphoria." But contrary to what we might expect, Columbus's crossing of the Atlantic was not the primary source of that euphoria; rather, it was the Castilian acquisition of the Muslim kingdom of Granada that was most celebrated. On New Year's Day, the queen of Castile, Isabella, and her husband, Ferdinand, the king of Aragon, rode through the gates and received the keys to the last great Muslim city in the peninsula.

We have been talking of Castile, Aragon, and Granada, rather than Spain, because Spain did not exist before 1492. Not since Roman times (218 B.C. to the A.D. 470s) had the Iberian Peninsula been politically united. A millennium before Isabella and Ferdinand's reign Visigoths from northern Europe had invaded. But their unstable kingdom was overrun by Islamic invaders (mostly Arabs and Berbers) who crossed from North Africa in A.D. 711. The Muslim rulers, like their Visigoth predecessors, were not able to stay united or control the whole peninsula. Iberia's political map shifted constantly over the next eight centuries as Muslim and Christian kingdoms grew, shrank, and merged. For the most part, Iberians of both faiths lived and traded in peace with each other and with the peninsula's sizeable Jewish population. Wars nevertheless broke out between 850 and 1250, resulting in a general Christian push southward, nearly always at Muslim expense. Portugal came into existence as an independent Christian kingdom in 1179, and had more or less assumed its present-day limits by 1250, when Castile took Seville. Until 1492, Granada remained as Iberia's sole Islamic kingdom.

The most precocious and aggressive Christian kingdom in medieval Iberia was Castile. While cosmopolitan kingdoms such as Portugal, Granada, and Aragon were looking outward from their long coastlines, initially small and landlocked Castile developed an intolerant pride as it expanded its frontiers. This mix of righteous intolerance and self-confidence would later blossom into an imperial philosophy. The Iberian Peninsula is surrounded mostly by sea and attached to the rest of Europe only by the rugged Pyrenees Mountains. There are plenty of mountain ranges in the peninsula, too, making Castile something of an "island within an island." The kingdom's emergence

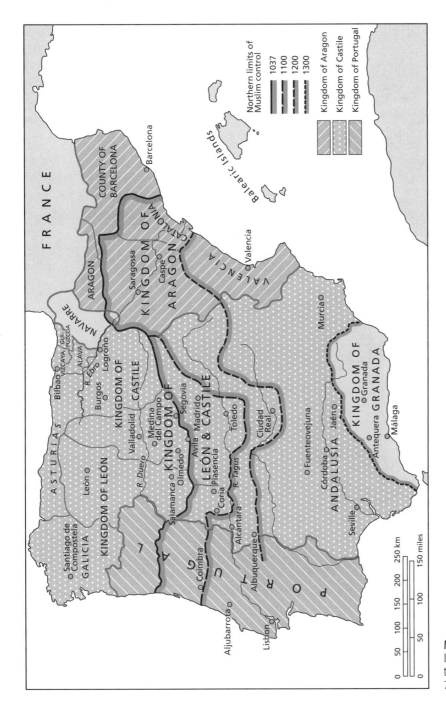

Map 2.1
Iberia in the Age of the Reconquista, 711–1492

from that isolation was a violent one marked by a cyclical pattern common to most early modern empires. Castilians who fought on behalf of their king received four kinds of rewards: booty, land, tribute-paying subjects (or slaves), and higher social rank. As newly conquered lands became consolidated and a new generation of young and restless frontier warriors emerged, the cycle was repeated. Territorial expansion thus became the normal avenue toward social and economic gain for Christian Castilians.

IN FOCUS 2.1

Figure 2.1. a. Life Of Raymond Lull, 14th Century (Reproduced in *An Illustrated History of the Knights Templar*, by James Wasserman) **b.** Alhambra Islamic details. © Jillian Pond / iStockphoto.com. **c.** The author presenting his book to Juana la Loca (Joan the Mad, 1479–1555) and Philip I the Handsome (1478–1506) of Castile. From the "Devocionario De la Reyna Da Juana a Quien Hamaron la Loca," by Pedro Marcuello. Ms.604, f.4 verso. Spanish manuscript illumination, 15th CE. Photo: R.G. Ojeda. Musee Conde, Chantilly, France. (Image Reference ART149479) © Reunion des Musees Nationaux / Art Resource, NY.

INSTRUMENTS OF EMPIRE

Antonio de Nebrija, author of the first vernacular grammar published in Europe (his was Castilian), famously wrote that languages were "instruments of empire." Indeed, the vernacular replaced Latin earlier in the Iberian kingdoms than it did elsewhere in Europe, and Castilian became the official language of Castile as early as the thirteenth century. Castilian would go on to become the official language of an empire that stretched around the world. But scores of languages and literatures flourished under that empire, just as many languages thrived in medieval Iberia. Galician poetry was widely composed into the thirteenth century, Hebrew literature survived and influenced Castilian poetry into the fifteenth century, and Arabic was being written through to Granada's fall in 1492. The great cultural vitality of medieval Catalonia was also expressed in its vernacular literature.

The images here show Ramón Llull's "autobiography," written in 1311 in Catalan; fourteenth-century verses written in Arabic by Ibn Zamrak, preserved on the walls of the Alhambra palace in Granada; and a Book of Hours in Latin, made for Juana of Castile (Ferdinand and Isabella's daughter; her son became the Emperor Charles V), shortly after she married Philip of Burgundy in 1496.

Preying on Muslim neighbors in the name of a Christian monarch may not sound noble, but most medieval Castilians believed otherwise. They cast their cyclical raids and resulting territorial expansion as essential parts of a Christian crusade aimed at cleansing the peninsula of infidels. A range of violent and unjust means, including theft, kidnapping, and murder, seemed warranted by this noble end, which they dubbed the Reconquest – *la Reconquista*. The Reconquest was a way of looking at Iberian history, whereby the past was reconstructed as a cosmic drama featuring Muslim villains and Christian heroes. The best known of these heroes was El Cid, the nom de guerre of Rodrigo Díaz. Díaz fought for both Muslim and Christian kings, winning the nickname "al-Sayyid," Arabic for "the master." El Cid's modest pedigree and mercenary tendencies got papered over as his legend grew. As the subject of Castile's most famous epic poem, he was cast as a crusading nobleman with an enormous beard, a trusty steed, and a sword capable of slicing "Moors," or infidels, in two. Upon arriving in the Americas, Spain's sixteenth-century conquistadors openly spoke of their desire to emulate El Cid. Cortés's official biographer could not avoid the comparison, and Spanish poets carried on for years eulogizing kings and conquerors as the Cids of their generation.

What matters most is not that the El Cid remembered since the fifteenth century was as much a mythical as a historical figure, but that Castile created his legend, putting it to the service of an expansionism that continued into the reign of Isabella and Ferdinand, Columbus's sponsors. Isabella became queen of Castile in 1479, ten years after marrying Ferdinand, who became king of Aragon. The two kingdoms retained their separate identities, but the fall of Granada in 1492 made it clear that Castile was the dominant partner. Granada added half a million people to Castile's roughly 4.5 million. By contrast, Aragon and Portugal's populations hovered around a million each. The tiny northern kingdom of Navarre's roughly two hundred thousand inhabitants would come under Castilian control in 1512.

It therefore makes sense of think of Iberia in 1492 as primarily consisting of two kingdoms, the larger Castile and the smaller Portugal. Despite being smaller and less populated than its hulking and aggressive neighbor to the east, Castile, Portugal was no stranger to expansion. It was just that most of it was overseas. The Portuguese spent the late medieval period fostering trade between the north Atlantic and the Mediterranean, with Lisbon as the key stopover. Accumulated revenues and borrowed sailing technologies were then used to push southward along the African coast, with the ultimate aim of finding a sea route to India. By the death of Prince Henry the Navigator (b. 1394) in 1460, the Portuguese had charted 1,500 miles of Africa's west coast. Henry, who spent much more time on land than his name suggests, set the pattern of royal patronage of shipping and exploration picked up by his grandson John II (r.1481–1495). In the last years of John II's reign, Portuguese sailors rounded the Cape of Good Hope, bringing India within reach.

Castile was by no means a mere landlubber kingdom, as Isabella's struggle for control of several East Atlantic islands would attest, but she and Ferdinand were always playing catch up to pioneering Portugal. The fact that Isabella chose to sponsor Columbus's ill-advised but ultimately fortunate western voyage after it was rejected by Portuguese royal cosmographers (a tale to which we return in Chapter 4) is emblematic of their differences in this period. The basic contrast was this: Castile in 1492 was riding a tide of land-based conquest and consolidation, whereas Portugal was beginning to enjoy the fruits of years of overseas exploration and trade.

Despite these and other differences, Castile and Portugal had much in common. Both were famous for their militant Catholicism and rising religious intolerance. Castilian expansion is usually blamed for the disappearance of medieval *convivencia*, or multifaith coexistence, but Portugal was a Reconquista kingdom, too. Portuguese kings were not only anti-Islamic crusaders, but also vocal and active anti-Semites. They participated willingly in Iberia's great anti-Semitic century that began with the horrific pogroms, or massacres of Jews, in 1391 and ended in the expulsion of all Jews from both kingdoms in the 1490s. Isabella of Castile has gone down in Spanish history as a heroic figure, but to Iberian Jews she was "the wicked Queen Isabella, she who has brought upon us all these evils." The Portuguese monarchy was no less "wicked" from a Jewish perspective; John II allowed tens of thousands of exiled Castilian Jews to migrate to Portugal in 1492 in exchange for a special tax payment, yet only five years later his successor, Emanuel I, followed Isabella's example and forced all Jews not willing to convert into exile. Iberia's monarchs seemed almost to be competing for the title of "most intolerant." Emmanuel added Muslims who were not slaves to the list of exiles in 1497, which example Isabella and Ferdinand followed in 1502. It was henceforth illegal, and deadly dangerous, to practice Islam or Judaism anywhere on Iberian soil.

The Castilian Reconquest gave rise to an intensely nationalistic Roman Catholicism, one requiring a more pious and ancient symbol than El Cid. St. James, or Santiago, known as the "Moor Slayer," was the obvious choice. According to local legend, the apostle James appeared on a white horse just in time to rally the armies of Ramiro I, the king of Asturias, and spare him defeat at Moorish hands. The saint was allegedly buried in the Galician town of Santiago de Compostela, helping the town to grow into one of medieval Europe's most visited pilgrimage sites. "Santiago!" became the standard battle cry of the American conquistadors, the Moor-slaying saint was seen saving Spaniards from indigenous warriors, and later paintings of the Conquest of Mexico had Cortés on a white horse in poses reminiscent of Santiago in battle. Many churches both in Spain and in Spanish America would be adorned with paintings and carvings in wood and stone of the mounted saint. Beneath his rearing horse there were usually depicted a half dozen decapitated, turbaned heads; Castilian religious nationalism was far from subtle.

It is hard to imagine that Castile and Portugal of the Reconquista and the expulsion of the Jews also participated in the Renaissance. But classical learning and humanist ideas did indeed spread to both kingdoms in the late-medieval period, helping to stimulate a flourishing in the written and visual arts. Although the Renaissance in Iberia was deeply rooted in local culture and history, the legacy of *convivencia* tied Iberians back to ancient Rome and Greece in unique ways. Muslim and Christian scholars, for example, collaborated to translate and interpret ancient Greek texts that had been preserved only in Arabic. The epitaph on the tomb of Ferdinand III – who ruled Castile, Galicia, and León, dying in 1252 and later canonized as Saint Ferdinand – was written in Castilian Spanish, Latin, Hebrew, and Arabic. His son and successor, Alfonso X, created a school of translators in Toledo. There Jewish scholars and other translators created Castilian versions of a wide range of Arabic texts, from scientific works to the famous Book of Chess, Dice, and Games.

Symbolic of what historian Angus Mackay has called "the ideal of combining 'arms' and 'letters'" are both the tomb of Martín Vázquez de Acuña (see In Focus 2.2) and the elegiac verses written by Jorge Manrique in 1476, shortly before the Vázquez tomb was built. Manrique's *Coplas por la muerte de su padre* (Couplets on the death of his father) idealizes his father's record of military service to the monarchy in wars against Muslims. At the court, arms and letters met, aristocracy and bureaucracy intermarried, and a new kind of warrior emerged, one who was also a cultivated courtier and who hoped to send his sons to university and at least some of his daughters to elite convents.

Figure 2.2 The Tomb of Martin de Arce, detail of bust. Cathedral, Siguenza, Spain. (Image Reference ART74459) © Scala / Art Resource, NY

CONQUISTADOR ROOTS: THE READING WARRIOR

Martín Vázquez de Acuña, dressed in armor but also reading a book, on his tomb in Sigüenza cathedral. The tomb was carved in the 1490s by Sebastián de Almonacid (c. 1460–c. 1526), recognized today as one of the most accomplished sculptors in Spain's history. The visual focal points of the sculpture are a book and a dagger. A symbol of the cultivated Castilian warrior of late medieval times, the image of Vázquez de Acuña evokes that of Hernando Cortés, born five years after Vázquez died and destined to write a veritable book of letters to the king describing his war against the Mexica (Aztec) Empire.

City and Country

Iberians were consummate city dwellers. The historian Felipe Fernández-Armesto has remarked that, "on a savage frontier, when two Englishmen meet they form a club; Spaniards found a city." We shall see that one of Cortés's first acts upon reaching Mexico's Gulf Coast was to found a city. This was a typical sixteenth-century practice, reflecting the fact that conquistador priorities stemmed from medieval Iberian perspectives on the world. In fact, the association of city-founding with imperialism goes as far back in ancient history as the Assyrians, and was deeply rooted in Iberia's Roman

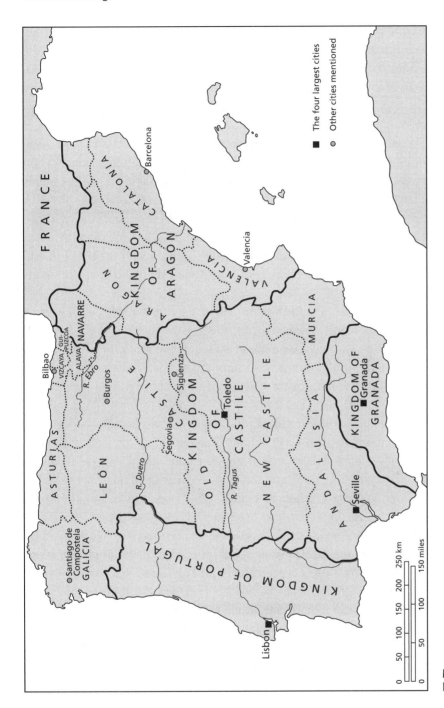

Map 2.2
Iberian Cities in 1492

past. "Roman Spain was a world full of cities," historian Michael Kulikowski has observed, "shaped by its hundreds of urban territories." Castilian urbanism also derived from a geographical logic. In a mostly dry and tree-less landscape, it made sense to cluster around rocky outcrops for defense and also to seize upon and defend rare sources of fresh water. The Spanish historian Juan Pablo Mártir Rizo (1593–1642) called seventeenth-century

Castile "a kingdom made of cities," a remark equally applicable to late medieval times.

Most Iberian cities were small – only four, Lisbon, Toledo, Seville, and Granada, had more than thirty thousand inhabitants by 1492 – but their identity as incorporated or chartered cities, with considerable legal autonomy and jurisdiction over the nearby hinterland, was vital (see In Focus 2.3). In the words of Fernández-Armesto, "city status was a habit of mind, rather than a function of size." Even though Barcelona was hit hard by the late-medieval crisis, and saw its population halved to twenty thousand by the fifteenth century, it functioned almost like a city-state, sending its own ambassador, with entourage, to the court. The rich merchant town of Burgos carried considerable political weight despite having a population of only five thousand people at the end of the fifteenth century. Most towns were home to no more than a thousand or two thousand inhabitants.

When it came to self-perception, size did not matter. Even inhabitants of the smallest Iberian towns viewed themselves as cultured urbanites; that is, city dwellers equated their mode of existence with civilization itself. Living alone in a country house or on a farm was considered barbaric, as well as unsafe. Cities and towns thus contained most of the Iberian population – even those whose lives tied them to the land. Owners of great estates and farm workers alike tended to maintain their primary residence in town. A city's charter was more than a coat-of-arms-like symbol, as it granted city dwellers a certain amount of independence from kings and other challengers, plus the right to collect regional taxes. Ambitious monarchs periodically sought to infringe on powerful or lucrative cities' rights, hoping to milk them for revenues or punish upstart citizens. Urbanites did not always stick together when faced with such pressures. At times kings and queens were able to play town councils and local nobles against each other, as in the cases of Burgos and Segovia. Despite the violence of late-medieval times, this strategy worked well for the Castilian monarchs, and it helped them to put in place the structures of governance that made Spain function as a unit.

Pacts between nobles and kings rarely benefited the Iberian masses, the vast majority of whom were landless peasants. How landless? In 1500, 95 percent of the land was owned by less than 3 percent of the population. Although no longer serfs (i.e., immobile rural servants tied to a landlord), Castilian and Portuguese peasants, who comprised 80 percent of the population, were free only in that they enjoyed – in the famous words of the Spanish historian Jaime Vicens Vives – the freedom "to die of hunger." Almost all Iberians were sedentary (in the sense of the categories discussed in the previous chapter with respect to Native Americans). But both Castile and Portugal suffered from a scarcity of arable land. Even those with access to arable land were vulnerable to crop loss and other

Figure 2.3 Pacheco, Francisco. View of the city of Seville, 16th century. Museo de America, Madrid, Spain. (Image Reference ART396737) © Scala/White Images / Art Resource, NY

SEVILLE: SPAIN'S CITY

Under its Muslim kings, Seville established itself as a commercial center drawing on its links to the surrounding agricultural lands and the markets of North Africa and the Mediterranean. It continued to grow after its conquest in 1248 by Ferdinand III, attracting migrants from the north during the late-medieval crisis. In the late fourteenth century, Seville's vibrant twenty-three-synagogue Jewish community used the courts successfully to resist anti-Semitic campaigns, although the community never recovered from the vicious pogrom that swept Spain in 1391. In the fifteenth century, Seville's commercial networks began to expand into the Atlantic, and a black African community developed in Seville and adjacent Triana, a mariners' quarter. Even before 1492, Seville had become Iberia's largest city (with close to one hundred thousand people).

This view of Seville, painted by Francisco Pacheco in the sixteenth century, captures the prominence of the cathedral, the largest medieval Gothic structure in the world, incorporating the minaret (Giralda) of the medieval mosque. Around the cathedral are the cramped buildings of the medieval and early-modern city, including the old Jewish quarter. To the far right is the Torre de Oro, a military tower built by the city's Muslim rulers in the early thirteenth century. In the foreground is the Guadalquivir River, which gave Seville access to the Atlantic, and across the bridge is the old port town of Triana.

damages thanks to the Mesta. Founded under Alfonso X, the powerful sheep raisers' guild enjoyed extensive territorial privileges and legal protection in exchange for providing the crown with tax revenues from wool exports, which were the biggest in Europe. The Mesta's flocks had grown to more than 3 million head of sheep by the time Isabella and Ferdinand married in 1469, a major environmental stress on Spain's already dry and rocky landscape.

Iberian peasants felt the brunt of the crisis that gripped the peninsula in the fourteenth and early fifteenth centuries. The Little Ice Age of shorter, wetter summers and colder winters compounded the problems created by endemic warfare, over-taxation, inflation, plague, unrest, and revolt. The Iberian population was smaller in 1492 than it had been in 1300, with declines most dramatic in the north. A quarter of northern Castile's villages became deserted. Catalonia's population was halved. Attempts to destroy Iberia's long tradition of peasant freedom, and to impose the kind of feudalism that tied men and women to lordly lands elsewhere in Europe, were successful in parts of Aragon – but only until peasant resistance ended the abuse in 1486. One of Ferdinand and Isabella's achievements was to curb the violence of local lords – the wolfish noblemen whom the poet Iñigo de Mendoza famously contrasted with "lamb-like" peasants.

Iberian artisans and professionals, who made up about 10 percent of the population, were somewhat better off than the peasant majority. Medieval port cities such as Barcelona, Valencia, Porto, and San Sebastian boasted numerous craft guilds, each with its own rules and privileges. Guilds could figure large in urban politics, especially when facing down a predatory monarch. On a day-to-day level, life in the city guaranteed steady work for artisans, physicians, and other professionals, and guild membership conferred a degree of status, usually reinforced by sponsorship of religious confraternities and charitable causes. Traditionally, craft shops both staffed and reproduced themselves by training apprentices and journeymen, but as some Iberian master craftsmen grew wealthy in late medieval times, it became possible to purchase slaves.

The expansion of the African slave trade in the fifteenth century meant that Iberian city dwellers, particularly in the south, became part of an increasingly multiracial society. Even as Jews and Muslims were being targeted for persecution and exile, and religious homogeneity was being imposed by force, the age-old Iberian practice of enslaving "infidels" was taking on a new dimension. Beginning in 1441, Portuguese explorers and merchants brought home black captives from West Africa – more than thirty-five thousand of them by 1492. At the same time, enslaved Africans and their descendants, all of them more or less forcibly converted to Roman Catholicism, became a modest but highly visible presence in numerous Castilian cities. Valencia was among the first to boast a thriving slave market and a sizeable black population. A new die was cast, and most Iberians who traveled to the Americas carried with them this pair of important ideas: (1) that a proper household was made complete only by the presence of male and female African slaves, and (2) a prosperous city required an enslaved black underclass working as artisans, mule drovers, porters, and so on. Even women housed in convents were routinely served by enslaved African women and girls.

* * *

Africans were increasingly crucial to life in late-medieval Portugal and Spain, particularly in the vibrant commercial cities of the south, and their growing presence and capital value helped spur further expansion into the Atlantic. Urban slavery overlapped with early plantation slavery in the East Atlantic islands and dovetailed precisely with the Iberian discovery of the Americas. But before exploring that sequence of events, we turn to Africa's Atlantic shores, and to the question of how West and West Central Africans came to inhabit the Iberian Peninsula in the first place.

SUGGESTIONS FOR FURTHER READING

Among the many textbooks on Spain and Portugal, one of the best is *Spain: A History*, edited by Raymond Carr (2000). Blackwell also publishes a series on Spain, including Teofilo F. Ruiz's excellent *Spain's Centuries of Crisis, 1300–1474* (2007) and *The Spain of the Catholic Monarchs, 1474–1520*, by John Edwards (2001). A recommended collection of translated primary sources is *Medieval Iberia: Readings from Christian, Muslim, and Jewish Sources*, edited by Olivia Remie Constable (1997).

With respect to Portugal, a dated but engagingly written classic is C. R. Boxer, *The Portuguese Seaborne Empire, 1415–1825* (1969); a more up-to-date survey is A. J. R. Russell-Wood, *The Portuguese Empire, 1415–1808: A World on the Move* (1998), and still more up to date and thorough is Anthony Disney's two-volume *History of the Portuguese Empire* (2009).

GLOSSARY

El Cid [el SID]: Castilian hero of the Reconquista celebrated in epic poetry

Reconquista [reh-kon-KEY-stah]: the Reconquest; the sporadic conflicts between Christian and Muslim kingdoms in Iberia, 711–1492

Convivencia [kon-vee-VEN-see-ah]: religious tolerance or the peaceful coexistence of Christians, Muslims, and Jews in medieval Iberia

La Mesta [la MESS-tah]: the Castilian sheep farmers' guild

Little Ice Age: A period of cooler and unpredictable weather that had a negative impact on Europe from the fourteenth to nineteenth centuries

3

TIMELINE

7th century: Islam begins its spread into sub-Saharan Africa

650–1600: era of trans-Saharan slave trade

1100–1500: West Africa's late-medieval dry period; rise of Mali and Songhai empires

1441–1870: era of transatlantic slave trade

1480s: Portuguese establish major trading posts along the West African coast

1506–1543: reign of Afonso I, the first Kongo king to convert to Catholicism

1571 on: increased Portuguese military presence and support of pro-Portuguese regimes in West Central African kingdoms

1591: Moroccan forces capture Songhai cities of Gao and Timbuktu

Atlantic Africa

Thieves and people of bad conscience [are selling my subjects as slaves] to obtain the coveted things and trade goods of that kingdom [Portugal].
(Kongo King Afonso I to Portuguese King João III, 1526)

THANKS IN PART to the Malian king Mansa Musa, sub-Saharan Africa was famous among late-medieval Europeans not for its slaves but for its gold. On his way home from a pilgrimage to Mecca in 1325, Mansa Musa spent so much of the yellow metal in Cairo that he caused its price to fall, thereby disrupting money markets throughout the Mediterranean. About a century later, as Europe and the Mediterranean were experiencing a commercial revival, African gold traded from the other side of the Sahara was in higher demand than ever. Historians refer to a bullion famine afflicting Eurasian and North African trade in the period leading up to Columbus's famous voyage, offset only partly by a revival of silver mining in Central Europe. Gold is what drew the first maritime explorers to Atlantic Africa from Portugal, but when gold was not available, war captives – also traded across the Sahara over the previous centuries – often were. It would take two centuries, but with the rise of Atlantic plantation agriculture, first off the coast of Africa and then in the Americas, the trade in African slaves slowly eclipsed the trade in African gold.

Before delving into the sad history of the Atlantic slave trade – and the related topic of African experiences in, and contributions to, colonial Latin American societies – it is necessary to explore key aspects of the western, or "Atlantic," African past. Neither the slave trade nor the many stories of African survival and cultural regeneration in the Americas can be understood without some sense of contemporary African modes of thought and strategies for living, as well as the numerous and dynamic historical processes under way throughout the continent.

As we will see in later chapters, slavery was in many ways at the heart of Iberia's colonial enterprise in the Americas, especially in the plantation zones and gold mines of Brazil and the Caribbean basin, and before it all ended around 1850, more enslaved Africans had been taken to Latin America than any other destination. Driven mostly by desire for commercial profit among its traders, the slave system would generate great tragedies and small triumphs. Africans in both Iberia and the Americas did not sit idly by, nor did they suffer humiliation and hard work in silence. Some rebelled violently, and many ran away. The vast majority of enslaved Africans, however, adapted to life in Iberia and its overseas colonies, and a considerable number found the means to purchase their children's freedom, if not their own. Atlantic Africa was itself deeply altered by the ever-growing slave trade. In the end, slavers of various ethnicities and national origins drained Africa of millions of people, exploited regional political feuds, sponsored violent raids extending deep into the interior, and in return gave almost nothing of lasting value to the continent's remaining inhabitants. It would be safe to say that Latin America's gain was Africa's loss.

Many Africas

Historians estimate that Africa in the age of Columbus was home to nearly 100 million people, about half of whom inhabited sub-Saharan West and West Central Africa, the primary regions from which slaves were be taken to Europe and the Americas. What we are here calling Atlantic Africa thus had a population similar to that of all the Americas taken together. African ways of life varied drastically from place to place, but as among Native Americans and Iberians, there were some commonalities. Perhaps most important, malaria and the tsetse fly that limited livestock raising were endemic throughout tropical Africa. As a result, most sub-Saharan Africans possessed a degree of acquired immunity to malaria, and because livestock could not survive to pull a plow, iron was used to make hand tools: hoes, axes, and machetes. Most Atlantic Africans lived as hoe farmers – village-dwelling growers of rice, millet, and sorghum. After contact with the Americas, many African farmers added maize, peanuts, and manioc to their repertoire of staple crops.

Sub-Saharan Africans lived primarily in chiefdoms in early-modern times, but others were subject to several dozen kingdoms and at least one large empire. Songhai, on the middle Niger River, was on the rise by the time of Columbus, and several city-states grew quite large near that river's mouth in what is today Nigeria. Still, Africa at that time had no tributary empires on the scale of the Aztecs or Incas, with their millions of subjects. Most common in western Africa were settled agricultural chiefdoms linked to one another and to the outside world by traveling merchants. Beyond the zone of the tsetse fly lived groups of pastoralists, and scattered bands of hunter-foragers inhabited

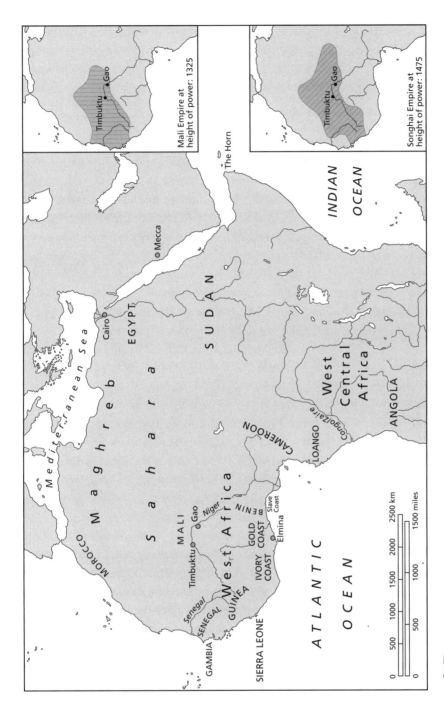

Map 3.1
Atlantic Africa in 1492

rain forests and deserts. Yet most western Africans, including nearly all those caught up in the transatlantic slave trade, were village farmers.

Islam was dominant in Africa's northern savannas and along the Indian Ocean down to Mozambique, but the vast majority of sub-Saharan Africans were not Muslims. Most commonly worshipped were local deities linked to fertility and martial prowess. Shrines similar to Andean *huacas* were also widespread, even in Islamic regions of upper West Africa. Before European arrival on the Atlantic seaboard, Christians and Jews were limited to tiny pockets in the northeastern Horn and Maghreb, or Mediterranean coast. More than two thousand languages were spoken in Africa, the majority derived from four major roots (Afro-Asiatic, Nilo-Saharan, Khoisan, and Niger-Congo; almost all Africans brought to the Americas spoke a Niger-Congo language). All told, Africa's cultural and linguistic diversity was comparable to that of native America in the era of Columbus – perhaps even exceeding it.

In the more Islamic, arid north, camels, donkeys, and horses served as beasts of burden. Some herders kept cattle in highland areas and in the far south, out of reach of the tsetse fly. West African kings and chiefs prized Arabian, or Barbary, warhorses, and a trade in them thrived south of the Sahara in this period. Other herders and households kept goats, swine, guinea fowl, sheep, and dogs. In general, domestic animals were far more common in precolonial Africa than in the Americas, and many enslaved Africans would later be put in charge of managing herds of livestock as cowboys and overseers.

Mining and metalworking were also widespread in Africa. Copper and copper-alloy metallurgy were quite sophisticated by 1500, at or above the level of the contemporary Andes. Gold working was also advanced, but gold was increasingly drawn away into commercial trade networks extending to the Mediterranean Sea and Indian Ocean. As we have seen, in West Africa it was gold, taken from ancient alluvial deposits near the headwaters of the Senegal, Gambia, Niger, and Volta rivers, that put the sub-Saharan region on the minds of European and Middle Eastern traders and monarchs. West Africa's mines were worked by agricultural peoples in the off-season, limiting somewhat the supply of gold available for trade.

Farther south, in West Central Africa, called by some historians the "land of the blacksmith kings," human relations were partly defined by long-term control of copper and iron deposits. As in West Africa, however, most people were engaged in subsistence agriculture rather than specialized metallurgy. Some grew yams and bananas in addition to sorghum and millet. Few people other than hunter-foragers, like the famous Pygmies, inhabited the most prominent geographical feature of the region, Africa's great equatorial, or Congo, rain forest. Most preferred instead to farm the surrounding savanna and to fish along the Atlantic coast and interior riverbanks.

Where Africans differed most from native Americans was in their use of iron. Whether in Mali or Angola (a name derived from *ngola*, or "smith"), African ironmongers were not only artisans but also priestly figures and often regional headmen. Rather like alchemy in the Eurasian tradition, forging metals in sub-Saharan Africa was a secretive and mystical business. Secretive or not, African smiths produced extraordinary quantities of tools, weapons, and artworks. Thus, it is no surprise that many enslaved African men took up the jobs of blacksmith, goldsmith, and even royal mint worker in the Americas. Many others, including a considerable number of African women, would work in the tropical Americas as miners.

African traders, usually organized into ethnic groups or clans, traversed vast distances to redistribute metal goods, textiles, and even basic commodities. Salt, mined in the Sahara or gathered along the seacoast, was widely traded. Manufactured goods like agricultural tools were generally exchanged for food, textiles, and livestock, but bits of gold, copper, and iron also served on occasion as currency. The cowry shell, rather like the cacao bean in Mesoamerica, also became a kind of money and was later imported in huge amounts by Europeans from the Maldive Islands off the coast of India. To some degree, Atlantic Africa's demand for shell and copper currency helped fuel the transatlantic slave trade.

Commercial ties between African chiefdoms and kingdoms sometimes fostered political alliances and at other times prompted raids and conquest wars. Droughts, pests, and other ecological stresses spurred some groups, especially vulnerable farmers, to join defensive confederations, whereas others united to raid for slaves, livestock, and other forms of portable wealth to trade away. Before the arrival of Europeans along the Atlantic coast, African traders routinely moved captives north across the Sahara to Mediterranean ports and east to the Swahili Coast to be sent to the Arabian Peninsula and across the Indian Ocean. Slavery and slave trading were thus well-established African customs. What changed with the arrival of Europeans was the slave trade's volume and scope. After a slow takeoff, both expanded exponentially.

Empire in West and West Central Africa

During what African historians call the late-medieval dry period (c. 1100–1500), dozens of West African kings established extensive tributary regimes, or paramount chiefdoms. Some kings relied on slave labor for export agriculture and gold mining, but similar to most of the precontact Americas, few of West Africa's petty kingdoms sustained a permanent class of bureaucrats, judges, scribes, and lawyers. This was true only of the empires of Ghana and the middle Niger River, which rose and fell in succession. A more common means of extending authority was by offering to protect vulnerable segmented or concentrated agricultural groups from semisedentary or nonsedentary raiders.

Sedentary imperial peoples also raided during the dry period, and when mounted on horses or camels, little could be done to stop them. The conquering kingdoms of Mali and Songhai rose along the shores of the middle and upper Niger River, both tied to the Mediterranean and Arab worlds by the caravan depot of Timbuktu. These empires were built by devout Muslim leaders drawn from local lineages, including the famous Mansa Musa (*mansa* means "conqueror") of Mali, whose story opened this chapter (also see In Focus 3.1).

IN FOCUS 3.1

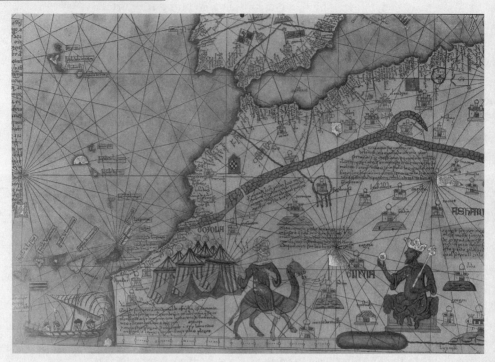

Figure 3.1. Credit: Detail from the Catalan Atlas, 1375 (vellum) by Abraham Cresques (1325-87) Bibliotheque Nationale, Paris, France/ The Bridgeman Art Library [Image # XZL 151844]

EPIC SCENES FROM AN AFRICAN EMPIRE

In the 1375 Catalan map shown here, an Arab merchant on a camel rides to meet Mansa Musa, emperor of Mali, who holds out a huge gold nugget, as if inviting traders to come and barter in his legendary capital city. Mali's emperors, such as Musa and Sunjata, received visitors on thrones such as the one pictured in the map – but beneath an arch of elephant tusks, surrounded by a vast retinue that included the official spokesman, executioner, cavalry officers, musicians, and women of the court.

Although Mali's rulers had converted to Islam in the eleventh century, by Mansa Musa's day, women were no longer veiled. Arab visitors were shocked by this and surprised by the prominent role of high-ranking women in Malian politics and society. This is also illustrated in the great epic Malian tale, the Sunjata. In the scene quoted here, Sogolon, mother of the legendary emperor Sunjata, prepares for marriage to King Naré Maghan. Throughout the Sunjata, women, characterized as both good and evil, exert extraordinary influence over succession and other affairs of state. Sogolon, a hunchback called derisively "Buffalo Woman," manages not only to marry a handsome king but also to outwit any number of scheming rivals. In the end, it is she alone who ensures that her son, Sunjata, fulfills his destiny as supreme ruler of Mali. He would go on to conquer in her name.

The royal drums of Nianiba announced the festivity at the crack of dawn. The town awoke to the sound of tam-tams that answered each other from one district to another; from the midst of the crowds arose the voices of griots singing the praises of Naré Maghan.

At the home of the king's old aunt, the hairdresser of Nianiba was plaiting Sogolon Kedjou's hair. As she lay on her mat, her head resting on the hairdresser's legs, she wept softly while the king's sisters came to chaff her, as was the custom.

"This is your last day of freedom; from now onwards you will be our woman."

"Say farewell to your youth," added another.

"You won't dance in the square any more and have yourself admired by the boys," added a third.

Sogolon never uttered a word, and from time to time, the old hairdresser said, "There, there, stop crying. It's a new life beginning, you know, more beautiful than you think. You will be a mother and you will know the joy of being a queen surrounded by your children. Come now, daughter, don't listen to the gibes of your sisters-in-law." In front of the house, the poetess who belonged to the king's sisters chanted the name of the young bride.

Just as Iberians were opening up the Atlantic, the Songhai Empire, centered at Gao (east of Timbuktu), expanded rapidly under Sonni Ali (1464–1492). Like the *mansas* of Mali, Sonni Ali embraced the role of conqueror, deploying great fleets of boatmen on the Niger River to complement his thousands of mounted warriors on land. By the time of Sonni Ali's death in 1492, Songhai encompassed a great swath of Sudanic West Africa, limited more by distance than resistance.

After Sonni Ali and his successor Mohammad Touré, Songhai's power diminished. Even so, the empire's defenders were much surprised when mounted attackers arrived from Morocco. Fresh from their defeat of the Portuguese king, Sebastian, at the 1578 battle of al-Qasr al-Kabir, the Moroccans under Sultan Mawlay Ahmad rode south across the Sahara. The key cities of Gao and Timbuktu were in their hands by 1591. The Moroccan conquistadors, including many exiled Andalusian Morisco musketeers, carried off slaves and considerable gold, but ultimately they could not keep hold of their distant colony. It seems the Sahara proved a mightier barrier to long-distance colonialism than any ocean.

Meanwhile, far to the south, in West Central Africa, warlords called *manikongos* forged a small kingdom that the Portuguese named Kongo, after its rulers. The *manikongos*, comparable in title to Andean *sinchis*, came to power in part by controlling copper deposits. By the late fifteenth century, Kongo commanded a large hinterland stretching south and east from the Zaire River, absorbing numerous villages, slaves, and tributaries along the way. Only a few independent kingdoms held out to the north and east. Eventually, their inhabitants, along with the Mbundu peoples of the Kwanza Valley to the south, challenged Kongo directly, partly in response to a Portuguese-inspired rise in slave raiding.

From an early date, Portuguese influence in West Central Africa was of major concern. Unlike Atlantic West Africa (sometimes referred to generically at that time as "Guinea"), which remained largely impenetrable to Europeans until the late nineteenth century, much of West Central Africa was deeply transformed by centuries of sustained and increasingly invasive Portuguese activity. This pattern was extended to Southeast Africa, as well, where the Portuguese took hold of Mozambique. Before long, there emerged in both regions a mixed, Afro-Portuguese elite capable of playing the roles of colonial intermediary and slave-raider proxy. Many such traders acquired the disease immunities that Europeans sorely lacked. For "whites," sub-Saharan Africa remained a malarial graveyard prior to the discovery of Andean quinine.

Beginning at the mouth of the Zaire River in the 1480s, the Portuguese gained a foothold in the region by blending trade, missionary outreach, and military alliances with local paramount chiefs and kings. Success was so quick that by 1491 most Kongo aristocrats were baptized Roman Catholics. The converts included Nzinga Mbemba, who ruled as King Afonso I (1506–1543). Afonso did more than convert: he learned to read; studied theology; and renamed Mbanza, the capital city, as São Salvador ("Holy Savior"). One of the king's sons was ordained as a priest in Lisbon and after consecration in Rome he returned to his homeland in Kongo. Despite what seemed like mutual political and spiritual gains, Kongo's alliance with the Portuguese soon foundered in the face of commercial realities. When Afonso complained to the king of Portugal in 1526 that "thieves and people of bad conscience" were selling his subjects, he noted that even Kongo nobility were being sold into slavery for "the coveted things and trade goods" of Portugal.

The Portuguese turned a blind eye to such abuses, as they benefited from them, but they showed a consistent and often violent commitment to sustaining Kongo as a political ally, ruled by a Christian king, and as a close partner in the larger slave trade. A parallel plan was to carve out a permanent colony in Angola, to the south of Kongo. Beginning in 1575 on the island of Luanda, just north of the Kwanza River mouth, the new Portuguese enclave soon became one of the busiest and longest-lasting entrepots for the transatlantic slave trade. Another similar post was established farther south along the coast at Benguela in 1617.

Centered on Kongo and Angola, West Central Africa would supply some 5 million slaves, or nearly half of all recorded slaves (about 11 million) sent to the Americas between the early sixteenth and mid-nineteenth centuries. These slaves, whom the Portuguese called *peças*, or "pieces," were nearly all peasants, poor farmers struggling to survive in a region prone to war and drought. Sometimes, as in the case of Kongo, they were renowned warriors or nobles. At least two-thirds of the captives were men, but another 3 million or more were women and children.

Before long, the Portuguese established a firm presence in Angola, which enabled them to procure slaves more easily from deep in the interior and also to house them in barracks in preparation for the Middle Passage across

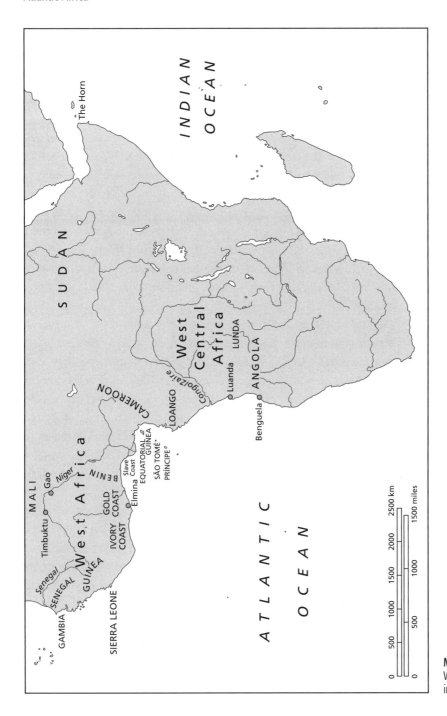

Map 3.2
West Central Africa
in 1492

the Atlantic. While being held on the coast, West Central Africans were baptized by Jesuits and other priests as Catholics, given new Christian names, and exposed to the Portuguese language. Most captives spoke Kikongo or Kimbundu, however, which could be understood despite wide differences in ethnicity and culture. Despite their differences, enslaved Africans who embarked from Angola or Kongo shared more cultural characteristics than groups from Upper Guinea or Senegambia.

Slavery and the Trade in Captives

We have just seen how the Portuguese involvement in African slavery dramatically affected the trade in human beings and profoundly altered West Central African history. In this final section of the chapter, we look in more detail at this institution throughout Atlantic Africa.

Although its scope and volume grew tremendously as a result of the transatlantic trade, the concept of chattel slavery was ancient in Africa. Like virtually all so-called traditional societies, including most native groups of the Americas, the chiefdoms and kingdoms of Africa made routine use of the labor of war captives and their descendants. Some surplus slaves were traded over long distances for commodities, such as salt or iron tools; others were retained to augment the households of paramount chiefs. Throughout Atlantic Africa, whole colonies of enslaved peoples were made to produce foodstuffs for the benefit of their owners, and also to mine gold, iron ore, and copper.

When Portuguese traders arrived along the Atlantic coast of Africa in the fifteenth century, they encountered mostly societies with slaves, and perhaps a few slave societies (a distinction historians make between cultures with slaves as household auxiliaries versus those that relied almost entirely on large-scale slavery for income). At first, the European newcomers raided coastal villages, Reconquista style, kidnapping a number of unsuspecting individuals. But the Portuguese, like the camel-caravan traders of the Sahara, soon shifted to an easier, safer, and more profitable strategy – exchanging foreign commodities for captives. Also like the caravan traders, the Europeans wanted gold more than slaves. Significantly, in the first two centuries after contact (roughly 1450–1650), the value of gold exported from West Africa exceeded the value of slaves. (West Central Africa did not produce gold at this time, although Mozambique, on the Indian Ocean side, did.)

In terms of origins, the seaborne trade in sub-Saharan African peoples began definitively when the Portuguese, spurred by Prince Henry, rounded Cape Blanco in 1441. By 1444, they had reached the mouth of the Senegal River, and by 1455, the mouth of the larger Gambia. On the Senegal, the Portuguese traded horses for captives with representatives of the Muslim Wolof kingdoms. On the wider Gambia, they sailed far inland, trading for gold and slaves with the outlying Djula traders of Mali. The warring Mandinka states of the region soon provided yet more captives.

The high demand for gold, rather than captives, prompted further reconnaissance. In 1471, Portuguese navigators reached what they called the Gold Coast, in present-day Ghana, and in 1482 they established a *feitoria*, or fortified trading post, called São Jorge da Mina. "St. George's Mine" was Portugal's major West African gold and slaving fort for more than a century afterwards. Columbus was an early visitor. In the seventeenth century, Elmina (as it was

STATISTICAL SHOCK: NUMBERS FROM THE SLAVE TRADE

The drawing here depicts captured West Africans, yoked in pairs, being transported to be sold as slaves. As the drawing shows, whole families were often sold into slavery. Note also that the overseer is himself a West African, for it was primarily Africans, not Europeans, who made the initial captures; Europeans then purchased slaves on Africa's Atlantic coast or in the Mediterranean. As the table here shows, from the seventh to fifteenth centuries, slaves were transported across the Sahara to Europe and the Middle East. Although that trade continued for a couple of centuries, it was dwarfed after 1450 by the new transatlantic trade.

Estimated number of slaves in millions	Transported from West and West Central Africa to . . .	Via	In the period
4	Europe and the Middle East	Sahara	c. 650–1450
1	Europe and the Middle East	Sahara	1450–1600
(5 million subtotal)			
0.3	Europe	Atlantic	1451–1870
0.5	British North America	Atlantic	1492–1870
1.7	Spanish America	Atlantic	1492–1870
4.7	Caribbean	Atlantic	1492–1870
4.2	Brazil	Atlantic	1492–1870
(11.4 million subtotal)			
(16.4 million total)			

Figure 3.2. Slave Trade, 19th Century. African captives yoked in pairs and force-marched by slave traders from the interior to the slave markets on the coast. Wood engraving, 19th century. (Image ID: 0009386.) Credit: The Granger Collection, New York

popularly known) fell, like Luanda, to the Dutch. Fierce competition from the French, English, and other Europeans soon followed.

As the market for slaves in the Americas grew, particularly after 1600, new "trading factories" were built along West Africa's Guinea coast. Mande and Mane peoples began invading parts of modern Guinea, Liberia, Sierra Leone, and Ivory Coast in the fifteenth and sixteenth centuries, yielding a nearly constant supply of captives for trade to outsiders through the seventeenth century. Subsequent developments in the interior, including an early-eighteenth-century Muslim expansion, periodically fed coastal ports like Conakry with still more slaves.

Much earlier, in the 1480s, Portuguese reconnaissance in the eastern Gulf of Guinea led to contacts with Benin and settlement of offshore islands like Príncipe and São Tomé, near present-day Gabon. Captives from Benin were initially sold to Akan traders at Elmina, but others were soon forced to grow sugar on the equatorial islands. Still more captives were brought to São Tomé's plantations from Kongo. It appears that the slave-based sugar plantation developed later in Brazil, and ultimately replicated throughout the Caribbean and lowland South America, had its beginnings here off the coast of Central Africa.

*   *   *

African societies in the regions most affected by the transatlantic slave trade were complex, varied, and dynamic when the Portuguese arrived in the fifteenth century, and they would continue to be so. Advanced gun-making and shipbuilding technologies gave Europeans some initial advantages over West and West Central African trading partners, but long-term African adaptation to tropical disease regimes and access to distant sources of gold generally offset them. European interlopers were thus literally held at bay throughout the period in virtually every part of Atlantic Africa. Meanwhile, local metallurgy, like statecraft, was on a par with or more developed than that practiced in the most densely settled parts of the Americas. These African skills were likely taken across the Atlantic along with belief systems, languages, musical styles, and many other traits, all to be rearranged, blended, and even reinvented in the "new world" of the Americas.

Why, we might ask, were so many Africans ultimately sent along this transatlantic "way of death" by fellow Africans? Like the puzzle of the "quick and easy" Spanish conquest of the great civilizations of the Americas, the answer may be in part quite simple when viewed from a more local, early-modern perspective. Just as before the arrival of the Spanish in the Western Hemisphere the category of "Indians" had no local meaning (nor did it in India, incidentally), before the arrival of the Portuguese there was no such category in Africa as "Africans," much less "blacks." These racial identities made no sense among ethnically, religiously, and politically diverse peoples engaged in their own internal and regional endeavors, peaceful and otherwise. Racism would prove useful only to those who stood to benefit, politically or materially, from European overseas expansion.

SUGGESTIONS FOR FURTHER READING

Two recommended books are George E. Brooks, *Landlords and Strangers: Ecology, Society, and Trade in Western Africa, 1000–1630* (1993) and Linda M. Heywood, ed., *Central Africans and Cultural Transformations in the*

American Diaspora (2002). A fine overall text is Robert O. Collins and James M. Burns, *A History of Sub-Saharan Africa* (2007).

On slavery in Africa, among the most scholarly but also most accessible publications are Paul Lovejoy, *Transformations in Slavery: A History of Slavery in Africa*, 2d ed. (2000); Patrick Manning, *Slavery and African Life: Occidental, Oriental, and African Slave Trades* (1990); and John Thornton, *Africa and Africans in the Making of the Atlantic World, 1400–1680*, 2d ed. (1999).

Two classic older works on aspects of West African history are Joseph Miller, *Kings and Kinsmen: Early Mbundu States in Angola* (1976), and Walter Rodney, *A History of the Upper Guinea Coast, 1545 to 1800* (1970).

GLOSSARY

Hoe agriculturalists: farmers dependent on metal-tipped hoes for tilling the soil

Afro-Asiatic, Nilo-Saharan, Khoisan, and **Niger-Congo:** Africa's four language families

Mansa Musa [MAN-sah MOO-sah]: emperor of Mali, made famous pilgrimage to Mecca in 1325

Morisco [moh-REES-coh]: descendants of conquered Muslims of southern Spain, most of whom were exiled to North Africa

Sunjata [soon-JAH-tah]: great epic tale from the Mali Empire passed down to the twentieth century by poets called griots

Griots [GREE-ohs]: the caste of professional oral historians in the Mali Empire

Gao [GOW] and **Timbuktu** [tim-buck-TOO]: major cities of the Mali and Songhai empires

Manikongo [mah-nee-KONG-go]: warlord and ruler in the Kongo kingdom

Peças [PEH-sahs]: Portuguese term for slaves, literally "pieces" or "units"

Feitoria [fay-tow-REE-ah]: Portuguese fortified trading post or "factory"

Elmina [el-MEE-nah]: Portuguese slaving fort on the coast of Ghana

Benin [be-NEEN]: major West African city-states in the era of the transatlantic slave trade

■ ■ ■ ■ ■ ■ ■ ■ ■ ■ ■ ■ ■ ■ ■ ■ ■ ■ ■ ■

THE LONG CONQUEST

The fascinating, varied, and often tragic dimensions of the great encounter among Iberians, Western Africans, and Native Americans is the focus of the five chapters in Part Two. Much of our discussion is about the Spanish Conquest in the sixteenth century, but these are not simply chapters about conquest in the traditional sense. For example, there are also native conquests in these pages – from the Aztec and Inca empires that flourished in the fifteenth century to the campaigns carried out by native forces under Spanish colonial auspices. Iberians neither conquered alone nor arrived alone; they brought African slaves and Old World diseases. Furthermore, the Iberian conquest of the Americas was a protracted affair that lasted for centuries – as reflected in the title of this part. Part Two thus focuses mostly on the 1490s to the 1570s, giving some attention, where relevant, to earlier and later decades.

The first stage of Iberian exploration, conquest, and colonization in the Americas was concentrated in the Caribbean islands in the three decades that followed Columbus's first voyage across the Atlantic Ocean. This story – from its Portuguese origins to the collapse of the native population on the islands – is the subject of Chapter 4 ("The Iberian Imperial Dawn"). We then return to the American mainland for Chapter 5, "Native American Empires," to examine the Aztecs (Mexica) and Incas. While Spaniards were conducting Caribbean conquests, these two great indigenous empires were themselves expanding through conquest – setting the scene for the clash of empires that is the subject of Chapter 6 ("The Chain of Conquest").

African slaves – and their free and mixed-race descendants in the Americas – quickly became an important and integral part of the story of conquest. Such roles are placed in the context of our presentation of the conquest in Chapter 6, which includes a narration of major events, a discussion of conquistador identities, and a brief exploration of conquest explanations. The final chapter here ("The Incomplete Conquest") elaborates our emphasis in Part Two on a multifaceted, prolonged, and complex conquest of the Americas by Iberians – one that was determined as much by negotiation as it was by brute force. These negotiations, and the communities they produced in the middle decades of the colonial period, are then the focus of Part Three.

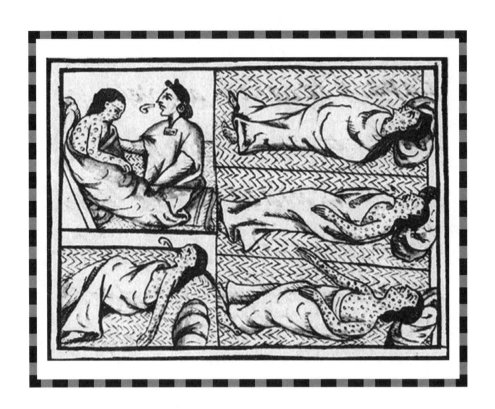

4

The Iberian Imperial Dawn

Make me the governor of some island, with, if possible, a little bit of sky above it.

(Sancho Panza to Don Quixote)

IN 1487, A FLEMISH NAVIGATOR named Ferdinand van Olmen sailed from Portugal, under license from the king, on a mission to cross the "Ocean Sea," as the Atlantic was then called, and reach the Spice Islands of East Asia. He stopped in the Azores, but thereafter his two ships disappeared over the horizon and were never heard from again.

Had better luck befallen the Fleming, there might today be a nation, even a continent, named Olmenia. But that luck fell instead, five years later, to Christopher Columbus. He set off from Spain, via the Canaries, likewise in search of a direct sea route to Asia. He survived the ocean crossing but did not attain his goal; it was Portuguese navigators, not Columbus, who discovered the Asia route a few years later, by sailing around Africa and across the Indian Ocean. However, Columbus was keen to convince Queen Isabella of Castile, the main sponsor of his voyage, that the islands he had found in the Caribbean were not only a short distance from the Asian mainland but also were themselves valuable territories to be settled. "I found numerous islands," he told the queen, islands brimming with animals and plants and "inhabited by numerous people," who were "submissive" and "trustworthy." The queen was sufficiently convinced to sponsor a far-larger second voyage, an expedition of fifteen hundred men whose purpose was to establish a colony. A few years later, when Portugal's second great expedition to India was blown off course, Pedro Álvares Cabral laid claim to Brazil, which he initially thought to be an island. Thus began a process of transatlantic expansion that would profoundly affect the "numerous people" of the Americas and result in a permanent, Catholic Iberian presence in the Western Hemisphere.

TIMELINE

1420s on: Portuguese explore and settle Madeiras, the Azores, and other Atlantic islands, and establish trading posts on the West African coast

1487: Portuguese (led by Bartolomeu Dias) round the Cape of Good Hope at the foot of Africa

1492: Columbus crosses the Atlantic; Granada, the last Muslim kingdom in Iberia, is conquered; Jews are expelled from Spain; Spain consolidates its control over the Canary Islands

1493–1498: first European settlement in the Caribbean, La Isabella, on Hispaniola

1498: Portuguese (led by Vasco da Gama) reach India, via the Cape of Good Hope

1500: Portuguese officially announce their discovery of Brazil

As we saw in Chapter 2, the Iberian kingdoms of Castile and Portugal underwent gradual but profound changes in the course of the fifteenth century, swelling to encompass a wider Atlantic world that included Africa's western shores. This chapter picks up that story in the year 1492 and explores the crucial decade of the 1490s on both sides of the Atlantic. Because Columbus made all four of his transatlantic voyages under license from the Spanish monarchs, we might expect him to have been Castilian or Aragonese. In fact, Columbus, or Cristofero Colombo, his real name, was a native of the Italian city-state of Genoa who spent his early years as a Lisbon-based navigator. In this chapter, we explain this Italian connection, as well as the crucial role of the Portuguese in the development of Atlantic exploration. As we will see, this is a tale with many protagonists – Genoese, Florentine, Castilian, Portuguese, Taino, and Tupi.

The Portuguese Initiative, the Creation of Spain, and the Opening of the Atlantic

Seeking to make a living as a navigator and cartographer, Columbus arrived in Lisbon in the 1470s, where he settled down with the daughter of a Portuguese Atlantic colonist. Why did Columbus choose to go to Lisbon? And why did it take him so long to win royal support for his Atlantic voyages, support that came eventually from Queen Isabella of Castile, not from the Portuguese crown?

Beginning in the early fifteenth century, Lisbon served as Europe's main springboard for Atlantic exploration. Portuguese navigators, some with crown sponsorship, explored and settled islands throughout the East Atlantic basin. Enterprising merchants, meanwhile, established *feitorias*, or fortified trading posts, all along Africa's west coast. The previously uninhabited Azores and Madeira islands were settled by Portuguese farmers as early as the 1420s. The peasant settlers of the cool Azores produced wheat for Portuguese consumption, whereas the warmer Madeiras yielded sugar for export to northern Europe – sugar produced not by Portuguese peasants but rather by enslaved Canary Islanders and West Africans working on plantations. Investment capital for Madeira's slaves and mills came from the cosmopolitan merchants of Lisbon, who profited handsomely when Madeiran sugar supplied the markets of London and other northern cities by 1450.

By the time Prince Henry the Navigator died in 1460, the Portuguese controlled the previously uninhabited Cape Verde Islands off West Africa and merchants had established forts in Senegambia to trade for gold and slaves. The Canary Islands, meanwhile, became the site of a special contest (see In Focus 4.1). By 1485, the Portuguese had passed the Equator to make

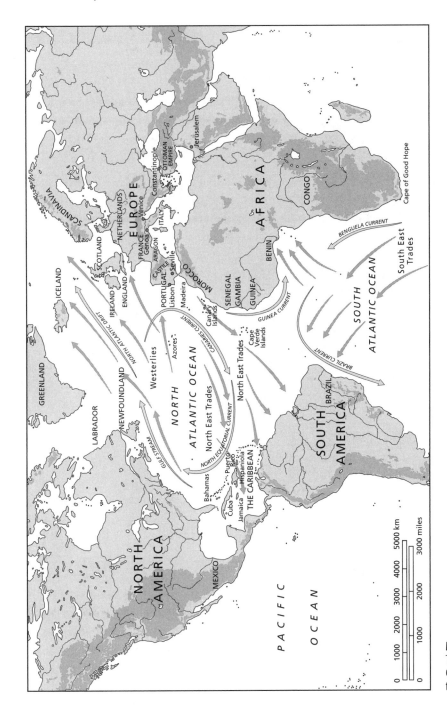

Map 4.1
The Wind and
Current System of
the Atlantic World

contact with the kings of Kongo, all the while searching for "lost Christians" such as the legendary Prester John and hoping to convert new ones. In 1487, the pope officially sanctioned Portuguese efforts in the Atlantic, laying the legal groundwork for Portugal's seaborne empire. Portuguese navigators rounded the Cape of Good Hope in the next year, opening the way to the long-sought sea route to the riches of Asia.

Figure 4.1. Credit: Eg 2709 fol.2 A ship crowded with armed men, from 'Le Canarien. A History of the Conquest of the Canary Islands', c.1420–1430 (vellum) by French School (15th century) British Library, London, UK/ © British Library Board. All Rights Reserved/ The Bridgeman Art Library [Image # BL 10432].

THE CONQUEST OF THE CANARY ISLANDS

Of the several volcanic island chains that dot the East Atlantic, only the Canaries, off the coast of Morocco, were inhabited when Iberians began to venture abroad. Europeans had known for many centuries that the islands existed, but they were not consistently visited by foreign sailors until the 1330s. Early visits by Catalan missionaries were interrupted by the Black Death in the late 1340s, but a French expedition under Jean de Béthencourt (shown in the illustration above) conquered the island of Lanzarote in 1402 for King Henry III of Castile. Béthencourt subdued a couple more islands and was proclaimed King of the Canaries (subordinate to Henry III). But the whole chain was by no means yet under Castilian control, and the Portuguese soon returned to the islands in search of slaves and gold.

The native Canarians were descendants of North Africans who had colonized the islands perhaps as early as Roman times. They had not been exposed to Islam, for example, a testament to their long isolation. Historians and archaeologists estimate a total Canarian population of about one hundred thousand when Europeans arrived, a population that subsisted on a mix of small-scale agriculture, fishing, and goat herding. The Canarians had no access to metal or horses, and they appear to have lacked the acquired immunity to many of the diseases carried by Africans and Eurasians.

The Portuguese were highly active all along Africa's East Atlantic coast in the fifteenth century, and they were the first Europeans to attempt conquest and settlement of all the islands. This course of action was a departure for the Portuguese, who tended to favor trading posts or uninhabited islands for settlement. The Portuguese campaign to conquer the Canarians was an expensive failure, and it was in the end the Spanish, mostly sponsored by the crown of Castile, who ended up in possession of the islands about the time of Columbus's first ventures in the Atlantic. The eastern islands fell first, and the larger western ones last, just a few years after Columbus's famous first voyage.

From the perspective of the conquered, the arrival of Europeans in the Canaries was a total disaster. The Canarians, never unified under one state or empire but rather organized under many chiefdoms, were initially baffled by Iberian aggression. Soon it became clear, however, that the invaders wished to plant sugarcane in the fertile volcanic soils of Gran Canaria and Tenerife, the two largest islands, and to force the Canarians to do the hard work of planting, harvesting, and processing cane for them. Resistance was stiff from the beginning, successfully defying the efforts of thousands of well-armed European men and their horses over the course of a century. Yet the Iberians had what might be called an unfair advantage: acquired immunity to smallpox, measles, and many other diseases. Once those took hold among the Canarians, there was no more holding out. In the 1490s, Tenerife and La Palma were fully subdued by Alonso Fernández de Lugo and the islands incorporated into the kingdom of Castile. Columbus set sail from the island of La Gomera in the fall of 1492, and the first Native Americans to greet him a little more than a month later would remind him of the Canarians.

How was it that tiny, rocky Portugal, with barely a million inhabitants in Henry the Navigator's day, took first place among Europe's overseas empires? To borrow the realtor's mantra: location, location, location. Partly because of their limited resources and handy coastline, the Portuguese had long looked outward. They were used to accumulating capital through trade rather than feudal rents, and the kingdom's economy was based not on internal-consumption products but rather on exports of wine, salt, and olive oil to northern Europe. Portuguese consumers in turn relied on imported wheat, textiles, metal goods, and other artisan products. Many more items passed through Lisbon as they were transshipped between the Mediterranean and north Atlantic, which gave rise to banking, insuring, and related financial service industries. As they ventured overseas, the Portuguese sought to compete with Italian and Flemish merchants who had long monopolized Europe's trade in high-value, exotic items such as spices, gems, gold, and sugar. As they pushed relentlessly into the Atlantic, the Portuguese also came to monopolize the growing trade in captive laborers taken from sub-Saharan Africa.

Portuguese expansion was not simply Portuguese. By the time Columbus reached Lisbon in the 1470s, the city was home to numerous Genoese,

Venetian, Florentine, Catalan, English, and Flemish merchant families, along with a host of cartographers, navigators, slave traders, and bankers' agents. One of these was Bartolomeo Marchionni, a figure far more illustrative of the developments of the time than Columbus, despite the fact that he is relatively unknown today. Marchionni came from his hometown of Florence to Lisbon in 1470 as *garzone* (junior agent) to the Cambini banking family. Within a decade he had gained a royal license to trade in slaves from Guinea and in spices, with a network of agents stretching from Florence to Seville, Lisbon to West Africa. For decades he bought slaves in Benin for use on his Madeira sugar plantations or to sell in Iberian and Italian cities. As Iberian interests expanded, so did Marchionni's merchant empire; he owned one of the ships that Vasco da Gama took to India in 1498 and one of the vessels on Cabral's larger expedition of 1500, which led to the official discovery of Brazil. His comment that Cabral had "discovered a new world" was one of the first uses of the phrase to refer to the newly "found" continents. If in the 1490s Marchionni was "the richest banker in Lisbon" and "in the best position to know all the secrets" of the Portuguese king (as one German traveler remarked), then his connections to the Spanish crown in the early years of the sixteenth century were almost as strong. The first royally licensed shipment of enslaved Africans destined for the "Spanish Indies," first claimed by Columbus, was sent by Bartolommeo Marchionni.

It was here in vibrant and competitive Lisbon that Columbus first sought royal sponsorship for his planned western voyage across the Atlantic to Asia. He failed due to a lack of social connections and a skewed sense of global geography. Columbus had married into a Madeira sugar family in 1478, but he lacked the connections at court needed to win the king's patronage. Without royal patronage, he risked gaining nothing even if his voyage proved successful. Columbus's heterodox geographical ideas were another hurdle. Portugal's kings employed the west's most knowledgeable cosmographers, and Columbus's claim that the world was relatively small and pear-shaped struck many as outlandish. An able navigator if not a born cosmographer, Columbus did not give up – displaying the strong will that later became central to his legend as a lone visionary surrounded by obscurantist doubters.

Columbus was fortunate in that Portugal's neighbors, the Castilians, shared his frustration at not being able to take full part in the great race into the Atlantic and beyond. Castile had laid claim to the Canary Islands – and as we have seen wrested them away from Portugal legally in the 1470s – but most of the fifteenth century was spent consolidating gains on the Iberian mainland. One could argue that Spain was born in 1479, when Ferdinand and Isabella took control of their kingdoms, effectively uniting Castile and Aragon. Or one could argue that Spain did not exist until the sixteenth century, when Castilians and other Spanish speakers began to refer to themselves primarily as Spaniards, or *españoles*. But a good argument can also be made for 1492 as the year in which four crucial events marked Spain's birth and its arrival on the European – indeed, the world – stage.

The first of these four events was the fall of the last Muslim kingdom of Granada, through whose gates Isabella rode in triumph on New Year's Day. The second was the consolidation of Castilian control over the Canary Islands in the 1490s, conquered and colonized along similar lines to Granada, and thus providing Castilians with an additional model and experience of imperial expansion to take to the Caribbean. The third event was the expulsion of the Jews, the climax of an anti-Semitism that had been building violently for a century and a religious intolerance that was rooted in the Reconquista and encouraged by the fall of Granada. The fourth event was Columbus's journey to Granada in April 1492 to seek another audience with Queen Isabella, the lucky timing of which led to royal sponsorship, the crossing of the Atlantic, and the discovery of the Caribbean islands – their discovery by a Genoese holding a Spanish license to explore and settle lands belonging to others.

Columbus and the Spanish Colonization of Hispaniola

On his second voyage, in 1493, Columbus founded the first European town in the Americas. He named it La Isabella, after his patron, the queen of Castile – and queen of Spain, as we can now begin to call her. The town lasted less than five years (see In Focus 4.2).

La Isabella's rapid rise and fall illustrates why the 1490s was both a beginning and a transition in the Iberian colonization of the Americas. Columbus arrived on Hispaniola in 1493 with fifteen hundred Spanish settlers packed, along with their livestock, clothing, and tools, into seventeen small ships. It appears at first glance that a Castilian model of land-based colonization was already under way, yet Columbus had something more Portuguese in mind: a trading post or *feitoria*. Anxious to establish trade with Asia, which he believed to be nearby, Columbus envisioned La Isabella as a royal trading settlement – in Spanish, a *factoría*. In lieu of Asian trade, the fort was to support itself through trade with Hispaniola's native Taino population. It would also serve as the capital of a hereditary governorship for Columbus's descendants and a base for further exploration.

La Isabella's failure has traditionally been blamed on Columbus and the supposed unsuitability of the site. But as the site's archaeologists have pointed out, "this first colony was, in fact, carefully and appropriately conceived, given the perceptions of America in 1493 and the experience of Spain in the late fifteenth century." The problem was that Columbus and the Spanish colonists who accompanied him did not understand that the Portuguese trading post model was unsuited to the indigenous economy of Hispaniola, the island on which all Spanish settlement focused in the first twenty years after contact. Whereas the Portuguese *feitoria* builders in West

Figure 4.2. a. Conjectural reconstruction of La Isabela, ca. 1494. Painting by Arthur Shilstone. Image#129537. © Arthur Shilstone / National Geographic Stock. **b.** Conjectural reconstruction of the Columbus house. Painting by Arthur Shilstone. Image#476539. ©Arthur Shilstone / National Geographic Stock.

THE "FIRST" HOUSE

Christopher Columbus "anchored in a large river port where there was an Indian village," wrote Bartolomé de las Casas in his *History of the Indies*, describing the first settlement made by Europeans in the Caribbean. Columbus "thanked God for the amenity of the land and rightly so, too, for the location is rich in stones, tiles, and good earth for the making of bricks, besides being very fertile and beautiful." That settlement was the town of La Isabella, on the island of Hispaniola. The site, and Columbus's residence, which was at the end of the town, looking out to sea, have both recently been excavated by the archaeologists Kathleen Deagan and José María Cruxent. These paintings reconstruct the town and the Columbus House as they would have appeared circa 1494. Today the site is one of the Dominican Republic's national parks.

Africa encountered local merchants already accustomed to exchanging gold, ivory, pepper, and captives for textiles, horses, ironware, and other goods, Columbus and his Spaniards were faced with indigenous peoples who practiced no such trade in luxury commodities or slaves. Hispaniola's semisedentary chiefdoms, with their wood and stone tools, were not at all like West Africa's sedentary, iron-producing kingdoms. Although they possessed some gold, the Tainos were local-minded subsistence farmers and fishing folk, not habitual consumers or producers of exports. The gap between native and settler expectations led to misunderstandings, then violence, then abandonment.

Spanish authorities seized upon Columbus's failure as a pretext to strip him of the ample rights and privileges he had won in his 1492 charter. In 1496, a new Spanish town, Santo Domingo, became Hispaniola's capital, and by 1500 Columbus was forcibly removed from the island. Although the "Admiral of the Ocean Sea" continued to sail for his Catholic Monarchs in search of Asia for a few more years, his governorship was gone. Columbus was replaced by the Spanish governor Nicolás de Ovando, who tried to rein in Hispaniola's unruly settlers who were forcing the Tainos to mine gold, feed them, and satisfy their sexual needs. Those without mines or access to indigenous workers rapidly fanned out to Puerto Rico, Jamaica, Cuba, and South America's north shore in search of new sources of mineral wealth and captives.

The model of colonization that prevailed was one the Castilians had recently followed in Granada and the Canary Islands. It consisted of two expectations: (1) Spanish invaders would settle and rule, with each province part of a new kingdom (making the Spanish Empire the sum of all its kingdoms; (2) the conquered local peoples would be converted to Christianity, allocated to work on the land or in the mines, and required to pay tribute (a basic head tax) to the Spanish crown. This essentially medieval European model for an American empire failed even more dramatically than La Isabella had, for the same reasons; it was not well suited to the region and its native peoples. The Taino produced no significant surpluses for tribute payment, did not use gold as currency, and had no experience with harsh labor regimes or religious persecution. These gaping cultural differences frustrated ambitious, wealth-seeking Spanish settlers to no end, leading them to violently enslave native peoples throughout the Caribbean in order to force them into a recognizably western economic system. Mass enslavement soon proved counterproductive.

The Portuguese groped their way toward a similar outcome in Brazil, though by a quite different path. Unlike the Spanish in the Caribbean, they did not immediately seek to colonize Brazil or conquer its Tupi-speaking coastal inhabitants. They had no illusions of being near Asia, and the Tupi had no gold or other obvious trade goods to offer. Worried by the arrival of

French interlopers as early as 1503, however, the Portuguese returned to reconnoiter their new American possession, and discovered that the Tupi were willing to trade tools and trinkets for a local dyewood (in Portuguese, *pau brasil*). Petty criminals were exiled from Portugal and dropped along the coast to establish trade relations with local tribes. Several of these unwilling colonists intermarried with the Tupi and founded lasting trade alliances. Tupi men, accustomed to clearing forest for women to plant manioc, were willing to cut and collect brazilwood in exchange for tools, and some also sought Portuguese aid in fighting hostile neighbors. It was only in the 1530s, when the French became a more serious nuisance, that Portugal's king launched his own "medieval" colonization scheme. Several of Brazil's early proprietary governors, or donatary captains, as they were called, soon took to enslaving native Brazilians to work on sugar plantations. The result was a social and demographic disaster that prompted the import of enslaved African replacements.

Questions of Numbers: Disease and Demographic Disaster

Bartolomé de las Casas, the most vocal Spanish defender of indigenous peoples in the era of contact and conquest, estimated that Hispaniola was home to between 1 million and 4 million Tainos when Columbus first reached the island in 1492 (see In Focus 4.3). Las Casas's lower figure is more or less accepted today, as is his second claim – that the Taino population dropped some 90 percent in his own lifetime (1484–1566). But what remains in doubt was the friar's assertion – made with resounding and polemic vigor in his 1552 book *The Devastation of the Indies* – that it was his fellow Spaniards' "egregious wickedness" that had caused this dramatic decline.

There is no doubt that Conquest violence, displacement, enslavement, overwork, and other brutal colonial impositions played a central role in devastating the Caribbean's native populations. What Las Casas ignored, however, was epidemic disease. What the friar and his fellow Spaniards did not understand was both the rapid and cumulative effects of Old World pathogens, such as those that caused smallpox and measles, on so-called virgin soil, or unexposed populations. Native Americans had normal immune systems, but they had been isolated from the rest of the world for so long that they lacked the acquired immunity shared by most Africans, Asians, and Europeans to a wide range of "ordinary" or childhood ailments. Smallpox, measles, and influenza killed Europeans and Africans, but not at the same drastic rates at which they affected the first colonized generations of Native Americans. Mortality was so high that within a century of 1492 the overall indigenous American population fell from at least 50 million to barely five million (In Focus 4.4).

IN FOCUS 4.3

 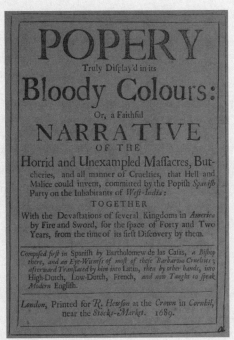

Figure 4.3. **a.** Credit: Friar Bartolomé de Las Casas defender of the Indians (oil on canvas) by Felix Parra (1845–1919) Museo Nacional de Arte, Mexico/ The Bridgeman Art Library [Image # REV346186] **b.** Popery Truly Display'd in its Bloody Colours: Or, a Faithful Narrative of the Horrid and Unexampled Massacres, Butcheries, and all manner of Cruelties, that Hell and Malice could invent, committed by the Popish Spanish Party of the Inhabitants of West-India. Credit: Washington University Libraries, Department of Special Collections.

LAS CASAS AND THE BLACK LEGEND

Bartolomé de las Casas first arrived in the Americas in 1502, at the age of twenty-eight, as one of the Spaniards accompanying the new governor of Hispaniola, Nicolás de Ovando. Bartolomé's father, a merchant from Seville, had come to the island with Columbus the previous decade. At first, Bartolomé helped his father in the business of supplying the conquistadors who had begun invading other Caribbean islands. But he was more interested in learning Taino and in the priesthood.

Ordained in Rome in 1507, Las Casas returned to the Caribbean a few years later, joining conquistadors in Cuba as a priest. This experience convinced him that Spanish methods of colonization were ineffective and immoral. Las Casas had received encomiendas, or grants of native labor and tribute, on both Hispaniola and Cuba. He now renounced those benefits and began a lifelong campaign to convince the crown to abolish the institution and to permit priests, not conquistador settlers, to create and govern the colonies.

Attempting to practice what he preached, he experimented with model settlements in Venezuela and Guatemala, with little success. Having joined the Dominican order, and having served briefly in the 1540s as bishop of Chiapas (in what is today southern Mexico), Las Casas was uncompromising and increasingly militant in his denunciation of Spanish mistreatment of native peoples. He was hated by settlers, denounced by the viceroy of New Spain, don Antonio de Mendoza, and recalled back to Spain by the Council of the Indies.

IN FOCUS 4.3

LAS CASAS AND THE BLACK LEGEND, *continued*

These were signs, however, that his persistence was paying off. The New Laws of 1542, which protected natives from enslavement and other abuses, reflected Las Casas's arguments. His *Brief Account of the Destruction of the Indies* and other such treatises were published and widely read. "A superb propagandist and quite astute at court politics," Las Casas enjoyed royal patronage and the right to make his case against colonial abuses until his death in 1566.

Las Casas's reputation has continued to grow over the centuries, in particular in two ways that can mislead the modern reader. First, his books were translated into other European languages and read widely for many centuries. Used as anti-Spanish propaganda, especially by the English (as illustrated above by the title page to a 1689 edition), Las Casas's works underpinned the Black Legend – the depiction of Spanish imperialism as excessively brutal and immoral, a negative stereotype that survives today in Protestant and Catholic countries alike. The Black Legend's implication that the Spanish were cruel because they were Catholic is ironic in view of Las Casas's insistence that the colonies should be run by priests.

The second way in which Las Casas's posthumous reputation can be misleading is his modern status as an icon of humanitarianism (as illustrated in the dramatic nineteenth-century painting above). His passionate denunciations of native suffering have often blinded modern readers to the fact that Las Casas was not a modern figure. Arguably, he is better understood as a medieval prophet. A onetime slave owner himself, he never argued for the abolition of African slavery, nor did he propose that native peoples be given the choice not to convert to Christianity. He questioned Spanish methods of conquest and colonization but not the existence of the Spanish Empire.

It became common around the time of the Columbus Quincentennial of 1992 to refer to the decline of the Native American populations as a holocaust. If the Holocaust of World War II claimed 6 million lives, according to this view, then surely the native population decline of tens of millions was a more than comparable genocide. The European invasion certainly caused demographic collapse in the Americas, both through the medium of disease and as a result of the disruptive impact of conquest and colonization. But wiping out native peoples was not a Spanish – or Portuguese – goal. On the contrary, Iberians were dismayed at how quickly native numbers fell in the Caribbean and coastal Brazil. In the Spanish case, Las Casas's arguments as to the cause of the disaster were widely disseminated in part because they amounted to a scathing and scandalous indictment of Spanish colonial methods – helping the book to find readers in England, the Netherlands, and other parts of Protestant Europe then fighting with Spain (see In Focus 4.3). But Las Casas was also taken seriously in the Spanish world itself because crown and settlers alike sought explanations in the hope of reversing the population crash.

The Spanish experience in the Caribbean – and the collapse of the native population – was significant, therefore, for several reasons. First, it did not

HOW MANY NATIVE AMERICANS WERE THERE IN 1492?

Region	Range of modern estimates (millions)	Probable population range (millions)
North America	1–18	4–6
Central Mexico	3–58	15–18
Central America	1–6	5–6
Caribbean	0.2–6	2–3
Andes	2–37	13–15
Rest of South America	1–11	7–8
New World total	8–100	46–56

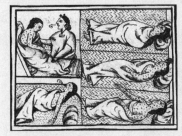

Figure 4.4. **a.** Florentine Codex (1540-1585), Book XII folio 54 [detail]. An illustrated panel appearing on fol.54 of Book XII of the en:Florentine Codex, the 16th-century compendium of materials and information on Aztec and Nahua history collected by Fray Bernardino de Sahagún. The drawing shows Nahuas infected with smallpox disease. **b.** Mummy from ancient peruvian culture. © Carlos Santa Maria / iStockphoto.com. **c.** Native woman in Northern Peru ill with smallpox, ca. 1785, from Bishop Baltasar Jaime Martínez Compañón, 2:197.

mean the abandonment of the "neofeudal," land-based Castilian model of colonization. As we will see, the basic institutions of that model survived and were central to Spanish settlement on the American mainland. But, second, the model was altered, most notably with respect to slavery. Spanish conquest campaigns on the mainland in the 1520s and 1530s were not slave raids, and in 1542, Spain's king decreed that his native subjects in the Americas could not be enslaved except in rare instances of sustained rebellion. Instead, the category of "slave" was almost entirely restricted to black Africans, who were sold as such by the Portuguese. Slaves from Africa's Atlantic shores had been a part of Spanish overseas endeavors since the conquest of the Canary Islands, but they became central to Spanish American colonization in the sixteenth century. On the Caribbean islands and in many coastal regions of the mainland, enslaved Africans and their descendants supplemented and then replaced indigenous populations altogether. Some Spanish colonial enclaves thus followed an earlier model, that of the slave-based sugar plantation first established by the Portuguese in the East Atlantic Islands and then taken to Brazil.

* * *

The watershed events of 1492 help us understand how Iberia's expansion into the Atlantic played out in the contact-era Americas. After 1500, however, the Iberians' trajectories split: the Spanish directed the bulk of their efforts toward the interior kingdoms and empires of the American mainland, whereas the Portuguese continued their push to Asia, only slowly encouraging Brazilian sugar production while supplying the mineral-rich Spanish with enslaved Africans. The new Ibero-American world slowly taking shape borrowed elements of Columbus's mercantile vision, focused on the extraction and sale of gold, gems, and spices – with reaching Asia a persistent dream – and some elements of Las Casas's vision of the Americas as a testing ground for Spanish morality focused on conversion rather than conquest. Even early Brazil would witness Catholic missionaries attempting to establish Las Casas–style utopias. It is safe to say, however, that it was Queen Isabella's vision of total conquest that inspired Castilian Spaniards such as Cortés and Pizarro, whereas most early Portuguese settlers in Brazil were more inspired by the entrepreneurial spirit of Bartolomeo Marchionni. Despite the intentions of its invaders, early colonial Latin America would take shape largely in response to the varied and often surprising actions and adaptive responses of its millions of Native American inhabitants. Where they became majorities, enslaved Africans and their descendants formed a similar counterweight to the Iberian colonizers' competing models of society.

SUGGESTIONS FOR FURTHER READING

Among the numerous books on Columbus we recommend Felipe Fernández-Armesto, *Columbus* (1991), and Nicolás Wey-Gómez, *Tropics of Empire* (2008). Also relevant is chapter 1 of Matthew Restall, *Seven Myths of the Spanish Conquest* (2003). On the topic of disease and demography, two readable syntheses are Suzanne Austin Alchon, *A Pest in the Land: New World Epidemics in a Global Perspective* (2003), and Noble David Cook, *Born to Die: Disease and the New World Conquest, 1492–1650* (1998). On Las Casas's career in context, see Rolena Adorno, *The Polemics of Possession* (2008).

GLOSSARY

Taino [tah-EE-no]: native peoples of **Hispaniola** [hiss-pan-YO-lah] and neighboring islands; sometimes also called Arawaks
Feitoria [fay-taw-REE-ah]: Portuguese permanent trading post
Madeira [ma-DEER-ah], **Azores** [a-SORE-eesh]: Atlantic islands settled by the Portuguese
Garzone [gar-ZOHN-eh]: junior agent in a mercantile or banking company (means "hotel servant" in modern Italian)

5

■ ■ ■ ■ ■ ■ ■ ■ ■ ■ ■ ■ ■ ■ ■ ■ ■ ■ ■

Native American Empires

TIMELINE

1325: the Mexica found their city of Mexico-Tenochtitlán

1427: Itzcoatl founds Mexica or Aztec Empire

1438: Pachacuti founds Inca Empire

1502–1520: reign of the Mexica emperor Moctezuma Xocoyotl (Montezuma)

1521: Aztec Empire falls with the capture of Tenochtitlán and the last emperor, Cuauhtémoc

Late 1520s: the Inca Huayna Capac dies, leading to civil war between his successors, Atawallpa and Huascar

1533: Inca Empire falls with Spanish execution of Atawallpa, although Inca resistance continues

We have priests who guide us and prepare us in the culture and service of our gods. There are also many others with distinct names who serve in the temples day and night, who are wise and knowledgeable about the movement of the heavenly bodies as well as about our ancient customs. They have the books of our forebears which they study and peruse day and night. These guide us and prepare us in counting the years, days, months, and feasts of our gods, which are celebrated every twenty days. These same priests are in charge of the histories of our gods and the rules about serving them, because we are in charge only of warfare, collection of tribute, and justice

(Aztec noblemen to the first Franciscan friars in Mexico, 1524)

THE STORY OF THE BRIDGING of the Atlantic up to 1519 gives a misleading impression of two very different worlds: on one side of the ocean, the two emerging imperial powers of the Iberian Peninsula, competing with each other in their ambition to discover unprecedented, overseas sources of wealth; on the other side, the isolated, semisedentary societies of the Caribbean and coastal Brazil, unprepared for the devastation of epidemic disease and foreign invasion.

But this is only part of the story, for the fifteenth century was an age of empires in the Americas as well as Iberia. By coincidence, at about the same time that Portugal embarked on the campaign of exploration that would lead to the great Iberian discoveries of the era, the two largest empires of the Americas were beginning their expansion. In 1425, the Portuguese began their efforts to conquer and settle Madeira and the Canary Islands, symbolic steps in the development of their overseas empire – and that of the Castilians, who would win the Canaries in that crucial decade of the 1490s. Meanwhile, in 1428, the Mexica seized control of the Valley of Mexico, laying the cornerstone for the future Aztec Empire. Exactly a decade later, in 1438, a Quechua prince came to power in Cuzco, high in the Andes of South America, and began an explosive campaign that forged the Inca Empire, one of the most extensive centralized states in the world at this time.

This chapter briefly explores the Aztec and Inca empires, as well as summarizing the state of other native societies (most notably the Mayas) on the eve of the Iberian invasions.

The Mexica

In 1790, native laborers paving the streets in downtown Mexico City came across an extraordinary piece of stone (see In Focus 5.1). The workers were descendants of the Aztecs (or Mexica) who had built the city on which Mexico City stood, the Aztec imperial capital of Tenochtitlán. The piece of stone, nearly twelve feet in diameter, had been buried in the rubble of Tenochtitlán when the city was destroyed in 1521. The carving depicted the earth god, Tlaltecuhtli, as the monstrous center of the earth. Placed in the central plaza of the city in 1427, the stone projected the Mexica capital as the fearsome center of its world.

What happened before 1427 that led to the carving of this stone and the development of this ideology? And in what ways did the Mexica of Tenochtitlán realize this destiny in the century that followed?

The Mexica, like many conquering peoples, had turned the history of their ancient wanderings and semisedentary lifestyle into an origin myth. Leaving a mythical far northern Lake Aztlán (hence the modern name *Aztec*, which grew popular in the eighteenth century), they moved around aimlessly until their patron god Huitzilopochtli advised them to head south. They were to settle on the site where they saw an eagle with a snake in its mouth alight on a prickly-pear cactus (see In Focus 5.2; the image is preserved today on the Mexican national flag). The ominous landing of the eagle was spotted in 1325 on an island in Lake Texcoco, where the Mexica then founded the city of Tenochtitlán.

On the shores of Lake Texcoco, now covered by Mexico City, were several highly competitive city-states, among them the mighty Azcapotzalco. According to their own history, the Mexica lived here on marginal marshlands for nearly a century, working primarily as mercenaries. After 1325, the Mexica went on selling their military services and paying tribute to Azcapotzalco, but they also began their own aggressive policies. They subjected weak neighboring towns to their own rule, and also sought to bolster the Mexica noble bloodline by marrying into the most eminent families in the Lake Texcoco region.

The year 1427 marked a major watershed in Mexica imperial history. In this year Itzcoatl, the fourth Mexica king, took the throne and set the Calendar Stone in Tenochtitlán's plaza. The following year, Itzcoatl formed an

IN FOCUS 5.1

Figure 5.1. Monolith of the Stone of the Sun, also named Aztec calendar stone (National Museum of Anthropology and History, Mexico City). Photograph by El Comandante.

THE AZTEC SUN STONE

The Sun Stone, or Calendar Stone, depicted a face at its center, believed for two centuries to be that of Tonatiuh, the sun god – although more recently scholars have argued that it is Tlaltecuhtli, the monstrous earth god. The date on the stone indicates that it was carved and placed in the central plaza of Tenochtitlán in 1427. Just as Tlaltecuhtli was presented in the stone as the monstrous center of the earth, so was Tenochtitlán thereby conceived as the fearsome center of its world. Tlaltecuhtli's tongue was carved as a flint knife, the symbol for war in the Aztec writing system, and extending from his ears were claws grasping human hearts. The concentric circles that surround this image represent the five creations of the world, extending back in time, as well as the twenty day signs that make up a month and a set of icons depicting the unceasing and all-important motion of the sun. Thus, Tenochtitlán's position in time and space was more than significant: it was sacred; it sanctioned and even required warfare and sacrifice; and it indicated a burdensome, if awesome, destiny.

alliance with the lakeside cities of Texcoco and Tlacopan, and led a successful campaign against Azcapotzalco. This victory marked not just the rise to regional dominance of the Mexica but also the birth of the Aztec Empire. For the next ninety years, until stopped by the Spanish invasion led by Hernando

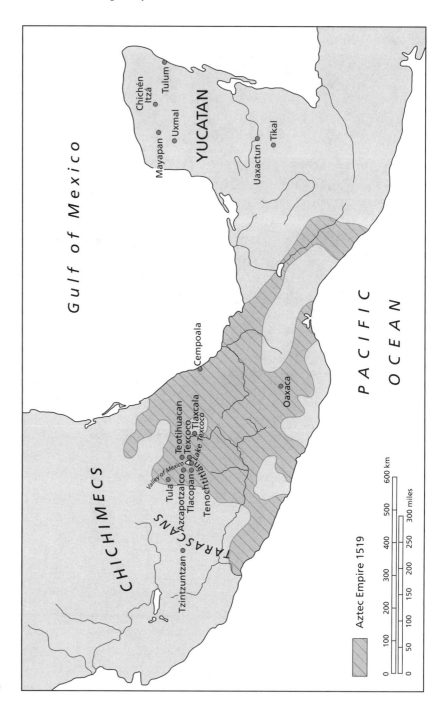

Map 5.1
Mexico at the Time
of the Aztec Empire

Cortés, the Mexica engaged in an aggressive imperial expansion, first across central Mexico and then toward Guatemala, to the southeast. The Aztec empire was not a bureaucratic state, nor did it rely on direct rule. Instead, local headmen were allowed to stay in office, provided that they were willing to accept Aztec sovereignty. This was not all, of course. In exchange for recognition, the Mexica required these subject headmen to collect and hand

IN FOCUS 5.2

 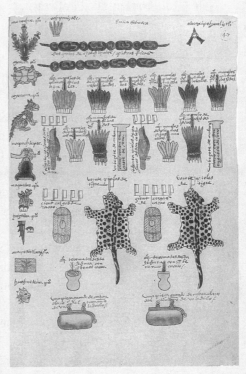

Figure 5.2. **a.** Folio 2r of the Codex Mendoza, a mid-16th century Aztec codex. Depicts the founding of Tenochtitlán, and the conquest of Colhuacan and Tenayucan. **b.** Folio 47r of the Codex Mendoza, a mid-16th century Aztec codex. Lists the tribute towns were required to pay to the Aztec empire.

PROMOTING THE PAST: THE CODEX MENDOZA

The Codex Mendoza is named after don Antonio de Mendoza, who arrived in Mexico City in 1535 as the first viceroy of the new kingdom of New Spain and commissioned the codex around 1541. Painted and drawn on European paper, and copied mostly from precolonial pictorial sources, the codex is an invaluable account of Mexica history, the economic structure of the empire, and daily life of the era. The image on the left is from the first part of the codex, which recounts Mexica history from the founding of Tenochtitlán to the empire's fall. The other image here is from the second part of the codex, which details the tribute that each province of the Aztec Empire owed to the Mexica rulers (this example includes feather headdresses; jaguar pelts; and sacks of cacao, or cocoa beans).

over significant tribute payments. These consisted of labor and a huge array of goods – from grains to warrior costumes (see In Focus 5.2).

In 1428, Itzcoatl and his chief minister and general, a nephew named Tlacaelel, collected and burned all hieroglyphic books that recorded the history of the region. That history was then rewritten with the Mexica at its center, as the heirs to the legacy of the Toltecs (whose city of Tula had dominated the valley four centuries earlier) and as the divinely sanctioned rulers of the known world. More political and economic authority was concentrated in the hands of Mexica royalty, as a relatively weak monarchy transformed into an imperial dynasty. The power that emperors would exercise for a hundred years over the Mexica themselves and their neighbors was justified by the claim of privileged access both to the regional great tradition of the Toltecs and to the will of the gods, especially Huitzilopochtli and Tlaloc, god of rain, of water, and of the fertility of the land.

A century after Itzcoatl became emperor, the Aztec rulers that had either survived the Spanish invasion or had assumed office in its wake met "the Twelve," the first Franciscan friars to reach Mexico. An exchange of speeches took place, and although the speeches were not written down for sixty years, the words of the Aztec lords give us some sense of a division of responsibility among religious and civil leaders in the Aztec Empire. The passage quoted in the epigraph to this chapter is a revealing one, but it needs to be read carefully. The division of responsibility between those governing religious and calendrical matters and those managing the empire through military campaigns and tribute collection did not amount to anything like a separation of church and state. On the contrary, the Aztec imperial rationale was framed as a cosmic struggle, with all subjects – and enemies – expected to play their assigned roles. Mesoamericans had ritually executed war captives and other select victims for millennia, but it appears that only in the fifteenth century, with the rise of the Mexica, that human sacrifice grew so vital to imperial expansion and maintenance. The Aztecs' patron god, Huitzilopochtli, was offered many thousands of war captives, who typically had their hearts removed and their heads placed on the skull rack in the plaza of Tenochtitlán. Much more rarely, Aztec children were sacrificed to the water god Tlaloc, an affair intended to provoke much sadness and offerings of tears. For visitors to the imperial capital, including the first Spaniards to arrive in 1519, the twin temples of the war god and rain god dominated the skyline, and must have been intimidating, if not terrifying (see In Focus 5.3). In one sacrificial ritual, an annual offering to the trickster god Tezcatlipoca, a specially chosen young captive was allowed to lead a life of luxury and privilege for a year before having his heart excised atop a pyramid. The Aztecs believed themselves responsible for carrying out all these sacrificial rituals in order to maintain cosmic harmony by paying debts to the gods.

This culture of ritualized violence was also found among other Nahuas (Nahuatl-speaking peoples of central Mexico), though to a lesser extent. Aztec neighbors and enemies such as the Tlaxcalans, for example, also excised the still-beating hearts from prisoners of war atop temple-pyramids. It even appears that such enemies as Tlaxcala and Tenochtitlán shared in larger ritual dramas. According to some sources, conventional warfare was finally replaced by the "flowery wars" (*xochiyaoyotl*), in which scattered red blossoms represented the blood of warriors and selected warriors were traded

Figure 5.3. Covarrubias, Luis. Vista de Tenochtitlán en el Lago de México. Museo Nacional de Antropología, Mexico City, D.F., Mexico. (Image Reference ART117086) © Schalkwijk / Art Resource, NY

THE IMPERIAL CAPITAL OF MEXICO-TENOCHTITLÁN

The first Europeans to set eyes on the Aztec capital were amazed at its size, setting, and beauty. The conquistador Bernal Díaz wrote that he and his fellow Spaniards were rendered speechless. The twin island-cities of Tlatelolco and Tenochtitlán – with their grid of canals, busy streets, and two plazas bounded by pyramids and palaces – seemed to float on the shimmering lake. European cities were cramped and chaotic by comparison (their grids, often associated with the Renaissance, actually came later and were in part influenced by Tenochtitlán). Lake Texcoco, divided by a great dike to keep salt water from the city and prevent flooding, was covered in canoes; its shores were studded with more cities, each with its own plazas and pyramids. There were about a quarter of a million people living in Tenochtitlán and several million in the whole valley (with the central Mexican population at an estimated 15 million or more).

Visitors to the city approached it either by canoe or along one of the three great causeways that connected it to the lakeshore and held the aqueducts that brought in fresh water. One first passed some of the small floating cornfields called *chinampas* that bordered the lake and city. Then one entered the outer neighborhoods, or *calpulli*, of the capital, which was divided into four quarters, each with eight or more *calpulli*. Closer to the center one reached the palaces where the royal family lived and where imperial administrators worked; one of the palatial compounds included a large zoo. At the heart of the city was the great plaza, dominated by twin pyramids devoted to Huitzilopochtli and Tlaloc.

as captives to be sacrificed. Tlaxcala was never conquered, but its inhabitants lived on constant alert, their daily existence hemmed in and overshadowed by the looming Mexica tributary apparatus that surrounded them. In the end, Tlaxcalan resentment of Aztec aggression greatly enabled the Spanish invasion.

Other states besides Tlaxcala managed to resist Mexica domination. West of Tenochtitlán lay the Tarascan kingdom, a modest empire in its own right with its capital city of Tzintzuntzan. Several other kingdoms stood firm against the Aztecs, reminders that the empire was not invincible. Even so, the Aztecs were becoming masters of highland Mexico thanks to the campaigns of Itzcoatl and the five emperors who followed him. In 1440, Moctezuma Ilhuicamina succeeded his uncle Itzcoatl. He was followed by three sons: Axayácatl, Tizoc, and Ahuitzotl. At Ahuitzotl's 1486 coronation, visiting rulers from many of the empire's tributary cities "saw that the Aztecs were masters of the world, their empire so wide and abundant that they had conquered all the nations and that all were their vassals. The guests, seeing such wealth and opulence and such authority and power, were filled with terror."

The last independent Aztec emperor, an aggressive and able ruler, was the namesake grandson of the first Moctezuma, Moctezuma Xocoyotl. This second Moctezuma consolidated and extended the empire from 1502 until 1520, when he was murdered by Spanish invaders. Despite his numerous successes as a ruler, Moctezuma Xocoyotl would be blamed by both Spaniards and natives for the Aztec Empire's rather sudden collapse. In the face of so many unforeseen calamities unleashed by the Spanish arrival on Mexican shores in 1519, it proved easy in retrospect to blame the last Aztec emperor for not reacting properly to the Spanish threat. History's Moctezuma thus became a myth, almost a caricature of ineptitude.

The Inca

Just ten years after the Aztec emperor Itzcoatl and his chief minister Tlacaelel rewrote the Mexica past as a foundation for Aztec imperialism, another emperor, thousands of miles to the south, achieved something similar. In 1438, a secondary Inca prince named Cusi Yupanqui repelled an attempt by his neighbors, the Chancas, to seize control of the Inca capital of Cuzco and surrounding territory. Exultant, Cusi Yupanqui forced his father to retire and took the Inca crown, with its distinctive fringe, from the designated heir. The first true Inca emperor, Yupanqui renamed himself Pachacuti, which means "earthquake" or "world-changer." The new emperor quickly established a mythological history that seemed to predict his arrival and also justified his aggressive vision of the future. Pachacuti reorganized the Inca system of rule from one centered on stability and reproduction to one that sought to encompass as much territory and as many subjects as possible. The justification for Inca expansion was ethnocentric but not unusual: Pachacuti claimed he wanted to "civilize" all Andean peoples after the Inca fashion. The fact that he began to do so at about the same time the Aztec Empire took off in Mexico was coincidental. There is no evidence of contact between the two, and in fact it appears neither knew of the other's existence. This helps explain why there are more differences between them than similarities.

Even at its height, the Aztec Empire covered much less territory than the modern Republic of Mexico and seemingly within its borders

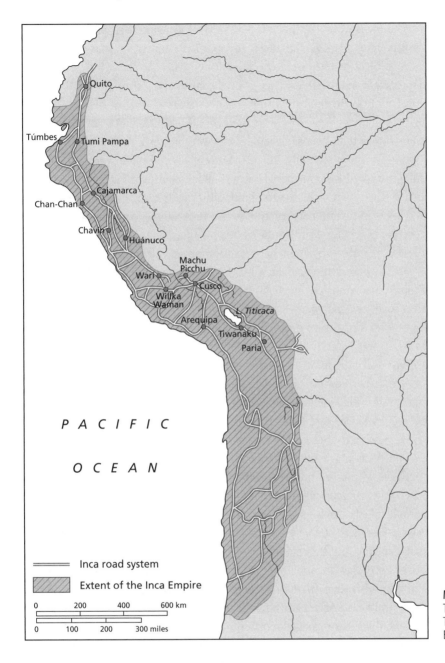

Map 5.2
The Andes at the Time of the Inca Empire

there remained many unconquered regions and city-states. By contrast, the Inca Empire at the time of the Spanish invasion encompassed some 2,600 miles of contiguous territory, limited only by the Pacific Ocean and Amazon rain forest, stretching from Ecuador to Chile (see Map 5.2). Inca was the emperor's title, a term we now use for the whole empire, but it was Cuzco-based Quechua-speaking peoples who conquered and administered what they called Tawantinsuyu, or the Union of the Four Quarters.

The Incas were like the Aztecs in quickly growing their empire by using threats and strategic alliances to augment violent military conquests. Once subject peoples were conquered, however, the Incas took a different approach from the Aztecs. They favored centralized control over indirect rule and tribute collecting. Inca rule was distinct from that of the Aztecs in at least four ways. First, the Incas preferred to extract tribute in the form of labor rather than goods, although both were important. The imperial labor system, or *mit'a* (literally "turn," a system revived under Spanish colonial rule), required local farmers to work lands taken over by the Inca state as well as their own plots. Male subjects also had to rotate into the Inca army and serve in various construction levies. Rotational labor systems existed in central Mexico, for example the *coatequitl* (literally "snake-work") draft, but these were not run by imperial officials or formalized for long-term purposes.

Mit'a workers supplied labor for the second key characteristic of the Inca Empire: its extensive, fourteen-thousand-mile network of royal roads. The Inca road, or *capac ñan*, included everything from broad desert avenues to grass-fiber suspension bridges spanning mountain gorges. The bridges had to be strong enough to sustain relay messengers, llama herds, streams of tribute-bearing porters, and even armies – everyone and everything that had to be transported from one end of the empire to the other. The Incas' unique road system also included a series of carefully located inns and warehouses. Stored goods were used to feed *mit'a* workers, supply troops, and keep luxury goods flowing to the wealthy Inca elite.

The Incas' third key characteristic, the forced migration of entire communities, also relied on the road system. These migrations could be temporary, but they generally required movement across great distances to meet specific needs, such as public works projects or defense against frontier rebels. The Incas officially required migrant communities to keep their original identities, but they also demanded that all subjects use the Quechua language for exchanges and imperial affairs. The Incas' system of imperial trade and administration marks the fourth key characteristic of the empire. In short, unlike the Aztecs with their large marketplaces dominated by regional traders, the Incas managed most exchanges at the state level in a redistributive way, suppressing free market activity. Also unlike their Mesoamerican contemporaries, whose writing systems varied tremendously, the Incas relied almost exclusively on the quipu (or *khipu*) system of knotted cords to store information. The special Inca imperial mold was set by Pachacuti, but his son Topa Inca and his grandson Huayna Capac carried on the Inca policy of constant military campaigns, aided by the continued building of roads, warehouses, and fortresses. Runners, carrying quipus, used the road system to relay information across thousands of miles with amazing speed.

While fighting on Tawantinsuyu's northern frontier near the modern Ecuador-Colombia border in 1525, Huayna Capac was told of an epidemic

Figure 5.4. **a.** Machu Picchu. Photograph by Fabricio Guzmán. **b.** A view of the entire site of Machu Picchu, seen from Huayna Picchu. Photograph by Steve Bennett.

THE RIDDLE OF MACHU PICCHU

One of the wonders of the world, the ruined and mysterious Inca city of Machu Picchu sits perched on a rocky ridge high in the Peruvian Andes. Machu Picchu was clearly built by the Incas, but what was it for? Why was it built here, amid sheer granite cliffs and cloud forest? The archaeologist Hiram Bingham, first led up the mountain from the banks of the Urubamba River in 1911, surmised that Machu Picchu was Vilcabamba, the lost city of Manco Inca and other rebels against Spanish rule. Later excavations of female skeletons suggested something else, a kind of Inca convent. Other evidence seemed to identify the city as a strategic outpost: part fort, part lookout.

These theories have been largely discarded thanks to new evidence. A number of early colonial documents suggest that Machu Picchu may well have housed *acllakuna*, or Inca "nuns," but it was most likely built late in Inca times to commemorate a series of military victories by the emperor Pachacuti. The "city" of Machu Picchu was apparently one of several sumptuous royal estates, some of which were built farther up the Urubamba and Vilcanota rivers, toward the Inca capital of Cuzco, and in neighboring valleys.

THE RIDDLE OF MACHU PICCHU, *continued*

Machu Picchu, despite its precipitous location, was likely planted with coca and maize, although not enough to sustain its inhabitants. The site is heavily terraced; supplied with carved stone irrigation works; and located in a lower, hotter, and wetter ecosystem than that of Cuzco. The estate's production could not have been great, given the limited farmable surface area, but coca and maize were both closely linked to Inca religious ritual, and therein lies the key, it seems, to Machu Picchu.

The site fits neatly into the Incas' sacred Andean landscape. Located above a dramatic bend in the Urubamba River, Machu Picchu is surrounded by many peaks, including two snowcaps more than twenty thousand feet high. The Incas revered mountains, especially glaciated ones, because they were linked to the seasonal hydrological cycle so critical to agriculture. Celestial patterns, including the path of the sun and movements of the stars, were also deeply imbedded in Inca religious thought. The Milky Way, for example, was conceived of as a heavenly river. From Machu Picchu and adjacent hills, a number of celestial risings and settings could be associated with notches and peaks in the mountainous horizon.

Why was Machu Picchu abandoned? Perhaps its maintenance became too costly or onerous following the death of Pachacuti Inca. Perhaps the estate fell into disuse during a succession crisis and civil war that broke out after the death of Huayna Capac. Whatever the case, we are fortunate that Machu Picchu was not looted. Today it provides stark and indelible testimony of Inca aesthetics and ingenuity at their height. From a more Andean point of view, it serves to remind us that human societies once believed in sacred symbiosis, in living in synchronicity with the motions of earth, water, and sky.

sweeping through the empire from the south and already ravaging the capital of Cuzco. Within a few years, possibly in 1527, the disease apparently killed Huayna Capac. Although descriptions of the symptoms are hazy, and were only related to the Spanish after the conquest, this was probably the first wave of smallpox to penetrate South America. It had most likely begun with the arrival of Europeans in the region of Buenos Aires. The disease also appears to have killed Huayna Capac's preferred heir – all this before a single Spaniard set foot in Tawantinsuyu. The deaths produced a succession crisis between two brothers, Atawallpa and Huascar, sons of Huayna Capac by different mothers. Their feud soon grew into a full-blown civil war, splitting the Inca Empire in half. When Francisco Pizarro sought to conquer the Incas in 1532 he had the problems of epidemic disease and internal division on his side.

Micropatriotism

In 1525, the year that the Inca Huayna Capac heard that smallpox had come to his empire, an expedition of some three hundred Spaniards and African slaves, and more than three thousand Nahua warriors, traveled across the base of the Yucatán Peninsula. The expedition was led by Hernando Cortés and included many of the protagonists in the Spanish Conquest of the Aztec

Empire (such as Bernal Díaz; Malinche; and Cuauhtémoc, the captive Aztec emperor). Our concern here is with the two Maya kingdoms that the expedition encountered – and whose hospitality, not hostility, permitted the expedition to survive and continue on its arduous six-month journey from Mexico to Honduras.

The first of these was the Chontal Maya kingdom of Acalan. The capital city, Itzamkanac, was located near the present-day border of Guatemala and the Mexican state of Campeche, but the kingdom stretched north to the Gulf coast and controlled modest territory in all the other directions. The king, Paxbolonacha, claimed to be the seventh ruler since his dynastic ancestor had founded the kingdom. To the east of Acalan was the second Maya kingdom that received Cortés and his expedition in 1525, that of the Itzá Maya. Its capital of Noh Petén was built on a small island at one end of Lake Petén Itzá (as it is now called). Its king, Canek, ruled a region that covered much of what is now northern Guatemala and a corner of Belize.

Both kingdoms had populations of around thirty thousand, but 90 percent of inhabitants lived scattered in farmhouses. These were thus modest polities, and their cities more like small towns. Compared to Tenochtitlán, or to Seville, they were unimpressive – hardly worth conquering, even if that had been on Cortés's agenda. They were likewise unimpressive compared to the kingdoms and cities that had once thrived in this very same region, most notably Tikal, which seven centuries earlier had been a spectacular, sprawling center of some 120,000 people. But that does not mean that we can dismiss these kingdoms as tribal or not fully sedentary or part of a civilization that was in decline. The Mayas were a fully sedentary people, and their civilization was still thriving when Spaniards first entered their cities and towns. Maya civilization (or the network of Maya cultures) was part of the larger Mesoamerican civilization. For example, the Mayas had developed one of the three Mesoamerican writing systems; the only one that was fully developed and complete, this writing system was still very much in use in the early sixteenth century.

However, what had disappeared by the time of the Spanish invasion was the political system of sacred kings and regal-ceremonial cities that had produced cities such as Tikal and Chichén Itzá. A combination of environmental and political factors – the so-called Maya Collapse – had destroyed that system in highland Guatemala in the ninth and tenth centuries A.D., and although it survived in a somewhat different form in the Yucatán for several centuries, by the fifteenth century, the whole Maya area was politically fragmented. In Chapter 1, we organized native societies into four categories – "concentrated sedentary," "segmented sedentary," "semisedentary," and "nonsedentary." The Mayas lived in segmented sedentary societies. At the time of Cortés's journey of 1525, the Yucatec Mayas to his north, perhaps 2 million in number, were divided into as many as two dozen city-states or polities. To his south, in what is today Chiapas and Guatemala, there were another 2 million, divided not only into numerous

Map 5.3
The Maya Area
at the Turn of the
Sixteenth Century

polities but also into dozens of separate ethnic or linguistic groups. Among them only the Cakchiquel and Quiché Mayas controlled significant territories; in the century before the Spanish invasion, and in competition with each other, the Cakchiquels and Quichés had developed networks of tribute-paying subject towns that were echoes of ancient Maya traditions and that mirrored on a far smaller scale contemporaneous Aztec imperial expansion.

In between the Yucatec Mayas and the Mayas of highland Guatemala lay the sparsely populated kingdoms through which Cortés passed. Their rulers, Paxbolonacha and Canek, seem to have quickly realized that Cortés's goal was not to settle permanently in their kingdoms. Their policies of response were similar: neither to risk the lives of their subjects through hostility nor to risk the future integrity of dynasty and kingdom through the surrender of political control or every available local resource. Instead, they chose to adopt a middle position of offering the Spaniards and their native allies sufficient hospitality to allow them to rest and resupply, so as to help them on their way (accompanied by Maya guides, who also acted as spies for their kings). At the root of this policy lay the simple fact that identities in the Maya region on the eve of the Spanish invasion were highly localized. Paxbolonacha and Canek saw their interests in personal and community terms, not larger ethnic or regional ones. We might be tempted to see the Chontal and Itzá Maya as part of a single larger group of Lowland Mayas, or Mayas in general, and Spaniards saw them in a larger category still, that of "Indians." But the Chontals and Itzás themselves shared no common identity with their neighbors, with whom they were in a state of almost constant conflict. In summary, we might call their identity and worldview micropatriotic.

Micropatriotism was not unique to the Mayas, or even to Mesoamericans. It was a common characteristic of the societies in much of the world at this time, including Iberians and Africans. Likewise, micropatriotism was equally evident in South America, only a mountainous sliver of which was controlled by the Incas when the Spanish arrived. In what is today Colombia and Venezuela, the Spanish encountered a wide range of nonimperial peoples whose material lives ranged from nonsedentary hunting and gathering to intensive maize farming, complex metallurgy, weaving, and pottery making. Some groups, such as the Tairona of the Sierra Nevada of Santa Marta, built stone palaces and temples of considerable size. The Muisca of the high plains surrounding Bogotá and Tunja also built stone temples, and they traded gold, emeralds, and fine cotton textiles with surrounding peoples. As in Maya country around 1500, warfare was common here, sometimes between complex chiefdoms, sometimes against more mobile hunters inhabiting the ecological fringes. In hot coastal and inter-Andean valleys, nonsedentary and semisedentary peoples proliferated, and their frequent belligerence and complex terrain made conquest difficult. To the east, the huge Amazon and Orinoco basins were still more diverse and daunting for any group with hopes of conquest.

Farther south, forest peoples whom the Incas had never managed to defeat – such as the Shuar, or Jívaro, of eastern Ecuador and Peru, and the Mapuche of Chile – proved still more indomitable. These semisedentary cultures sometimes recognized chiefs and other authority figures, but mostly they prized independence of individual warriors and their extended families. Only when faced with outside threats did they come together for defense. In general, sedentary Andeans such as the Incas and Muisca of Colombia felt that these and other neighboring forest, desert, and mountain peoples were barbarians whose dietary and other customs were despicable. Such hostile feelings were mutual.

A more complex micropatriotism prevailed in coastal Brazil, where several hundred thousand Tupi speakers subsisted on a rich variety of marine, agricultural, and forest resources. Despite close cultural and linguistic similarities spanning hundreds and even thousands of miles of coastline, the Tupi were constantly at war with one another. Instead of giving rise to an empire, as had happened with the Aztecs and Incas, the warrior ethic in Brazil led to cultural splintering. When Portuguese and French traders and missionaries encountered the Tupi in the early 1500s, they found themselves quickly drawn into alliances with one group against another, usually a near neighbor whom Europeans perceived as nearly identical. Once again, the generic term *Indians* proved a woefully inadequate misnomer in light of such localized identities and cultural variations.

* * *

One might expect that the two great empires of the Americas in the early sixteenth century, that of the Mexica and the Inca, would prove formidable hurdles to Spanish invaders, whereas smaller polities – from the Mayas to the Jívaros to the Tupis – would easily succumb to conquistadors, missionaries, and Iberian settlers. In fact, it was the opposite. As the following chapters show, although no native groups succumbed "easily" to the invaders, empires fell within a matter of years, and smaller polities, including those that had resisted Mexica or Inca incursions, resisted incorporation into the Spanish or Portuguese empires for decades – if not centuries. In the next chapter, we therefore turn to this great encounter – the clash of empires – between the invading Spaniards and the native kings and emperors of the American mainland.

SUGGESTIONS FOR FURTHER READING

Thames and Hudson carries an impressive catalog of accessible and well-illustrated volumes on the Mexicas, Mayas, and Incas, including Michael Coe's *Mexico* (5th ed., 2002) and *The Maya* (6th ed., 1999), David Webster's *Fall of the Ancient Maya* (2002), and Michael Moseley's *The Incas and Their Ancestors* (2d ed., 2001) – although note that none of these focus exclusively on the century before the Spanish invasion. Inga Clendinnen's *Aztecs: An Interpretation* (1991) does have such a focus but is best suited to upper-level courses. Terence D'Altroy's *The Incas* (1999) is a first-rate overview with many useful maps. A fantastic source on the Tupi is Jean de Léry's eyewitness *History of a Voyage to Brazil* (1987), edited by Janet Whatley. The larger view is detailed by John Hemming in *Red Gold* (1978).

Serge Gruzinski, *The Aztecs: Rise and Fall of an Empire* (1992), and Carmen Bernand, *The Incas: People of the Sun* (1994) (both in the Abrams Discoveries series), are also appropriate for a survey class; they are brief, well illustrated, include an appendix of documents, and give as much attention to the Spanish conquest as they do to the empires themselves – making them particularly relevant to a course on colonial Latin America.

GLOSSARY

Mexica [me-SHEE-ka]: popularly called Aztecs in modern times; the native group that created the city of **Mexico-Tenochtitlán** [me-SHEE-ko tenoch-teet-LAHN] and the Aztec Empire

Inca [ING-kah]: the ruler or emperor of the empire of the same name

Tlaltecuhtli [tlal-teh-KOO-tlee]: the Mexican monstrous earth god

Huitzilopochtli [weets-eel-ope-OCH-tlee] and **Tlaloc** [TLAH-lok]: the gods of war and rain, patron gods of the Mexica and their capital city

Azcapotzalco [ahs-kah-pot-ZAL-koh], **Texcoco** [tesh-KOH-koh], **Tlacopan** [tla-koh-PAN]: cities in the Valley of Mexico

Itzcoatl [eets-koh-ATL] and **Tlacaelel** [tla-kah-EL-el]: the Mexica ruler, and his chief minister and nephew, who effectively founded the Aztec Empire

Nahuas [NAH-wah]: Nahuatl-speaking central Mexicans

Tlaxcala [tlash-KAH-lah]: central Mexican city-state that resisted conquest by the Mexica

Xochiyaoyotl [zoh-chee-YAH-oh-yotl]: the flowery wars, or ritual mock battles of fifteenth-century central Mexico

Moctezuma Xocoyotl [mock-teh-ZOO-mah shoh-coy-YOTL]: also known as Moctezuma II or Montezuma, the Aztec emperor at the time of the Spanish invasion

Pachacuti [pach-ah-COOT-ee]: Inca ruler who effectively founded the Inca Empire

Tawantinsuyu [tah-wahn-teen-SOO-yoo]: Union of the Four Quarters, the name the Incas gave to their empire

Mit'a [MEE-tah] and **Coatequitl** [kwa-tek-EETL]: rotational labor systems in the Andes and central Mexico, respectively

Quechua [KECH-wah]: native language of central Peru, made the language of the empire by the Incas

Quipu [KEY-poo]: Andean system of record-keeping and communication using knotted strings

Huayna Capac [WHY-nah KAH-pahk]: grandson of Pachacuti; Inca emperor who expanded the empire into what is now Ecuador and died shortly before Spaniards invaded, perhaps from smallpox

Machu Picchu [MAH-choo PEEK-choo]: royal palace and city built in the high Andes by Pachacuti and his successors

Acllakuna [ahk-yah-KOO-nah]: Inca sacred virgins, or "nuns of the sun"

Paxbolonacha [pash-boll-on-ACH-ah]: ruler of the kingdom of **Acalan** [ack-al-AN], whose capital city was **Itzamkanac** [eets-am-kah-NAK]

Polity: a state or society governed by a single ruler or body of rulers, and thus functioning as a single political entity

Tairona [tie-ROAN-ah], **Muisca** [MWEE-skah], **Jívaro** [HE-vah-roh], **Mapuche** [ma-POO-chay], and **Tupi** [TOO-pee]: native groups in South America

6

The Chain of Conquest

TIMELINE

1493–1519: Spanish exploration and colonization of the Caribbean

1519–1521: the Spanish-Mexica War, culminating in the Cortés-led Spaniards and their Tlaxcalan allies destroying the Mexica/Aztec imperial capital of Mexico-Tenochtitlán

1520s: Spanish consolidate control over central Mexico, make initial invasions of Guatemala and Yucatán, and explore the northern Pacific coast of South America

1532: the Inca Atawallpa captured by Pizarro at Cajamarca in northern Peru, executed in 1533

1534: Inca capital of Cuzco captured; Spaniards found a new capital at Lima in 1535

1536: revolt by the Inca Manco Capac, who besieges Cuzco before retreating to Vilcabamba (which is not conquered until 1572)

1537–1548: civil war between Spaniards in Peru

More than forty years ago he entered this province and since then he has served us with his weapons, especially in helping to place that province under our command and afterwards, in things relating to our service, according to the orders of our governors acting as a guard in various places as necessity required, without drawing any salary or receiving any reward.

(King Philip II, in an edict on Sebastian Toral, 1578)

THOUSANDS OF INTRICATELY WORKED plates, ornaments, and sculptures were melted down into bars of gold and silver and divided into piles. To them were added "the pearls and emerald stones," counted and divided up. The men, 168 in all, were grouped into only two categories, "persons on horseback" and "persons on foot." A notary wrote down a record that ran to more than sixty pages of the names of the men and the precise nature of their reward.

This was the great *fundición* and *repartimiento*, the "melting down" and "dividing up" of the ransom of the Inca ruler Atawallpa, received in the northern Peruvian city of Cajamarca in 1533. This event was viewed by Spaniards for centuries afterward as a symbol of the fantastic successes of the conquistadors; when a century later a Spanish official lamented the loss of silver when Dutch pirates seized the colonial fleet (see Chapter 12), his assertion that the enemy had taken five times as much "treasure" as had been won from Atawallpa at Cajamarca would have been a shocking image indeed to Spaniards of the day.

This chapter explains and explores the various aspects of the Spanish Conquest suggested by this event at Cajamarca – how and why Spaniards got there and into other corners of the Americas, who these Spaniards were, what the significance was of their apparently small numbers, how they acquired "treasure," and why its division was made and recorded in the manner just described. The chapter's focus is the half century from 1500 to about 1550. The Conquest has often been portrayed both as a simple act of military boldness made possible by European "superiority" over Native Americans and as a phenomenon so historically unique as to defy explanation. This chapter counters these perspectives with explanations that debunk old myths.

From Cuba to Mexico and Beyond

Although Columbus's first two voyages explored only islands in the Caribbean, his third voyage of 1498 touched on the American mainland (at Venezuela) for the first time. During his final voyage of 1502–1504, the Genoese navigator reconnoitered Central America, from Honduras to Panama. But by that time, Columbus had lost not only his governorship of Hispaniola but also his primacy as an explorer. Alonso de Ojeda and Amerigo Vespucci, a Castilian and a Florentine, had explored the northern coast of South America in 1499, and the Portuguese navigator Cabral had claimed Brazil for Portugal in 1500. Within twenty-five years of Columbus's first voyage, the Caribbean was largely known and claimed by Spain, with colonies established on the four largest islands of Hispaniola, Cuba, Puerto Rico, and Jamaica. The coast of Florida had been provisionally mapped and a small settlement planted in Panama.

It is therefore important to remember that the Spaniards did not simply jump from their Caribbean discoveries to the conquest of the Aztecs or Incas. A full generation passed between Columbus's first voyages and the exploration of the Mexican coastline in the late 1510s, and another passed before the Incas fell. This Caribbean interval allowed hundreds of Spaniards to practice conquest and colonialism. They steadily explored new territories, subdued new peoples, and established the institutions of church and state. Those who, like Las Casas and other missionaries, sought to establish peaceful relations between Europeans and Native Americans found their idealism thwarted by the widespread enslavement and brutal treatment of Caribbean natives. But when island populations dramatically declined, a high-level debate over how to treat indigenous subjects yielded a ban on "Indian" slavery. (No such ban on enslaving Africans was pondered.) After 1512 or so, Spaniards hoping to penetrate the American mainland searched not for slaves but for wealthy kingdoms to conquer in the name of their king and transform into tribute-paying, Christianized colonies.

Thus, Columbus's initial notion, borrowed from the Portuguese, of a network of trading posts was replaced by Spanish ideas of total territorial control and tribute extraction. These ideas had developed in Spain and the Canary Islands, but they were adapted to the Caribbean in the form of key institutions such as the encomienda (the allocation of native labor and tribute to Spanish settlers, dubbed *encomenderos*) and *congregación* (the

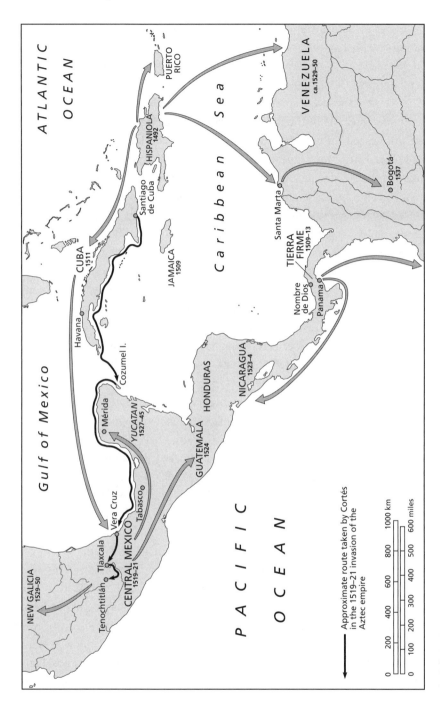

Map 6.1
Mexico, Central America, and the Caribbean in the Conquest Period

resettlement of native peoples into concentrated towns). Despite the frequent failure of the encomienda and congregación as tools of governance and taxation, Spaniards fully expected to impose such institutions on whatever new native societies they encountered on the mainland. After about 1570, they attempted to apply the same model in the distant Philippines, where they also referred to native peoples as *indios*.

Cuba – where the encomienda had quickly decimated the native population – served as the springboard for Mexican conquest. Voyagers set out in 1517 and 1518 to reconnoiter the Yucatán, as it was the closest mainland point to Cuba, and even sailed part way up the Gulf coast of Mexico. These expeditions were sponsored by Cuba's governor Diego Velázquez, who commissioned one of the island's *encomenderos*, Hernando Cortés, to lead a third expedition in 1519. Velázquez held the coveted title of *adelantado*, the official license to invade, so Cortés was supposed to explore only, not march inland. Once given command of an expeditionary force, Cortés knew well that he might be able to extend the chain of Spanish conquest that linked each new settlement to the next one – Hispaniola to Cuba to Mexico, for example. As we have seen in the case of Columbus, this was not a stable system, but rather one that bred competition and betrayal. It was tempting for each would-be conqueror to work back down the conquest chain to the king in Spain and simply bypass local patrons in favor of direct royal sponsorship. Worrying that Cortés would do just that, Velázquez vainly tried at the last minute to prevent his sailing from Cuba.

Upon reaching the Mexican mainland, Cortés had his five hundred men ground most of their eleven ships and swear direct allegiance to the king. Cortés's next move was to found a city, not an act of construction but a ritual act, which created a town council whose votes of support lent a veneer of legality to his actions. The expedition's captains were appointed officers of the town council; Francisco de Montejo became an alcalde, for example, and Pedro de Alvarado a regidor. Over three hundred men signed the foundational petition (a document that disappeared into the Spanish archives for centuries, and remains unpublished). It would be six years, well after his conquest war against the Mexica had been won, before Cortés received royal approval, in person in Spain, for his revolt against Velázquez.

Invading Spaniards on the Mesoamerican mainland (and in South America) frequently faced stiff resistance from native warriors. This was Cortés's experience, first on Mexico's Gulf Coast and then inland as the Spaniards made their way toward the Mexica capital. What factors enabled these vastly outnumbered Spaniards to withstand repeated attacks? One was the advantage of their steel swords, helmets, and armor, which allowed them to kill native warriors quickly without much fearing projectiles or obsidian-bladed daggers and clubs, the typical weapons of Mesoamerica. This led to the second factor: quick alliances with Mexica rivals. When Spanish forces proved unbeatable and continued resistance costly – as happened with the kingdom of Tlaxcala – native lords moved to accommodate the invaders through alliance.

Cortés and native rulers thus found common ground in identifying a shared and distant foe, Moctezuma Xocoyotl, the Mexica emperor, and they soon marched together to the Valley of Mexico to confront him. It is clear from later native testimonies that local rulers were anxious to see the Spaniards leave their communities and were hopeful that the invaders would bring about the collapse of the Mexica (or Aztec) Empire. Some, like the Totonacs, deeply resented their subjection to the Mexica Empire and were quick to rebel against it. Others, like the Tlaxcalans, had successfully resisted Mexica subjection, but were finally convinced that this new alliance with outsiders might destroy their longtime enemies.

These two factors – the advantage of steel weapons and a growing number of native allies – kept the Spanish forces alive. Cunning and treachery would soon help them win. Cortés and his men continued toward the Mexica capital of Tenochtitlán and, in November 1519, entered the city as guests of the emperor. Moctezuma, speaking through Cortés's Nahua interpreter, Malinche (see In Focus 6.1), delivered a welcoming speech. Cortés interpreted it in a letter to his king as a speech of surrender, but Moctezuma appears to have been acting in accordance with custom by receiving foreign dignitaries with regal hospitality. The increasingly fearful and isolated Spaniards, however, soon resorted to terror and betrayal. Cortés had his followers seize Moctezuma by surprise and imprison him in his own palace. He then ordered through interpreters that anyone resisting the Spanish and their allies would be hacked to pieces and fed to the conquistadors' dogs. Ransoming chiefs and terrorizing their subjects were stock Spanish tactics developed in the course of decades of Caribbean slave raiding, tactics that all but crippled mainland imperial peoples, whose sacred kings' wellbeing was essential to the continuance of life itself.

The Spanish-Tlaxcalan invaders spent the next eight months engaged in periodic looting and guerrilla-style warfare in Tenochtitlán. In the midst of the violence, disease, the third Spanish advantage (along with steel weapons and native allies), struck the Mexica. Within this first wave of diseases, a smallpox epidemic caused massive mortality in the city and across central Mexico. This land of plenty that gave the world maize, chocolate, tomatoes, and so many other vital and pleasurable foods was receiving only the Old World's most deadly germs in these early phases of the Columbian Exchange. A bloody stalemate settled over the metropolis.

Meanwhile, Cortés had images of the Virgin Mary placed atop Aztec temples to assert the primacy of the invaders' religion. He then left with a number of Spaniards and native allies for the Gulf coast, where he confronted a company of Velázquez supporters sent from Cuba to challenge him. Cortés and his followers quickly forced them to surrender, then convinced most to join in the conquest of Mexico. By the time Cortés returned to Tenochtitlán, the advantage had shifted to the Mexica, who now held the Spaniards, led by Pedro de Alvarado, under siege.

In desperation, the Spaniards murdered Moctezuma, later claiming that he was stoned to death by his own people. After dark on June 30, 1520 – which

IN FOCUS 6.1

Figure 6.1. **a.** Credit: Ms Palat. 218–220 Book IX Marina interpreting for the Spaniards at a meeting between Hernando Cortés and Montezuma (1466–1520), from the 'Florentine Codex' by Bernardino de Sahagún, c.1540–85 by Spanish School (16th century) Biblioteca Medicea-Laurenziana, Florence, Italy/ The Bridgeman Art Library (Image # XTD 82721) **b.** Cortés and Malinche, as portrayed in the Lienzo de Tlaxcala, a sixteenth-century native pictorial account of the Conquest. **c.** Orozco, José Clemente, © ARS, NY. Hernan Cortez and "la malinche". 1926. Mural. Escuela Nacional Preparatoria San Ildefonso, Mexico City, D.F., Mexico. (Image Reference ART27199) Image provided by Schalkwijk / Art Resource, NY. © 2010 Artists Rights Society (ARS), New York / SOMAAP, Mexico City.

MALINCHE'S WORDS

The little girl's birth name was probably Malinal, the twelfth day in the Nahua calendar. In her teens, she was baptized Marina, then called Doña Marina in recognition of her noble status. The Nahuas rendered Marina as Malina, giving it a reverential suffix (again, to recognize status) to make it Malintzin. The Spaniards in turn heard this as Malinche. By that time, the young woman's role in what was happening in Mexico was so important that Nahuas began to call the Spanish leader Cortés "Malinche"; her name rubbed off on him.

For Malinche to undergo so many transformations in so few years – from being sold as a slave to being one of the best-known and highly regarded women in the land – was testimony to both extraordinary times and an extraordinary personality.

Around the year 1510, Malinche had been sold to a noble family in Tabasco, on Mexico's Gulf coast. She herself was allegedly of noble lineage, a native speaker of Nahuatl. Maya was the language of her new masters, and soon she learned the local dialect of this language.

From Malinche's arrival in Tabasco, stories circulated there of bellicose strangers traveling in what looked like floating houses. Several had attacked Maya settlements and kidnapped fishermen and traders. One day in 1519 (the year One Reed by the local calendar) the strangers came ashore in Tabasco and quickly defeated the people who held Malinche. In suing for peace, the people offered servant girls, including Malinche.

The strangers' Maya interpreter was called Gerónimo, a Spanish castaway who had survived several years' captivity in the Yucatán. In conversing with Malinche, he discovered that she knew Nahuatl, the language of Mexico. As a result, Hernando Cortés, the strangers' leader, took a special interest in Malinche.

Sailing west, the foreigners' flotilla reached a tiny island. Here "don Hernando" ordered his followers to go ashore. Soon, Cortés's men made contact with local townsfolk, and through them, a conversation was opened with group of traveling Aztec representatives who spoke only Nahuatl.

Malinche's linguistic skills were now critical: she rendered into Nahuatl each phrase the castaway gave her in Yucatec or Chontal Mayan. Then she did the reverse for each of the Mexica ambassadors' replies. Gerónimo interpreted the Mayan responses in the Castilian language for don Hernando. Soon, Cortés wrote to his king, the castaway Gerónimo proved unnecessary. Malinche had learned Castilian.

Malinche went on to serve as Hernando Cortés's key to Mexico, helping him and his swelling number of native allies bring down one of the world's most fearsome and populous empires. In the process, Malinche bore Cortés a son. Because of her roles as conquistador helpmeet and mistress, Malinche came to be regarded in Mexican mythology as a traitor. At best, she is depicted ambiguously as the mother of modern Mexico (which, in Orozco's mural, lies prostrate at hers and Cortés's feet). Scholars have recently shown these characterizations to be false. Malinche was not an "Aztec," although she spoke their language, and she was not regarded as a "sell-out" in her own day, not even by the Mexica. Instead, her drastic transformation from exiled servant to Mexico's most powerful woman struck many as just another trick of the gods. Nahua artists working shortly after the Conquest routinely depicted Malinche at the center of key encounters, her all-important speech emanating in scrolls (as in the first image above). For a people whose kings were called *tlatoque*, or "speakers," Malinche's linguistic fluency and intervention mattered deeply. Debates on character aside, Malinche's words made history.

The images above are Cortés and Malinche, as portrayed in the Florentine Codex, Book 12 of which is an account of the Conquest of Mexico written in Spanish and Nahuatl by a Franciscan friar and his informants from Tlatelolco; the Lienzo de Tlaxcala, a sixteenth-century native pictorial account of the Conquest; and a 1930s mural by the Mexican painter José Clemente Orozco.

the Spaniards would dub the *la Noche Triste*, the Tragic Night – they attempted to secretly exit the city. But Mexica warriors were ready for them. They killed about half the Spaniards and thousands of Tlaxcalan and other native allies. The survivors of Cortés's company escaped and eventually regrouped with Tlaxcalan assistance, but over a year would pass before they managed to recapture Tenochtitlán and its twin city of Tlatelolco. Cortés ordered that brigantines be built on Lake Texcoco's shores, each armed with light cannon. The brigantines and guns were used to cut the Mexica off from the mainland, and also to hammer Aztec warriors in canoes and on land. As the residents of Tenochtitlán and Tlatelolco fell victim to starvation and disease, Cortés and his allies landed and marched ashore. As they proceeded block by block, the invaders found no treasure, only bodies and dying victims. In disgust, Tenochtitlán was razed, its rubble later used in the building of Spanish Mexico City.

By 1521, the fabled center of the Mexica Empire lay in ruins. Yet the empire's extensive infrastructure and ruling apparatus, including trade routes, tribute agreements, and diplomatic ties to regional nobles, survived. The conquering Spaniards moved quickly to transform this preexisting imperial framework and productive capacity into the basis for their own Mesoamerican empire – which they called the Kingdom of New Spain. And just as the Mexica had created their own chain of conquest in the region, the Spaniards followed suit, extending that chain into new frontiers in the 1520s – often using surviving Mexica warriors as auxiliaries.

Still hungry despite his success, Cortés led an expedition to distant Honduras (executing the last Mexica emperor, the captive Cuauhtémoc, on the way). His relative Francisco Cortés went west, beginning the long and difficult conquest of that Mexican region. Others ventured north into what is today the U.S. South and Southwest. As speedily as these early "conquest chains" were started, creating lasting colonies proved a protracted and highly contested process. Toppling the Mexica of the Mesoamerican center had taken several years, but truly subduing the fringes would take centuries. Equally challenging – perhaps more so – was turning millions of former Mexica subjects into subjects of the king of Spain. This battle for native Mexican hearts and minds would continue throughout the colonial era and beyond.

What of Cortés? Was he more fortunate than Columbus? Returning to Spain, Cortés was well received by the first Habsburg king of Spain and, by that time, the Holy Roman emperor, Charles V. But the king, having just faced off against Castilian nobles, was reluctant to make conquistadors into viceroys. Cortés was bought off with an illustrious new title – Marquis of the Valley of Oaxaca – and given enormous encomienda holdings to match. It was not what the Americas' most famous conquistador had expected, so he returned again to Europe to fight for his king. In 1547, after participating in a failed expedition to North Africa, Cortés died in Seville.

From Panama to Peru and Beyond

One chain of conquest thus ran from Hispaniola to Cuba to Mexico. Another extended from Hispaniola to Panama – and from there, along South America's Pacific coast to Peru. Spaniards began conquering native Panamanians and establishing lasting towns in 1508, and by 1514 Panama boasted the first Spanish bishop appointed to the American mainland, or "Tierra Firme," as it was called. Also in 1514, Vasco Núñez de Balboa and one of his black slaves sighted the Pacific Ocean, or "South Sea." Though nothing new to Native Americans in the region, this first sighting of the Pacific by a European and an African went some way toward fulfilling Columbus's dream of finding a westward route to Asia.

Meanwhile, the newcomers focused on nearer objectives. After founding Panama City on the Pacific shore of the isthmus, the Spaniards began to reconnoiter long stretches of coast, as well as offshore islands. The early settlers included the Pizarro brothers, natives of Extremadura, which was also Cortés's home region (see In Focus 6.2). In 1522, one of the brothers, Francisco, sailed south in search of "Pirú," a mythical chieftain. His dream, shared by many other Spaniards who had spent years in the greater Caribbean basin, was to repeat the success of Cortés. The Pizarro brothers alone were

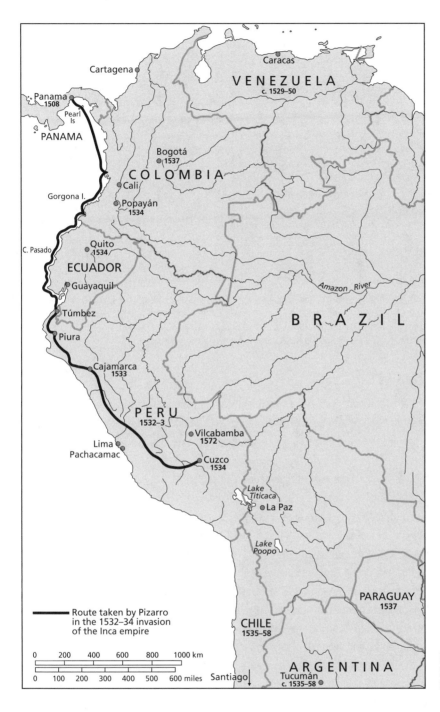

Map 6.2
South America in
the Conquest Period

fated to do so, helped in large part by events taking place in the high Andes, far away. Even so – as Cortés and the other Spaniards who had invaded Mesoamerican kingdoms found out – the conquest of Native American empires was not to be a simple, miraculous, overnight affair.

In the end, it took a decade of coastal reconnaissance and humiliating failure before Francisco Pizarro led his legendary 168 men into what is today

IN FOCUS 6.2

Figure 6.2. a. This portrait of the "invincible" Cortés as a 63-year-old conquistador was first published in 1588 as the frontispiece to Gabriel Lasso de la Vega's flattering *Valiant Cortés*. Courtesy of the John Carter Brown Library at Brown University. **b.** Drawing 148. The conquistadors Don Diego de Almagro and Don Francisco Pizarro. From The Guaman Poma manuscript (GKS 2232 4°) at the Royal Library, Copenhagen, Denmark. Credit: The Royal Library, Copenhagen, Denmark.

CONQUISTADOR COUSINS

The portrait here of the "invincible" Cortés as a sixty-three-year-old conquistador was first published in 1588 as the frontispiece to Gabriel Lasso de la Vega's flattering *Valiant Cortés*, and the depictions of Diego Almagro and Francisco Pizarro were included in Felipe Guaman Poma de Ayala's 1615 *Nueva corónica y buen gobierno*.

Hernando Cortés was born in the early 1480s in Medellín, Extremadura, a dry, poor region of western Spain. He was the son of an illegitimate lesser nobleman, Martín Cortés. He studied law at Salamanca University for a couple of years, later working as a notary. He went to Valencia, with the intention of seeking his fortune with the Spanish forces fighting in Italy, but changed his mind and went to the Caribbean instead – arriving in his early twenties. He thus had more than a dozen years' experience as a conquistador-settler on Hispaniola and Cuba before he invaded Mexico. After a decade of exploration and conquest in Mesoamerica, Cortés returned to Spain; in 1529, not long after meeting with the king in Toledo, Cortés ran into Francisco Pizarro, who was there seeking a license from the king to invade Peru.

Cortés's mother was a Pizarro, and he was therefore a distant relation of the Pizarro brothers – Francisco, Gonzalo, Hernando, and Juan, all of whom participated in the Spanish invasion of the Inca Empire. Like Cortés, the Pizarros were from Extremadura – from the town of Trujillo. Their father was a lesser nobleman and a veteran of the wars in Italy. Francisco was an illegitimate son by a local farmer's daughter. Francisco was never legitimated; he remained all his life illiterate, a consummate gambler, and a man more at home fighting or working with his hands than governing or discussing matters of law (in this respect, he was very different from Cortés, whose letters to the king are artfully composed). Pizarro briefly visited Italy and may have come close to following in his father's footsteps there. But, as did Cortés, he chose "the Indies" over Italy – and instead sailed with an uncle to the Caribbean. Just as Cortés won encomiendas in Cuba, so did Pizarro in Panama. It is not clear how close Francisco was to his much younger brothers in childhood, but they were ready to follow him after 1529 – including Hernando, the eldest and only legitimate brother. In that year, Francisco added to his two and a half decades of conquest experience in the Americas a royal license to invade Peru.

That license gave Pizarro the right to be governor of whatever he conquered in South America; it excluded his junior partner for the second half of his years in Panama, Diego de Almagro. Pizarro never accepted Almagro as an equal, and Almagro never forgave Pizarro, claiming all of southern Peru for himself in 1537, in defiance of Pizarro's authority. The Pizarros organized an army against Almagro, defeating and executing him. His son took revenge, assassinating Francisco Pizarro in 1541 in Lima. In the subsequent conflicts, Almagro's son and Gonzalo Pizarro were executed. Juan Pizarro had died earlier, during the siege of Cuzco. Of the four Pizarro brothers, only Hernando would die like Cortés – as a wealthy but bitter old man, back in Spain.

Peru, the heartland of the Inca Empire. In the meantime, Pizarro had acquired Quechua-speaking translators, a small army of men with horses, armor, and state-of-the-art weapons, and a license from Charles V that excluded one of his early partners in Panama, Diego de Almagro (see In Focus 6.2). By late 1532, when Pizarro's forces began their inland march, Inca "Peru" seemed ripe for the taking.

As we have seen, the Inca empire, or Tawantinsuyu, was in deep crisis in 1532. The Inca Huayna Capac had apparently died of smallpox, leaving his heirs, Atawallpa and Huascar, to battle for the right to succeed him. By chance, Pizarro and his Spaniards got the opportunity to meet Atawallpa in the northern highland city of Cajamarca just as he was returning from a victory over his brother's forces. Like Moctezuma in Mexico, Atawallpa seems to have believed that he might employ the well-armed foreigners as mercenaries to help him consolidate power. There is no evidence that Atawallpa or any of his subjects mistook the Spaniards for gods, although their weapons, horses, and physical features (particularly their hirsute bodies) were cause for amazement. According to chroniclers, some African slaves were closely examined to see if they had been permanently painted for war.

As we have seen, the conquistadors had learned to follow a script: it began by initiating a false diplomatic encounter that would enable them to seize a headman – preferably the king or emperor – and hold him hostage. Thus, according to a carefully rehearsed plan, Pizarro and his men sprung their trap at Cajamarca and seized Atawallpa in November 1532. The Inca's men were unarmed, many of them assembled to view a Spanish demonstration of horsemanship and gunplay. The attack, reminiscent of Cortés's seizure of Moctezuma, crippled resistance before it began. Atawallpa, like Moctezuma, had no reason to suspect such treachery from guests whom he had supplied with safe passage, food, and lodging. The humiliated emperor, to his subjects a divine king and "son of the Sun," now spent almost a year as a captive, awaiting a huge ransom in gold and silver brought in from all over Tawantinsuyu. Aztec gold was justly famous, but the Incas were true masters of gold and silver metallurgy, and the hoard of treasure amassed to free Atawallpa was staggering. Once it reached Seville's counting houses, Atawallpa's ransom gave rise to a new saying: "vale un Perú," or "worth a Peru." The subsequent discovery of the world's richest silver mines would reinforce the legend. In a second, scripted act of treachery, the Inca Atawallpa was executed – strangled with a garrote on Pizarro's orders – in July 1533. And yet the conquest of Tawantinsuyu had only just begun.

Subsequent stages of war included the capture of Cuzco, then Quito, the empire's distant, twin capitals. Both fell to the Spanish and their newfound allies, such as the Cañaris of southern Ecuador, by 1534. Even so, their hold was tenuous; in 1536 an heir of the Incas once friendly to the Spanish, Manco Capac, nearly managed to retake Cuzco. One of Francisco Pizarro's younger brothers and several other Spaniards were killed in the siege, but Manco's forces finally retreated to the northwest past Machu Picchu, where they established a new but much reduced capital at Vilcabamba. It survived, complete with its own line of emperors, until 1572.

As if following yet another act in the unofficial conquistador script, Peru's conquistadors soon began to fight bitterly with one another, and with the Spanish crown, for control. There were disagreements between the followers of Pizarro and those of Diego de Almagro, each of whom claimed preeminence. There were other contenders, too. One was the latecomer Pedro de Alvarado, associate of Cortés and decorated conquistador of Guatemala. Despite command of a large and well-equipped expedition, Alvarado lost his way in the jungles of coastal Ecuador and arrived in Quito too late to share in the plunder. Sebastián de Benalcázar, one of Pizarro's captains, had beat him there in a highland march from the south. Benalcázar continued north beyond Cali, in what is now Colombia, where he met still other conquistadors heading south from the Caribbean coast and Venezuela in search of a mythical chieftain (later an imaginary city) the Spanish called El Dorado.

Soon after the conquistadors won control of the Andean highlands, Charles V sent representatives to establish order and collect taxes on precious metals coming out of the former Inca mines of Carabaya and Porco. There were also new proclamations issued in 1542 that sharply reduced conquistador access to and retention of encomiendas. Another decree promised that anyone enslaving or physically abusing Native Americans would be tried and punished. The conquistadors were aghast, but Bartolomé de las Casas had won his day at court.

Conquistador resentment of what were known as the New Laws sparked a conquistador revolt and civil war in Peru that lasted until 1548. In the end, the crown won out, but not before a viceroy was killed in battle and Gonzalo Pizarro, another of Francisco Pizarro's younger brothers, was captured and executed as a rebel. Unhappy conquistadors continued to rebel against crown authority throughout the Americas until the 1570s. The problem of reining in upstart Spanish subjects abroad would require a complex bureaucratic solution, in Peru and elsewhere.

Who Were the (Spanish) Conquistadors?

Hernando Cortés and Francisco Pizarro achieved a legendary fame that has barely diminished since the sixteenth century. But they stand out from the thousands of other conquistadors only by their good fortune and ability to do well what other company captains also did. In other words, in most respects, Cortés and Pizarro were typical conquistadors.

So what defined a typical conquistador? The identities, experiences, and life stories of the Spaniards who participated in the Conquest in the Americas were varied. Nevertheless, an archetype can be reconstructed from the patterns of conquistador biographies: A young man in his late twenties, semiliterate, from southwestern Spain, trained in a particular trade or profession, seeking opportunity through patronage networks based on family and hometown ties. Armed as well as he could afford, and with some experience already of exploration and conquest in the Americas, he would be ready to invest what he had and risk his life if absolutely necessary to be a member of the first company to conquer some wealthy and well-populated polity.

This archetypal conquistador was not a soldier in the armies of the king of Spain. Although the conquistadors are often misleadingly referred to as soldiers – and they were certainly armed, organized, and experienced in military matters – they acquired their martial skills not from formal training but from conflict situations in the New World. Expedition members were usually recruited in recently founded colonies, as the patterns of the chains of conquest meant that most participants already had some experience in the New World. For example, among the Spaniards who participated in the famous capture of Atawallpa at Cajamarca, over two-thirds had prior Conquest experience and more than half had spent at least five years in the Americas. But none of that amounted to formal training.

The conquistadors' lack of formal training was paralleled by a lack of formal ranking; Spanish forces in Europe at the time were led by commanders from the high nobility and organized into various ranks. In contrast, conquistador groups were headed by captains, the sole named rank and one that varied in number. The record of the division of spoils at Cajamarca listed the men in two categories only: men on horseback and men on foot.

Conquistadors were motivated by a search for economic and social opportunity. The letters Cortés wrote to the king, published in the conquistador's lifetime and still in print today in many languages, give the impression that Spaniards were driven by a sense of loyalty to crown and church. This image was constructed for the benefit of the king, who was well aware of the personal ambitions and motives of the conquerors. But nor should Spaniards be seen as totally obsessed with gold; they sought precious metals because they were the only nonperishable, easy-to-ship item of value that could pay the merchants and creditors who funded conquest campaigns.

Conquistadors "were neither paid nor forced but went of their own will and at their own cost," in the words of one of them, Francisco de Jérez. Gaspar de Marquina, like Jérez, followed Pizarro into the Inca Empire. Marquina wrote to his father that he went to Peru because it was a place where "there's more gold and silver than iron in Biscay, and more sheep than in Soria, and great supplies of all kinds of food, and much fine clothing, and the best people that have been seen in the whole Indies, and many great lords among them." Marquina was not a professional soldier but a page, a fully literate, high-ranking servant to two of the early conquistador-governors of Spanish American colonies (Governor Pedrarias of Nicaragua and Francisco Pizarro). He came to "the Indies" of his own free will, hoping to return to his father in Spain a wealthy man and, most likely, to take up a career as a notary or merchant. He pursued that opportunity through his connection to important patrons. However, like most Spaniards who fought in the violent invasions of the early sixteenth century, he died before he could return to Spain (in Marquina's case, he was killed in a skirmish with native Andeans by the time his father had received his letter and the gold bar accompanying it).

Spaniards, then, joined conquest expeditions not in return for specified payments but in the hope of acquiring shares of booty and status according to their contributions. Spaniards called these ventures "companies." Although powerful patrons played important investment roles, it was the captains who primarily funded companies and expected to reap the greatest rewards. The spirit of commercialism infused conquest expeditions from start to finish, with participants selling services and trading goods with one another throughout the endeavor. Conquistadors were, in other words, armed entrepreneurs. The members of a successful conquest company hoped to be granted an encomienda, which would afford them high status and often a superior lifestyle among fellow colonists. As there were never enough encomiendas to go round, the most lucrative grants went to those who had invested the most in the expedition – and survived to see it succeed. Lesser investors received lesser grants (a few dozen, instead of thousands, of indigenous "vassals") or simply a share of the spoils of war.

Conquistadors were overwhelmingly middle-ranking men, from occupations and backgrounds below the high nobility but above the commoner masses (as was true of Cortés and Pizarro – see In Focus 6.2). Documents show that the conquerors of the New Kingdom of Granada (today's Colombia) were mostly skilled men of some means or property. Likewise, those Spaniards at Cajamarca in 1533 who recorded their occupations were not career soldiers but professionals and artisans who had acquired various battle experience and martial skills. A third of those who stated their occupation were artisans – including tailors, farriers (horseshoers), carpenters, trumpeters, a cooper, a sword smith, a stonemason, a barber, and a piper or crier. The same kinds of artisans had also accompanied Francisco de Montejo on his first expedition into the Yucatán in 1527, along with the usual professional men – merchants, physicians, a couple of priests, and a pair of Flemish artillery engineers. An unspecified number of the artisans and professionals invested in the company were confident enough of its outcome to bring their wives (although, following customary practice, the Spanish women probably remained with the merchants at the last Caribbean port before Yucatán was reached).

We also know the age and birthplace of more than twelve hundred conquistadors who participated in the original invasions of Panama, Mexico, Peru, and Colombia. The makeup of each expedition was similar, with an average of 30 percent from the southern Spanish kingdom of Andalusia, 19 percent from neighboring Extremadura, 24 percent from the core kingdoms of Old and New Castile, and the remainder from other regions of the Iberian Peninsula. Among these, Basques stood out. Other Europeans were rare among the conquistadors, restricted to the odd Portuguese, Genoese, Flemish, or Greek individual. In age, the conquerors ranged from teenagers to the occasional sixty-year-old; the average age of the men who went to both Peru and Colombia was twenty-seven, with the vast majority in their twenties or early thirties.

In terms of education, the range was broad, from men who were completely illiterate and uneducated to the occasional man of considerable learning. Despite the impression given by conquistador chronicles, the fully literate were in the minority in conquest companies – although the paucity of farmers among conquistadors meant that literacy rates were slightly higher than back in Spain. Eyewitness narratives such as those by Bernal Díaz and Cortés on Mexico, and Francisco de Jérez on Peru, are classics partly because they are rare. Most conquistadors wrote or dictated "merit" reports in a formulaic style. Despite the common misconception that literacy gave Spaniards an advantage over Native Americans, members of conquistador companies could probably read and write no better than the most literate Native American societies, such as the Mayas.

Nor was there a close correlation between social status and literacy among conquistadors; the colonial chronicler Juan Rodríguez Freyle, a Bogotá native, claimed that some city council members of the New Granada settlements used branding irons to sign documents. Among the four Pizarro brothers and the other six leaders of the 1532–1534 invasion of Peru, four were literate, three were semiliterate (they could sign their names), and three were illiterate (including Francisco Pizarro).

Who Were the (Other) Conquistadors?

In 1578, King Philip II of Spain signed a royal edict in Madrid and dispatched it to the governor of the province of Yucatán. The edict (quoted at the start of this chapter) stated that the governor was to cease demanding tribute payments from one Sebastián Toral, a resident of Merida, the colony's capital. Toral's wife was also to be spared the burden of tribute, as were their children when they reached taxable age. The edict was a response to petitions sent to the king from Toral, whose pleas were based on his citation of service to the crown during the Spanish conquest of Yucatán.

Such a story was not unusual. As we have seen, Spanish conquistadors were never salaried, holding at best a license to conquer and promises of future royal favors. Thus, Spanish kings in the sixteenth century were besieged by – and often responded favorably to – requests for privileges and rewards from those who had carved out Spain's empire in the Americas. However – and this is what makes the edict unusual – Sebastián Toral was neither a native nobleman nor a Spaniard. He was a black African. Toral had entered Yucatán as a young teenage slave owned by one of the conquistadors on the failed campaign into Yucatán of the early 1530s; he returned in 1540, possibly already free, along with the Spaniards who came to try to subdue the Mayas of the peninsula for the third time. Once a colony was founded in the early 1540s, Toral lived among Yucatán's new settlers as a Christian Spanish speaker with, eventually, a family. When a law was passed that required all those of African descent in the Spanish colonies to pay tribute (three pesos a year, equivalent to a laborer's monthly salary), Toral wrote a letter of protest to the king. Then, when he received no reply, he sailed to Spain, where he won the edict described earlier. In 1580, he crossed the Atlantic for the third time; the last we hear of him is in Mexico City, but presumably he died in Yucatán, among his family, in the 1580s.

Toral was a conquistador, then, but he was never granted the status of a Spanish conqueror. His post-Conquest occupation was that of guard, one commonly associated with blacks and mulattoes in the Spanish colonies. He remained, despite his free status and his freedom to travel to Spain and back, in the subordinate category of a *negro*. His decision to travel to Spain was in some ways extraordinary, as the voyage involved several weeks of expense, risk, and discomfort, and Toral was almost sixty (an old man for the sixteenth century). He must have been thinking not of himself and his own pocket but of his children and of the principle of the thing – paying tribute put him in the same category as the Mayas he had fought against in his youth; being exempt categorized him with the Spaniards he had fought beside.

In what ways was Sebastián Toral typical, and how was he exceptional? He was typical in the sense that he represents the hundreds of thousands of sub-Saharan Africans brought to the Americas in the sixteenth century, many of whom fought in Conquest wars and played vital roles in Spanish victories over native armies and in the defense of new colonies (see In Focus 6.3).

Figure 6.3. **a.** Credit: Fol.208v Meeting of Hernando Cortés (1485-1547) and Montezuma (1466-1520), miniature from the 'History of the Indians' by Diego Durán, 1579 (vellum) Biblioteca Nacional, Madrid, Spain/ Giraudon/ The Bridgeman Art Library [Image # XIR 227180] **b.** Arrival of Cortés in Mexico, followed by his black servant and preceded by La Malinche, his mistress and translator. 16th CE. Codex Azcatitlan. Ms mexicains n°59-64. Bibliotheque Nationale, Paris, France. (Image Reference ART170224) © Snark / Art Resource, NY

BLACK CONQUISTADORS

Sebastián Toral, black conquistador in Yucatán, was not the only African to fight alongside Spaniards against native warriors in the Americas. There were dozens of such fighters in the early Conquest campaigns in the Caribbean and Mexico. After 1521, the wealth and credit generated by the acquisition of the Mexica Empire funded auxiliary forces of black conquistadors that could number as many as five hundred. Spaniards recognized the value of these fighters. Although they usually chose to forget black contributions in written accounts of Spanish campaigns, Spaniards occasionally admitted that African men were outstanding soldiers (because so many African men became slaves by being captured on battlefields back in Africa, they already had military experience before coming to the Americas).

One of the black conquistadors who fought against the Aztecs and survived the destruction of their empire was Juan Garrido. Born in Africa, Garrido lived as a young slave in Portugal before being sold to a Spaniard and acquiring his freedom fighting in the conquests of Puerto Rico, Cuba, and other islands. He fought in the Spanish-Mexica War as a free servant or auxiliary, participating in Spanish expeditions to other parts of Mexico (including Baja California) in the 1520s and 1530s. Granted a house plot in the new Mexico City, he raised a family there, working at times as a guard (as Toral did in Merida) and town crier. He claimed to have been the first person to plant wheat in Mexico. Garrido or one of his black fellow conquistadors is portrayed in various early colonial drawings illustrating the Spanish invasion of Mexico. The image above left shows Moctezuma welcoming Cortés – whose horse is held by a black slave or servant, drawn small perhaps to indicate his subordinate status (from Diego Durán, *The History of the Indies of New Spain*). The other image is from the *Codex Azcatitlán*, showing a black soldier clearly visible among a groups of Spaniards, led by Cortés and Malinche, with native porters bringing up the rear.

He was exceptional in that most of these men and women remained slaves until they died in Spanish America or Brazil, never acquiring freedom or the chance to sail to another colony or back across the Atlantic Ocean. In another way, however, Toral was typical of those of African descent in the Americas. Just as he fought to survive the Conquest, win his freedom, and then go to great lengths to spare his family the burden and ignominy of tribute-paying status, so did black slaves never reconcile themselves to their bondage; as we will see in subsequent chapters, during the course of our exploration of the African experience in early-colonial Latin America, Africans and mulattoes sought to improve their lives in numerous ways; to resist the subordinate, involuntary circumstances of their passage to the New World; and to forge the bonds of family and community.

Spanish and African men were not the only people who fought with invading conquest companies. First of all, a small number of Spanish women accompanied the conquistadors. Of the thousand-odd Spaniards who entered Mexico with Cortés in 1519 or with other companies in the 1520s, nineteen Spanish women participated to the degree that we might call them *conquistadoras*. There is evidence of at least five of them actually fighting. Second, the title of *conquistador* was appropriated soon after the conquest by Maya, Zapotec, and other Mesoamerican elites who had allied with Spanish invaders and won certain privileges in the new colonial system. Their role was crucial, as without the many thousands of indigenous soldiers who fought as *indios amigos*, or "Indian friends," the Spanish conquistadors would not have lived to found colonies in the Americas; we return later to these native conquistadors.

The Habit of Winning

Francisco de Jérez, conquistador of Peru, asked, "When in ancient or modern times have such huge enterprises of so few succeeded against so many?" The question of how the Spanish Conquest was possible is arguably one of the great questions of human history. For centuries, the answer was thought to be either providential (the preferred Spanish view) or the result of Spanish depravity and greed (the Black Legend view preferred by Spain's enemies, along with some Native Americans). The modern view of the Conquest is more complex and contested, periodically reinterpreted by scholars of various disciplines.

Throughout colonial times, Spaniards believed that their conquests in the Americas were made possible by their moral superiority. Even Las Casas believed that God had chosen the Spaniards as his agents to bring the true faith and the benefits of civilization to the pagan barbarians of the New World. As a result, many Spaniards felt there was something miraculous about military triumphs over great empires such as those of the Aztecs and Incas. Gaspar de Marquina, in the letter to his father quoted earlier, remarked of the capture of Atawallpa that "God gave us the victory miraculously over him and his forces."

But divine intervention did not detract from the credit due to the conquistadors; for, in the words of Cortés, "Spaniards dare face the greatest peril, consider fighting their glory, and have the habit of winning." Santiago, the patron saint of the Reconquest, and the Virgin Mary may have been seen coming to the aid of the Spaniards during crucial Conquest battles, but Spaniards still insisted that the skill and confidence with which they wielded their swords and other weapons made all the difference. These two factors – military superiority and "the greater self-confidence of the civilization that produced the conquistadors" (as the historian J. H. Elliott put it a half century ago) – have been dominant explanations of the Conquest for much of the past five centuries (see In Focus 6.4).

But although technological disparities clearly played an important role in military encounters, the Conquest is better understood and explained if the military factor is placed within the context of a nexus of the following four factors. The first factor, which Las Casas ignored and Europeans underestimated for centuries, was disease, specifically the deadly impact of Old World epidemics, such as smallpox and measles, upon the Native American population. Germs traveled faster than Spaniards did, killing Native Americans before they ever saw a European face, but the conquistadors were nevertheless greatly outnumbered among sedentary societies such as the Aztecs and other Nahuas, the Mayas, and the Andeans. This numerical imbalance was largely offset by the second factor, native allies. The highly localized nature of Native American identities fostered native disunity. This made possible the Spanish recruitment of large numbers of native warriors under their own leaders, the acquisition of native interpreters (of whom Malinche is but the most famous), and the collaboration of indigenous elites in conquest campaigns and colony building.

Combined with the impact of these two factors, the third factor is that advantages of Spanish weaponry were significant. The weapon that was most useful to the conquistadors, the one that killed more native warriors and saved invaders more often than any other, was the steel sword. Of secondary importance were guns, horses, and war dogs or mastiffs; these were not available to all Spaniards and were useful only under particular circumstances, although Spaniards greatly prized horses. Yet despite the benefit to Spaniards of epidemic disease, native allies, and the steel blade, there remained moments in the history of the Conquest when the invaders perished anyway – and moments when they would have perished were it not for a fourth factor.

The fourth factor was the circumstances of the Spanish invasion. Spanish invaders risked nothing beyond their own skins. Pressing on into unknown

IN FOCUS 6.4

Figure 6.4. a. Built in the 16th century for Hernando Pizarro. The carved busts represent Francisco Pizarro, Inés Huylas Yupanqui, Francisca Pizarro, and Hernando Pizarro. Photograph by Ángel M. Felicísimo. **b.** Francisco de Montejo's house in Mérida, Yucatan. Photograph by Bonnie Miluso.

CONQUISTADOR SUPERIORITY – CARVED IN STONE

Few conquistadors were more successful than Hernando Cortés and Francisco Pizarro. Yet many others were proud enough of their accomplishments in defeating indigenous kingdoms and empires to want to memorialize them on their private residences, either in the colonies or in Spain. Francisco de Montejo, conqueror of Yucatán and Honduras, ordered his likeness carved on the portal of his palatial residence on the central plaza of Merida, the capital city of the new colony of Yucatán, built in the 1540s (above right). He and his son were depicted standing on open-mouthed severed heads – perhaps those of defeated Maya lords, perhaps those of potential Spanish rivals.

Hernando Pizarro, meanwhile, Francisco's older brother and heir to the unambiguous title of Marqués de la Conquista, built a palatial residence on the central plaza of his native Trujillo, Spain (above left). There in the center of town one can still see Hernando's head carved in stone, and beneath him that of his mestiza wife, Beatriz, also the daughter of his brother Francisco. In a touch that would have outraged Las Casas, the couple is surrounded by a string of small, identical, and nearly nude native Andeans chained about the neck. Even if the Spanish crown proved ambivalent in rewarding the deeds of its American conquistadors, these men themselves sought to prove their merit through lasting monuments to their bloody triumphs. In adopting symbols of conquest in their homes and coats of arms, they appealed to medieval notions of knightly service.

territory held the promise of great wealth and social prestige; turning back ensured debt, ignominy, and perhaps the retribution of a betrayed patron. Native leaders, in contrast, were defending more than their lives. At stake were the lives of their families, the future status of their descendants, possession of fertile lands and irrigation works, the welfare of whole communities.

Symbolic of these concerns was the Mesoamerican view of war as a seasonal activity; like many peoples in West Africa, they waged it when it was not time to plant or harvest. Natives were thus motivated to seek compromise and accommodation with an invader willing – and often able – to keep fighting until such an accommodation was reached. Indigenous leaders could not possibly have known that such compromises would result in three centuries of Spanish colonial rule.

* * *

In the following chapter, we extend our discussion of the Conquest chronologically and geographically, as well as conceptually – detailing the protracted nature of the Conquest; examining the perspective of indigenous leaders; and showing how the Spanish invasion was, from most native viewpoints, only the beginning of a long process of negotiated relations. We also fill in some important further gaps in the story, explaining Brazil's particular experience of conquest.

SUGGESTIONS FOR FURTHER READING

This chapter is designed to accompany Matthew Restall's *Seven Myths of the Spanish Conquest* (2003), but we also recommend the following texts: Stuart B. Schwartz, ed., *Victors and Vanquished: Spanish and Nahua Views of the Conquest of Mexico* (2000), which neatly juxtaposes Spanish accounts, chiefly that of Bernal Díaz, with Nahua and other native accounts; and Matthew Restall, *Maya Conquistador* (1998), which presents Maya accounts of the Conquest of Yucatán.

For those seeking fuller access to primary Spanish sources in translation, we suggest the following editions: Bartolomé de las Casas, *The Devastation of the Indies* (1992); Hernán Cortés, *Letters from Mexico*, edited by Anthony Pagden (1986 ed.); Bernal Díaz, *The Conquest of New Spain*, edited by Davíd Carrasco (2008); Pedro de Cieza de León, *The Discovery and Conquest of Peru*, edited by Alexandra Parma Cook and Noble David Cook (1998); and James Lockhart and Enrique Otte, *Letters and People of the Spanish Indies* (1976), especially part 1.

Accessible secondary works on aspects of the Spanish Conquest include Inga Clendinnen's *Ambivalent Conquests: Maya and Spaniard in Yucatan, 1517–1570* (2d ed., 2003), which pairs well with Restall's *Maya Conquistador*; Anna Lanyon's books *Malinche's Conquest* and *The New World of Martin Cortes* (2000 and 2004); and Camilla Townsend's thoughtful and probing *Malintzin's Choices: An Indian Woman in the Conquest of Mexico* (2006). On the Andes, see John Hemming's *The Conquest of the Incas*, originally published in 1970 but still a gripping read (available in various editions). On Colombia, see J. Michael Francis, ed., *Invading Colombia* (2007). Instructors using Matthew Restall, Lisa Sousa, and Kevin Terraciano, *Mesoamerican Voices: Native-Language Writings from Colonial Mexico, Oaxaca, Yucatan, and Guatemala* (2005) might assign chapter 1 of that book here.

GLOSSARY

Fundición [foon-dees-YOAN] and **Repartimiento** [rep-art-eem-YEN-toh]: the melting down and dividing up of precious metals

Encomendero [en-kom-en-DARE-oh]: holder of an encomienda or grant of native labor and tribute

Adelantado [a-de-lan-TAH-doh]: "invader" or holder of a royal license to invade and conquer

Malinche [mal-EEN-chay]: Nahua noblewoman who acted as Cortés's interpreter during the Spanish invasion of the Aztec/Mexica Empire

Columbian Exchange: the exchange of plants, animals, viruses, and bacteria between Old and New Worlds that followed Columbus's voyages (further explained in Chapter 7)

Cajamarca [ka-ha-MAR-kah], **Cuzco** [KOOZ-koh], and **Quito** [KEY-toh]: the principal cities of the Inca Empire

BVEN GOBIERNO

ATOPA AMARO LE COR

TANLA CAVESẽ ELCVZCO

yncauanacauximaytamtinquisapraaucachicchomanahuchayocta
concayquita cuchon

en el cuzco   fue

S I 453

7

The Incomplete Conquest

They were all decorated with feathers according to their custom, and they bit their arms, threatening me that they wanted to eat me in this way. A king walked in front of me, carrying the club with which they kill their captives. He preached and told them how they had captured me, their slave, the Perot (that is how they name the Portuguese). They would now avenge the deaths of their friends on me. And as they brought me to the canoes, several among them beat me with their fists.

(Hans Staden's *True History*, 1557)

Thus did a young German gunner named Hans Staden describe his 1550 capture by native Brazilians. Staden had been shipwrecked in 1549 while on a Spanish vessel bound for the fledgling colony of Buenos Aires. Thanks to his knowledge of cannon, he was hired by the Portuguese in a small coastal fort near São Vicente, southwest of Rio de Janeiro. While out hunting one day, Staden was seized by Tupinamba warriors allied with the French, who were then competing with the Portuguese for control of the lucrative trade in Brazilian dyewood. Sugar production for export was also under way. The Tupinamba planned to execute Staden, and possibly to eat him. But thanks to a lucky series of events he survived, and after nine months of captivity, he was rescued by French traders. He published his story in Germany in 1557.

Staden's tale, along with many contemporary French and Portuguese accounts, remind us of how tenuous European claims to Brazil were, and this was true not only of the sixteenth century. For most of the colonial period, the vast portion of South America claimed by the Portuguese remained in the hands of native Brazilians. Conquest was slow and uneven, carried out over the course of three centuries by small troops of colonists, slaves, and indigenous and mixed-race auxiliaries. Driven by the prospect of "lost" empires and emerald-studded mountains, these *bandeirantes* (from

TIMELINE

1524–1529: Spanish invasion of highland Guatemala under Pedro de Alvarado fails; native warriors from Mexico and Oaxaca, including Nahuas from Quauhquechollan, play major role in invasion under Jorge de Alvarado

1527–1542: Spaniards under the three men named Francisco de Montejo invade Yucatán three times, failing to establish a permanent colony until the 1540s

1571: execution of the rebel Inca emperor Túpac Amaru Inca, in Cuzco, Peru

1684–1687: native rebellion in the Chocó (in today's Colombia) forces Spaniards to reconquer the region; resistance continues through the eighteenth century

1697: Spanish conquest of the Maya kingdom of Petén Itzá (in today's northern Guatemala); Itza resistance continues through the eighteenth century

1540s–1880s: Almost continuous failure of Spanish colonial (and then Chilean national) authorities to subdue the Mapuche

1760s–1810s: Portuguese conquest of the Botocudo and other native groups in the *sertão*

Map 7.1
The Protracted
Conquest in South
America

bandeira, or "banner") survived mostly by capturing or bartering for indigenous slaves in the backlands, or *sertão* (Map 7.1). Much like African slavers, they then sold their captives to coastal sugar planters, most of whom lived concentrated along a narrow strip of coast in the far northeast. "We cling like crabs to the seashore," was one Portuguese refrain. Eventually, the *bandeirantes* were hired to destroy runaway slave communities, including the largest one to ever form in Latin America, at Palmares, in the modern state of Alagoas. Only when *bandeirantes* discovered gold in the southern highlands around 1695 did the Portuguese shift their attention to colonizing the Brazilian interior. Even so, the unconquered "Indian" frontier persisted until well after independence in 1822.

Was Brazil's slow conquest totally different, then, from that of Spanish America? The answer is not a simple yes or no. The surprising fall of the Aztec and Inca empires in the 1520s and 1530s has led many to believe that the Spanish Conquest was a dramatically rapid affair (hence the capital *C*), and that swift, follow-up campaigns by Spaniards allowed Castile to lay effective claim to all but the most unpopulated fringes of the American continents and islands. This chapter explores how the conquests of both Spanish and Portuguese America were in fact long, drawn-out affairs in two ways, in terms of political consolidation of claimed territories and geographical barriers to expansion into new ones. In the first sense, like the Portuguese in the *sertão*, it took Spaniards decades in some areas, centuries in others, to consolidate their control over native peoples they claimed to have conquered. And in the second, some regions were not invaded until decades or even centuries after Cortés attacked Moctezuma's empire. We then turn to native views of European invasion. Although some indigenous leaders remained committed to resisting colonial rule, most preferred to accommodate Iberian demands in ways that inverted the Conquest or muted their subordinate status within the new colonies.

The Myth of Pacification

The Spanish conquistadors themselves laid the foundations for what we might call the myth of pacification or the myth of completion. For example, Francisco de Montejo, after a two-year conquest campaign, claimed in 1539 to have brought peace to the new colony of Honduras. "Since my arrival," he wrote to the king, "everyone mines gold, [and] the land is so tranquil and so in repose, and the Indians are so quiet, that whoever sees it marvels, because it seemed impossible that the province should ever come to be in the state it is." Montejo had once written similar words about Yucatán, which in 1539 remained unconquered after two Spanish invasions. Montejo's rival for control of Honduras, Pedro de Alvarado, had painted a similarly rosy picture of Guatemala in the midst of a conquest war marked by excessive violence and more Spanish failures than successes. He abandoned Guatemala to try his luck in Peru in 1533, where he also foundered before returning to Central America. Montejo's Honduras letter was typical in that it contained all the hallmarks of conquistador spin: an emphasis on the docile nature of the local indigenous peoples; a reference to plenty of gold; and an overoptimistic view of the colony's stability and its future.

Why did Spaniards do this? Did they simply wish to disguise failures and disappointments with claims of success? The answer is yes, but for greater reasons than mere pride. As we have seen, Spanish conquistadors (like Brazil's *bandeirantes*) were not salaried employees of the crown. Through their own initiatives, they created companies of investors who funded armed settlers, who were in turn aided by African slaves and native warriors. Conquistador captains could only hope to pay off their debts and rule new provinces of the empire if the crown rewarded them for their accomplishments and sacrifices. To be sure, those who fought in the Conquest's campaigns made much of their personal sufferings (not all pictures painted were rosy), but conquistador spin usually presented those sacrifices as productive, as leading to the enlargement of His Majesty's dominions.

Conquistador spin therefore began in the official reports submitted to the crown by Spanish, black, and native conquerors (reports called *probanzas de mérito*, or "proofs of merit"), and in other related documentation (the Spaniards, more than the Portuguese, produced voluminous records on everything). Thus, the captain with the license to invade and the title of *adelantado* ("invader"; literally, "the advance man") was motivated to declare as soon as possible that a land worth settling had been found and subdued. Ideally, such a land was characterized by its docile natives and abundance of gold or silver, and its conquest completed by the process of what the Iberians called pacification. Pacified natives were those who had accepted the permanent presence of settlers, administrators, and priests – who had accepted that they would henceforth be Christian subjects of the king and that the king and his representatives would tax native labor and produce.

However, we know from numerous documents that Native Americans had their own views on Spanish conquest and pacification, and they were never as simple or "black-and-white" as Montejo and other conquistadors claimed. There are many examples, but we have chosen three regions: the first is the Maya area, stretching from highland Guatemala north into Yucatán (Map 7.2); the other two are regions of South America – the Chocó (in present-day Colombia) and southern Chile (see Map 7.1).

Pedro de Alvarado was one of the Spanish captains who, under Cortés's leadership, had invaded Mexico in 1519. It was in the wake of the destruction of the Aztec imperial capital of Mexico-Tenochtitlán in 1521 that Cortés and Alvarado heard of two prosperous kingdoms to the south – those of the Quiché and Cakchiquel Mayas of highland Guatemala. An embassy of Nahuas, accompanied by two Spaniards, was sent to investigate. They returned to Mexico City with more than a hundred Quiché and Cakchiquel envoys, whose declarations of friendship were described by Cortés as an acceptance of Spanish sovereignty – a classic case of conquistador spin. Nevertheless, when Cortés heard that the Maya envoys had supposedly harassed natives in Soconusco, a region close to Guatemala that had declared loyalty to the Spaniards, he asked Alvarado to assemble an invasion force as soon as possible.

Alvarado left Mexico City in December 1523. His three brothers and two cousins were among the eight Spanish captains of the company. Pedro's pregnant Nahua wife, doña Luisa Xicotencatl (from Tlaxcala's royal family), also came with him. The roughly three hundred Spaniards were accompanied by a number of armed African slaves, with the bulk of Alvarado's forces Nahuas from central Mexico – as many as six thousand of them. Nahua survivors testified that, in addition to the thousands of Mexica, Tlaxcalteca, and other Nahua warriors fighting with the Spaniards, Alvarado also picked up thousands of Zapotec, Mixtec, and other native soldiers as he traveled south toward Guatemala.

Map 7.2
The Protracted Conquest of the Mayas

During his campaign, Alvarado wrote letters to Cortés. One was written in the Quiché capital of Utatlán, after Alvarado and his native forces had attacked and destroyed much of it, capturing and burning alive the two rulers – the king (*ah pop*) and king-elect (*ah pop qamahay*). Amid the violence in Utatlán, Alvarado's half-Tlaxcalteca daughter was born, baptized doña Leonor after the conquistador's mother. Alvarado then continued in the stepping-stone fashion that the Spaniards had been using in Mexico for five years (a method that originated in part in the chain of conquest described earlier and in part borrowed from the Aztecs, who had used it to build their empire over the previous century). His native army reinforced with Quiché warriors, Alvarado moved against the Cakchiquel Mayas, seizing their capital of Iximché. Then with the help of Cakchiquels, the invasion force subdued the Tz'utujil Mayas at Atitlán, continuing south against the Pipil and into what is now El Salvador. By July, Alvarado was back in Iximché (which he renamed Santiago), where he wrote again to Cortés. Although on one level the letters are personal messages to a friend and patron, they are also intended to promote and justify Alvarado's actions to a larger audience (including, he hoped, the king). The rapid publication of letters to patrons and monarchs by the likes of Columbus and Cortés meant that Alvarado might even have imagined the possibility of his letters seeing print – as indeed two of them did, in 1525.

Despite the optimistic tone of many passages in the letters of 1524, a bitterness creeps in at the end of the last letter. Alvarado's ambition was to see Santiago rise from Iximché just as Spanish Mexico had begun to rise from Tenochtitlán, with the Cakchiquels harnessed to the machine of Spanish empire building just as the Mexica, Tlaxcalteca, and other Nahuas were. But such hopes were soon dashed, partly as a result of Alvarado's own impatience, frustration, and impulsive violence, but more so because of persistent indigenous resistance. Alvarado's energetic six-month campaign of 1524 had left him in tenuous control of small pockets of the Guatemalan highlands – yet even this was achieved only through a level of violence and brutality that was excessive even for a Spanish conquistador. When Alvarado departed for Spain in 1526, he left behind devastated Maya kingdoms, ongoing hostilities, and the mere semblance of a new colony. In short, the conquest was a failure, saved only by the return of Pedro's brother Jorge in 1527 at the head of a second invasion force (see In Focus 7.1). As one Spaniard who fought in Guatemala testified, "When the captain Jorge de Alvarado came to conquer this land . . . the country was at war and was unconquered, for there were few people [i.e., Spaniards]."

Jorge de Alvarado brought somewhere between six thousand and ten thousand native warriors from central Mexico. They not only fought side by side with Spaniards but also engaged in their own battles against Mayas, making it possible for Jorge de Alvarado to subdue most of highland Guatemala by the summer of 1529 – and allowing Spaniards to begin building a colony there in the 1530s. However, the Alvarado legacy of violence persisted. During the 1530s, Pedro and Jorge were periodically back in Guatemala, putting down Maya "revolts" and imposing new mechanisms of colonial exploitation until Pedro's death in 1541. The Dominican fray Bartolomé de las Casas, who lived in Guatemala in the 1530s, claimed that in sixteen years the Alvarado brothers and their conquistador colleagues had killed 4 million native Guatemalans. Although this figure cannot be taken too literally, it illustrates vividly how the myth of pacification often masked decades of struggle and violence – and it illustrates the high price that native Guatemalans paid for the privilege of being placed (in Pedro's words) "under the dominion of His Majesty."

Meanwhile, Francisco de Montejo, together with his son and nephew and their Spanish partners, embarked on a series of invasions of the Yucatán Peninsula. The first, of 1527, was a complete failure, and the Spaniards, many of whom had died of disease and wounds received in battles with local Mayas, were forced to return to highland Mexico in 1529. The second, begun later that same year, seemed at first to be more successful, with a base established at Campeche and military victories followed by the granting of encomiendas to members of the invasion company. But the premature allotment of Mayas to Spaniards, indicative of the Spanish rush to make real the myth of pacification, served only to exacerbate tension between Spaniards and Mayas. By 1534, the Conquest was in disarray, and when word of Pizarro's discovery of the Inca Empire reached Yucatán, almost all the surviving Spaniards left the peninsula for South America. The third Spanish invasion began in 1540. This time the Spaniards were able to establish bases that remained permanent – at Campeche, refounded in 1541, and Mérida, founded on top of the Maya city of Tiho in 1542. How were the Spaniards finally able to found a colony despite such an incomplete conquest? First, their previous invasions had planted epidemic disease (see In Focus 7.2) and sparked local wars that weakened the Maya capacity to resist invasion. Second, Maya political disunity allowed the Montejos to forge alliances with several important dynasties, such as the Pech (to whom we return shortly). Finally, the Spaniards did not conquer the entire Yucatán. In fact, the colony of the late sixteenth century comprised little more than the northwest corner of the peninsula, and although the colonial frontier did slowly move south and east over the following two centuries, there remained independent, unconquered Maya communities through to the turn of the twentieth century.

One community that remained unconquered for a century and a half after the Montejos founded Spanish Yucatán was the capital of a substantial independent Maya kingdom – that of the Itzas. As late as the 1690s, a vast area lay unconquered between the colony of Yucatán in the north and the colony of Guatemala in the southern highlands. Spaniards referred to much of this area as *despoblado* (uninhabited), but in fact it contained numerous independent Maya settlements and small kingdoms. The largest of these (which indeed expanded considerably during the seventeenth century) was the Itza Maya kingdom of Petén Itzá. The capital of the Itzas was Noh Petén, a city located on an island in a lake (rather like Tenochtitlán, but far more modest in scale). After several years of negotiations between Itza ambassadors and Spanish officials broke down, the Spaniards – who all along had been building roads and preparing invasion forces both in Yucatán and Guatemala – invaded Petén Itzá, occupying Noh Petén and defeating Itza warriors in 1697. Many of those warriors were descended from Mayas that had fled Yucatán during the Spanish invasions of the previous century. For more than a century after 1697, Spanish attempts to establish a viable colony

IN FOCUS 7.1

NAHUAS VERSUS MAYAS: AN INDIGENOUS SPIN ON A "SPANISH" CONQUEST

This extraordinary painted account of a military campaign during the era of the Spanish Conquest was thought for centuries to depict episodes in the Conquest of Mexico. The painting is from a Nahua town in central Mexico called Quauhquechollan, and the alphabetic glosses beneath the place-name glyphs (the symbols identifying the towns attacked in the campaign) have long ceased to be legible. However, the painting was recently identified by Dutch art historian Florine Asselbergs as an account of the 1527 invasion of highland Guatemala by thousands of Quauhquechollan warriors. Ultimately under the command of their Spanish *encomendero*, Jorge de Alvarado, the Nahua warriors engaged in independent military actions against local Mayas – primarily Cakchiquels defending their homelands. Most died in battle, but the survivors settled their own communities, primarily in and around the Spanish capital of Santiago. As the original Spanish invasion of Guatemala in 1524–1526, under Jorge's brother Pedro, had resulted in failure, the role played by warriors from Quauhquechollan was crucial in bringing some semblance of Spanish colonial authority to the highlands in the 1530s.

Made of fifteen sheets of cloth sewn together, the painting is almost eight feet tall and nearly eleven feet wide. Its narrative map illustrates the departure of the warriors from their hometown of Quauhquechollan, where an alliance with the Spaniards, against the Aztec/Mexica Empire, had been established in 1520 (the large scene depicted on the left, beneath the double-headed eagle naming the town). Seen from the Quauhquechollan perspective, the Spaniards helped them throw off domination by the Mexica and expand their local territorial control, in return for which Quauhquechollan paid tribute to the new invaders. Their 1527 journey into Guatemala was a peaceful one, initially following routes that warriors from Quauhquechollan had taken in Aztec times. Once in the highlands, the Quauhquechollan forces engaged in a series of victorious battles against Cakchiquels (shown in the central part of the painting). The Nahuas appear in the painting as fearsome fighters, crushing Maya resistance; Jorge de Alvarado, in contrast, appears sitting in a chair, setting war dogs on captive Mayas. The Quauhquechollan warriors swept through more than a dozen towns, culminating in a successful but costly attack on the Pipil (a Nahuatl-speaking group), before returning in triumph to the highland town of Chimaltenango – where ritual dances (three dancing scenes are found in the painting) honored slain warriors and celebrated a victory that was clearly considered a Quauhquechollan conquest of Guatemala, carried out with mere assistance by Spaniards. Indeed, this surviving painting was probably a copy sent back to Quauhquechollan to share this triumphal narrative with those back home.

Figure 7.1. Lienzo de Quauhquechollan. Digital Restoration; Universidad Francisco Marroquín, Guatemala. Sponsored by Banco G&T Continental, Guatemala. © Universidad Francisco Marroquín.

Figure 7.2. a. Brazilian shaman with sick natives, from Jean de Léry, Histoire d'un voyage fait en la terre du Bresil (1578), p. 174. **b.** Detail from an early 18th-century tile painting showing a chocolate party or chocolatada in the Spanish town of Valencia. Used with permission of Museu de Ceràmica, Barcelona, Spain.

THE TWO FACES OF THE COLUMBIAN EXCHANGE

The images here show the Columbian Exchange's two faces: a Brazilian shaman, or native healer, with Tupis dying from epidemic disease, as depicted in Jean de Léry's 1578 *Histoire d'un voyage fait en la terre du Bresil*; and detail from an early-eighteenth-century tile painting showing a chocolate party, or *chocolatada*, in the Spanish town of Valencia.

In 1972, the historian Alfred Crosby threw a bombshell when he argued that the most profound changes brought about by 1492 were biological. Using the term Columbian Exchange, Crosby examined the massive transfer of plants, animals, and diseases begun by Columbus. Many such transfers – like the introduction of smallpox and certain weeds to the Americas – were unintentional, yet their consequences were often devastating. Other transfers were more beneficial. When potatoes from the Andes reached Northern Europe after 1532, for example, populations expanded considerably (although over-dependence on potatoes sometimes led to famines). Tomatoes, chocolate, and tobacco were gradually but deeply absorbed into European cultures of cuisine and consumption. Asian cuisines quickly adopted American chili peppers, and in some cases, peanuts. Many Africans became dependent on maize.

In the Americas, European livestock, including sheep, cattle, pigs, horses, goats, and other large domestic mammals, quickly altered vast landscapes, displacing local species but also offering new opportunities for predators and carrion eaters. Large animals often benefited indigenous farmers and long-distance traders, but their food and water requirements were high, and a serious problem in fragile desert environments. In central Mexico, for example, sheep populations exploded soon after they were introduced in the 1520s, leading to widespread overgrazing and desertification. Indigenous farmers constantly struggled, meanwhile, to keep Spanish cattle from eating their crops. Thus, a kind of slow environmental and cultural conquest was achieved by the spread of Old World plants and animals.

Even more tragically, Native American populations were devastated by Old World pathogens such as smallpox, measles, and influenza. Because Africa and Eurasia had long been connected by trade and warfare for thousands of years, diseases such as smallpox, measles, and mumps had become endemic. That is, the repeated epidemic spread of these and other pathogens helped create a substantial and frequently replenished pool of people with acquired immunity, or helpful antibodies, often gained in early childhood. Epidemics were often destructive in Europe, Asia, and Africa, but never to the extent that they would be in long-isolated regions overseas. Only the sexually transmitted disease syphilis appears to have had American origins, although this remains a matter of scientific debate.

What is painfully clear is that in the decades following Columbus's arrival in the Americas, unwittingly introduced diseases, compounded by conquest wars, labor drafts, displacement, and malnutrition, caused rapid population decline. Both Native American and European medical practices were too rudimentary to slow the process. In most parts of the Americas population losses reached ninety percent (see Chapter 4), bottoming out by the early seventeenth century. Population rebound after such a catastrophic decline was slow, and was not much helped by the everyday demands of life under colonial rule.

in the Petén region sputtered, and many Mayas continued to live in small settlements in the tropical forests, unconverted and "unpacified."

Even indigenous peoples inhabiting regions abundant in precious metals proved capable of resisting Spanish attempts at conquest. Such was the case in the Chocó region in what is now western Colombia. Spaniards first entered the Chocó in 1510 from Caribbean shores, but their desire for gold and indigenous captives soon sparked resistance. Surviving Spaniards moved on, mainly to Panama, but attempts to penetrate the region from the Pacific side beginning in the 1520s met with no more success. Invading Spaniards such as Francisco Pizarro were met with poisoned arrows, abandoned villages, and war cries from the forest. Pizarro moved south to drier shores in Ecuador, before setting off for the Peruvian highlands to conquer the Incas.

Meanwhile, the less glamorous conquest of the Embera, Citará, and other native peoples of the Chocó region was left to ambitious men following in the footsteps of Gonzalo Jiménez de Quesada, conqueror of the Muiscas near Bogotá, and Sebastián de Benalcázar, conqueror of Quito and Cali. Despite repeated expeditions from the central highlands, the native peoples of the greater Chocó, which stretched from northern Ecuador to eastern Panama, resisted all attempts at conquest and settlement until the seventeenth century. Beginning in the 1610s, concerted campaigns to "reduce" the people of Chocó to encomienda status began to compensate for heavy losses, as gold-mining camps were established and soon staffed with a mix of indigenous and enslaved African workers. First, the Barbacoas region of southwest Colombia fell to creole conquistadors and their indigenous and enslaved African allies in the 1630s. Then came the Raposo region west of Cali, where the Spanish maintained a tenuous hold on the port of Buenaventura. Last to fall was

Colombia's present-day Chocó Department, which had been penetrated by Franciscan and Jesuit missionaries as well as highland conquistadors by 1660. The abundance of gold in the region's many rivers was astonishing, but the conquest of its inhabitants was far from a sure thing.

Although increasingly decimated by disease, the Citará and other native groups refused to give up. Between 1684 and 1687, they led a coordinated rebellion that killed 126 Spaniards and their African slaves and put the rest to flight. But the lure of gold was too much, and by 1700, creole highlanders had reestablished control of the central gold-mining zones and had made peace with unconquered groups, such as the Kuna near the mouth of the Atrato River. Most of the Chocó's indigenous peoples were reduced to tribute-paying status and subjected to priestly efforts at conversion. They adopted some Spanish imports (e.g., metal tools, pigs; see In Focus 7.2) but remained largely separate from incoming African slaves, who mined the bulk of the region's gold. The Chocó natives lost most of their autonomy in the end (with the exception of the Kuna), yet the "pacification" of the Chocó was a textbook case of protracted conquest: it was a violent conflict that lasted for most of the colonial period.

A third example of a region where conquest never ended is south-central Chile, in the temperate Southern Cone of South America. The fertile Andean piedmont south of Santiago is the homeland of the Mapuche, a cluster of peoples with shared cultural and linguistic features, and it is there perhaps more than anywhere in the Americas that Spanish conquistadors met their match. Though not known for their unity, the Mapuche repelled numerous attempts at conquest by the Incas, the Spanish, and even the independent Republic of Chile. Only modern weapons changed the balance of power in the 1880s, when the Mapuche were finally forced at the point of a Gatling gun to live under state control. Yet there remain a half million Mapuche today, and they are still proclaiming their independence. So what happened five centuries ago? As in the Chocó, there was substantial gold in Mapuche territory, and the Spanish knew it. Yet they failed to conquer them. Why?

In fact, Spaniards at first succeeded in subduing the Mapuche. Chile's first conquistadors, headed by Pedro de Valdivia, managed to convince many chiefs to surrender by 1550. Gold-rich streams were soon discovered, however, and Mapuche men found themselves working in them against their will. Once it was obvious that the primary Spanish goal was to procure laborers for the gold mines, the Mapuche rebelled, and with great violence. Drawing from their warrior tradition, they not only killed Governor Valdivia, but also ate portions of his corpse in a public ritual. Mapuche cannibalism, rather like that of the Tupinamba who captured Hans Staden in Brazil, was clearly meant to intimidate.

A general Mapuche uprising lasted from 1553 to 1557. Mapuche raiders were still attacking Spanish towns in their heartland in 1598, when they killed and ritually consumed another governor, Martín García de Loyola. A new native confederacy was able to drive the Spanish out entirely, fully extinguishing a string of Spanish towns south of the Biobío River by 1600. All attempts to reconquer the Mapuche and occupy their lands failed despite troop reinforcements from as far away as Ecuador and the construction of a series of forts.

How had the Mapuche succeeded against the Spanish when even great empires had failed? Oral, written, and even archaeological records suggest that successful Mapuche resistance owed much to a combination of deep cultural patterns and wily adaptability. Mapuche culture appears to have valued military skill long before the arrival of the Spanish, and successful warriors could expect great gains in status. Mapuche boys were raised to fight and take captives from an early age, and girls were taught to prepare and stockpile food and other supplies.

Taking advantage of their homeland's varied topography, the Mapuche patiently watched how the Spanish fought, and then they adapted. Much like the Great Plains tribes of North America and the Argentine pampas, the Mapuche quickly adopted horses, which gave them enhanced mobility and enabled very long-distance raiding. Some Mapuche warriors also used knives, swords, and guns taken in raids and skirmishes, and some made Spanish-style leather armor and helmets from slaughtered Spanish cattle. Yet despite these adaptations and borrowings, Mapuche warring techniques did not fundamentally change. A culture that valued successful captive taking was simply different from one aimed at battlefield domination. Thus, the Mapuche continued to hone established tactics such as the ambush and night raid that inspired the Spanish term *guerrilla* (little war). Long, native-style lances remained the most favored weapon despite access to guns and swords, and Mapuche men continued to fight barefoot, even in winter.

Native alliances were another key to success. We have seen how the disunity of native peoples in Mesoamerica allowed Spaniards to bring Nahuas to conquer Mayas and to divide Maya groups against one another. In southern Chile, Spaniards initially benefited from a comparable local disunity. But that advantage was lost during the late sixteenth century. When the Mapuche formed a confederacy of formerly warring tribes in 1599, they proved unbeatable. The Spanish referred to them as the Indomitable State. As a result of sustained Mapuche resistance, southern Chile became a permanent frontier of Spanish South America, a region of defensive rather than offensive operations. Throughout the Spanish world, the fiercely resistant Mapuche became legendary.

Disappearing Defeat

Once it became clear that Iberian invaders had come to stay, native rulers and nobility sought to accommodate, modify, or resist their demands in various ways. Whatever their response to colonial rule, they all made decisions on the basis of their evaluation of the best interests of their dynastic family and the community they governed – not the interests of native peoples as a whole (as neither "Indians" nor Andeans, or even Mayas, shared a sense of common identity). From the perspective of native leaders, including that of the Tupinamba chief who held the captive Hans Staden, the outcome of the European invasion was to be negotiated – negotiations that were to last, in one form or another, for the three centuries of the colonial period.

We have already seen an example of how the leaders of one Nahua town responded to the Spanish presence (see In Focus 7.1). The rulers of Quauhquechollan formed an alliance with Cortés in 1520, negotiating their incorporation into the new Spanish colony in Mexico. In return for agreeing to Spanish tribute and labor demands, the town's ruling nobility were confirmed in office and participated in subsequent wars as conquistadors themselves – helping defeat the Mexica in 1521 and playing a major role in the conquest of highland Guatemala in 1527–1529. In the Andes, the Cañaris of southern Ecuador and the Chachapoyas of northern Peru played similar auxiliary roles and were similarly rewarded. It was a Cañari who served as executioner of the rebel Inca Túpac Amaru, captured at Vilcabamba in 1572, and a special Cañari neighborhood survived in Cuzco throughout the colonial period (see In Focus 7.3).

Another common pattern, found especially in rugged backcountry or isolated regions of the Americas, was accommodation followed by armed rebellion. In places such as the Maya Petén, northern New Mexico, and the Brazilian *sertão* local indigenous leaders typically accommodated some armed invaders, priests, and settlers, then rose up against them, usually in response to punishing labor demands, sexual abuse, and other intolerable behaviors. One example comes from eastern Ecuador. Soon after the Spanish conquest of the northern Inca highlands in the 1530s, settlers began to move into the lowland jungle province of Quijós, east of Quito. At first, they were aided by a local headman named Jumandy, but once the newcomers' desire to make their new allies mine for gold in the tributaries of the upper Amazon became clear, Jumandy led a violent revolt. The Spanish were entirely expelled in 1579. Only a few intrepid missionaries returned in subsequent decades.

Millenarian or messianic revolts constitute yet another pattern of accommodation followed by resistance. In Yucatán, initially compliant Maya elders fused indigenous and Catholic religious ideas and ceremonies in hopes of throwing off the Spanish yoke in 1564. A similarly syncretic or hybrid movement called Taqi Onqoy, or "Dancing Sickness," swept through portions of highland Peru at about the same time. In northeastern Brazil, meanwhile, a religious rebellion called *santidade* emerged by the 1590s, drawing not only indigenous but also African and mixed-race adherents. Inquisition officials visiting from Portugal were totally confounded by

THE PLEASURE OF CONQUEST: AN EYEWITNESS TO THE EXECUTION OF TÚPAC AMARU

In 1610, Captain Baltasar de Ocampo, a veteran Peruvian conquistador, addressed to the viceroy of Peru a lengthy *probanza* – a report, or "proof," of his services to crown and colony. The letter included an account of the Spanish assault on Vilcabamba – the capital of the small Inca kingdom that had survived forty years of the Spanish presence in the Andes. Shortly after the new Inca, Túpac Amaru, came to power in 1571, a Spanish priest was tortured to death – and then a Spanish ambassador from Cuzco was killed in Vilcabamba. In response, a Spanish force, accompanied by native warriors from the colony, attacked the rebel kingdom and took Túpac Amaru prisoner. Ocampo's account shows how the Spaniards followed the same procedures used in earlier decades of the Conquest – such as resettling native peoples (*congregación*), assigning them in encomienda, and ritually executing resistant native leaders as rebels.

In the wake of the battle, wrote Ocampo: "The Inca and the other Indians were collected and brought back to the valley of Hoyara. Here the Indians were settled in a large village, and a city of Spaniards was founded. It was called San Francisco of the Victory of Vilcabamba for two sacred and honest reasons. The first was because the victory was on the 4th of October, 1571, the day of San Francisco, and the second being the name of the viceroy [don Francisco de Toledo] to whom the victory was due. Great festivities were held in the city of Cuzco when the news of the victory arrived." Ocampo described how the Spanish officer who led the attack, General Martín Hurtado de Arbieto, "began the foundation of the city" – the one named after San Francisco – "and named citizens to receive encomiendas, among whom he divided more than 1500 Indians for personal service." The site of the city was later moved to be nearer "important silver mines" discovered in the hills.

General Hurtado "then marched to Cuzco with the Inca Túpac Amaru and his captains," who were chained together but dressed in full regalia – the Inca's "crown or headdress, called *mascapaycha*, was on his head, with fringe over his forehead, this being the royal insignia of the Inca, in the same way as a crown is used by kings." Arriving in Cuzco, "in form of an ordered force, the General and his captains marched in triumph, and presented their prisoners to the viceroy. After his Excellency had felt the pleasure of conquest, he ordered that the Inca and his captains should be taken to the fortress" at Colcampata, a former Inca palace. A few days later, the governor of Cuzco, in his capacity as magistrate of the local court, sentenced the prisoners to be beheaded. "The captains were led through the streets to the place of execution, while the town crier proclaimed their offences. Three died in the public streets, and two at the foot of the gallows, because they had been tortured in prison until they were dying. Notwithstanding their condition their bodies were taken to comply with the law, while two . . . were hanged when still alive."

Ocampo claimed that two Mercedarian friars were sent in to convert Túpac Amaru and were "such great adepts in their office" that the Inca became a Christian. On the day of his execution, "the Inca was taken from the fortress, through the public streets of the city, with a guard of 400 Cañari Indians, having their lances in their hands. The Cañaris were great enemies of the Incas." Ocampo wrote that two friars accompanied the Inca "until they reached the scaffold, which was reared on high in the center of the great square, facing the cathedral," where the friars "remained with the Inca, comforting his soul with holy preparation."

"The open spaces, roofs, and windows" of the adjacent neighborhoods "were so crowded with spectators that if an orange had been thrown down it could not have reached the ground anywhere, so closely were the people packed. When the executioner, who was a Cañari Indian, brought out the knife with which he was to behead Túpac Amaru, a marvellous thing happened. The whole crowd of natives raised such a cry of grief that it seemed as if the day of judgement had come, and all those of Spanish race did

IN FOCUS 7.3

THE PLEASURE OF CONQUEST: AN EYEWITNESS TO THE EXECUTION OF TÚPAC AMARU, *continued*

not fail to show their feelings by shedding tears of grief and pain. When the Inca beheld the scene, he only raised his right hand on high and let it fall. With a lordly mind he alone remained calm, and all the noise was followed by a silence so profound that no living soul moved, either among those who were in the square or among those at a distance. The Inca then spoke with a self-possession unlike one about to die. He said that now his course was run, and that he merited death." According to Ocampo, the Inca then advised parents never to curse their children for bad behavior, because his mother had once cursed him, saying he would not die a natural death, hence his execution. The priests rebuked the Inca, saying his death was God's will, and Túpac Amaru then "repented of what he had said." Eight of the most senior friars and priests in the colony then came forward and, on bended knee, requested clemency for the Inca from the viceroy, "urging that he should be sent to Spain to be judged by the king in person."

The viceroy, however, stood firm, and one of his officers "was sent on horseback to clear the way, galloping furiously and riding down all kinds of people. He ordered the Inca's head to be cut off at once, in the viceroy's name. The Inca then received consolation from the padres who were at his side and, taking leave of all, he put his head on the block, like a lamb. The executioner then came forward and, taking the hair in his left hand, he severed the head with a knife at one blow, and held it on high for all to see. As the head was severed the bells of the cathedral began to ring, and were followed by those of all the monasteries and parish churches in the city. The execution caused the greatest sorrow and brought tears to all eyes."

Although Ocampo describes Túpac Amaru's executioner as a Cañari, this illustration, drawn about the same time (for Huaman Poma de Ayala's *El primer nueva corónica y buen gobierno*), shows a Spaniard beheading the Inca. Ocampo was probably correct, as the Spanish rarely served as executioners, usually leaving this task to indigenous subordinates or enslaved Africans. The Andeans are lamenting the last Inca's death.

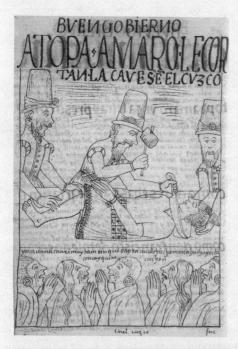

Figure 7.3. Drawing 182. The execution of Tupac Amaru Inka by order of the Viceroy Toledo, as distraught Andean nobles lament the killing of their innocent lord. From The Guaman Poma manuscript (GKS 2232 4°) at the Royal Library, Copenhagen, Denmark. Credit: The Royal Library, Copenhagen, Denmark.

this colonial religious brew. Far away at the northernmost margins of Spanish control, the great Pueblo Revolt of 1680 in New Mexico was led by an indigenous prophet who had been trained by Franciscan priests. As a result of this messianic uprising, the Spanish were driven from power for over a decade. Most of the revitalization movements in Spanish America and Brazil were violently crushed, but they serve to remind us that indigenous peoples did not lose their will to fight even as their religious faith was transformed by the introduction of Catholicism and certain African beliefs.

Flight to the margins was yet another alternative to colonial subjection. As In Focus 7.3 describes, numerous Inca refugees established the independent kingdom of Vilcabamba to the north of Cuzco in the upper Amazon basin following the Spanish conquest of the coast and central highlands. This "rump Inca Empire," as some historians have called it, survived until 1572, when Spanish forces captured and executed Túpac Amaru I. This "last of the Sapa Incas" had in fact accommodated Spanish missionaries and traders, and several predecessors had done the same. Túpac Amaru's capture was not the result of sudden Spanish strength in the region, but rather a swift and unexpected change in crown policy as dictated by the new Peruvian viceroy, Francisco de Toledo. The change was so swift that the last Inca's capture and gruesome death came as a great surprise to everyone, and was widely perceived as an act of deception rather than bravery.

Accommodation followed by messianic resistance did not end in the sixteenth century in the Andes. In the Gran Pantonal, or Great Swamp, of eastern Peru, a Jesuit-educated indigenous leader calling himself Juan Santos Atahualpa led a deadly uprising beginning in 1742. A charismatic leader – who borrowed elements of Catholicism in his call for the expulsion of the Spanish and their dependents of African and mixed-race descent – Juan Santos hoped to turn the tables on those whom he felt had most betrayed his people. A similar mixture of indigenous and imported ideas resurfaced in the greatest and deadliest native uprisings of them all, those led by Túpac Amaru II and Túpac Katari that swept violently across highland Peru and Bolivia from 1780 to 1783.

From a modern perspective, almost any indigenous choice to accommodate the Spanish and Portuguese appears perplexing, and in the long term self-defeating. It is therefore crucial to seek native sources that can help explain these actions. Some native language accounts of the Conquest's events confirm Spanish sources – such as Guaman Poma's depiction of Andeans lamenting Túpac Amaru's execution, which echoes Ocampo's description. Just as often, however, they entirely reshape our understanding of such events. For example, we would know nothing of Paxbolonacha's role in Cuauhtémoc's death were it not for the Chontal Maya description of the affair, as Spanish sources ignore the Maya king's involvement altogether. Also, the traditional view of the conquest of Guatemala as the achievement of Pedro de Alvarado in 1524–1525 is undermined by the Quauhquechollan pictorial account (see In Focus 7.1), which supports the impression given by other sources that it was not until later in the decade that the region was subdued – by Spanish, African, and Nahua forces under the (often indirect) leadership of Pedro de Alvarado's brother, Jorge.

A final example comes from Yucatán, two decades later, where the Maya Pech dynasty decided to adopt an appeasement strategy and permit the Spaniards to settle in their corner of the peninsula. In 1542, the Pech town of Tiho became the Spanish capital of Mérida. Pech lords were baptized and confirmed as noblemen and rulers of the surrounding towns, and they participated in campaigns in other regions of the peninsula. As a result, they more than willingly identified themselves as conquistadors; for example, Nakuk Pech and Macan Pech both styled themselves in Maya-language accounts of the Conquest as *yax hidalgos concixtador en*, combining Maya words with Spanish terms for *nobleman* and *conqueror* to mean "I, the first of the noble conquistadors."

Yet as with the Spanish conquistadors' accounts of their own deeds, we must be careful not to take all indigenous claims or testimonies at face value. When writing to the king of Spain, a Tlaxcalan, Maya, or Cañari lord had as much reason to "spin" events in his favor as any Spanish *don*. Indeed, the Castilian culture of merit and service proved surprisingly attractive to some native peoples, especially those who saw something to gain in the new system. Unlike in Portuguese Brazil, indigenous chiefs and lords possessed special rights and protections under Spanish law thanks in part to the efforts of Las Casas. Thus, instead of the riskier practices of rebellion, religious subversion, and flight, participating in the new regime as loyal, Catholic subjects was something to brag about in writing – and at length. If done properly, one could win tribute concessions and other rewards. Guaman Poma even imagined he could persuade the king to reorder colonial society altogether. Even in Brazil, where native peoples had fewer opportunities to win concessions from the Portuguese monarch, service against the French and Dutch after 1600 was proclaimed and in a few cases recognized. In learning to either write for themselves or to hire others to do it for them, indigenous Latin Americans immediately set about challenging the invaders' "Conquest narrative." The more we read of their writings, the less perplexing the persistence of colonial rule becomes.

*　*　*

The Iberian conquest of the Americas was neither as quick nor as easy as the Spanish conquistadors and Brazilian *bandeirantes* hoped it would be or as later chroniclers and historians suggested. Still, native empires fell, smaller kingdoms eventually crumbled, and local chiefs and rulers more often than not sought accommodation with the invaders. In the meantime, native cultures were not only affected by the demographic disaster of disease but also altered by the introduction of Old World plants and animals – a kind of protracted conquest itself. Although backland conquests rumbled on through the eighteenth century, by the mid-sixteenth century, most of we now call Latin America was characterized by day-to-day, nonmilitary interaction between Iberians and Native Americans. But this, too, was an incomplete conquest.

SUGGESTIONS FOR FURTHER READING

On Hans Staden and indigenous relations in sixteenth-century Brazil, see Neil Whitehead and Michael Harbsmeier, eds., *Hans Staden's True History* (2008), and Alida Metcalf, *Go-Betweens and the Colonization of Brazil, 1500–1600* (2005). See also the superb essays by John Hemming, Stuart B. Schwartz, Frédéric Mauro, and others in Leslie Bethell, ed., *Colonial Brazil* (1987).

The three books we recommended at the end of Chapter 6 – Schwartz's *Victors and Vanquished*, Restall's *Seven Myths of the Spanish Conquest*, and Restall's *Maya Conquistador* – are also highly relevant to this chapter, especially the last of the three. Also of particular relevance are chapters 1–3 of Matthew Restall, Lisa Sousa, and Kevin Terraciano, *Mesoamerican Voices: Native-Language Writings from Colonial Mexico, Oaxaca, Yucatan, and Guatemala* (2005).

The definitive books on the Quauhquechollan map and the Spanish Conquest of the Itzas are suitable for advanced undergraduates only; they are, respectively, *Conquered Conquistadors: The Lienzo de Quauhquechollan, a Nahua Vision of the Conquest of Guatemala*, by Florine G. L. Asselbergs (2004), and Grant D. Jones's *The Conquest of the Last Maya Kingdom* (1998).

On the Chocó, see Caroline A. Williams, *Between Resistance and Adaptation: Indigenous Peoples and the Colonization of the Chocó, 1510–1753* (2005), and on the Shuar, see Kris Lane, *Quito 1599: City and Colony in Transition* (2002). For the Mapuche, see Kristine Jones, in *Cambridge History of the Native Peoples of the Americas III: South America*, vol. 2, edited by Schwartz and Salomon. On Guaman Poma, see Rolena Adorno, *Writing and Resistance in Colonial Peru*, 2d ed. (2000), and *The Polemics of Possession* (2008). The full text of Guaman Poma's *El primer nueva corónica y buen gobierno* has also been placed on line by the Royal Library of Denmark, where the original text is housed (http://www.kb.dk/elib/mss/poma/).

GLOSSARY

Sertão [sair-TAH-oh]: a huge and vaguely defined desert region, mostly in the northeast and inland from the coast

Chocó [cho-KOH], Citará [see-tah-RAH], and Noanamá [no-wah-nah-MAH]: the gold-rich northwest Pacific lowlands of Colombia and two of the native groups of the region that resisted Spanish rule through most of the colonial period

Ah pop and ah pop Qamahay [kam-ah-HIGH]: the king and king-elect of the Quiché Maya kingdom in highland Guatemala

Petén Itzá [pet-EN eets-AH] and Noh Peten: the name of the kingdom and capital city of the Itzas or Itza Mayas, conquered by Spaniards in 1697

PART THREE

■ ■

THE COLONIAL MIDDLE

The period that we have called the colonial middle stretched from the late sixteenth century through to the early eighteenth century. This was a period of relatively little change, at least compared to the period before it (the era of contact and conquest, covered in Part Two) and the period after it (the crises and changes of the eighteenth century, culminating in independence in the 1820s, covered in Part Four). The five chapters of Part Three are thus more thematic than chronological.

Having examined various aspects of the long-term native response to Iberian invasions in Chapter 7, in Chapter 8 ("Native Communities") we continue to focus on native responses. The chapter's primary purpose is to show how the colonial system both exploited indigenous labor and permitted – in fact, depended on – the survival of self-governing Mesoamerican and Andean towns and villages. Chapter 9 ("Black Communities") picks up the topic of African slavery and develops it into the related topic of community formation among people of African descent. The chapter takes the Afro-Iberian experience into the eighteenth century, comparing the different types of communities that slaves and free coloreds (free people of African descent) created in city and countryside, on plantations and near mines, and even at sea.

The Spanish Inquisition finally makes an appearance in Chapters 10 and 11. The first of these ("The Religious Renaissance") begins with the Spiritual Conquest (as Spaniards called their early conversion efforts). We go on to look at church building, religious literature, middle-colonial campaigns against native "idolatry," and other aspects of Catholicism in the colonies. Then "Defining Deviancy," Chapter 11, examines the roles played by Inquisitors, other officials, and colonial society as a whole in defining and policing belief and behavior – from general questions of religious orthodoxy to witchcraft and homosexuality. The chapter includes a discussion of sociracial identity, arguing that expectations of behavior based on gender, parentage, and other forms of identity appeared rigid but could often be bent.

The final chapter of Part Three, "Daily Life in City and Country," pulls together many of the threads of social and cultural history introduced in previous chapters.

8

■ ■ ■ ■ ■ ■ ■ ■ ■ ■ ■ ■ ■ ■ ■ ■ ■ ■ ■ ■

Native Communities

TIMELINE

1495–1510: first American gold boom-and-bust cycle takes place on Hispaniola

1505–1540: rise and fall of pearl beds off the Venezuelan coast

1542–1543: implementation of New Laws restricting the encomienda system

1545: discovery of silver in Potosí (soon followed by Zacatecas and Guanajuato in Mexico)

1549: Jesuits arrive in Brazil and begin creating *aldeias*, or indigenous mission communities

1572: creation of *mita* labor draft in Potosí's silver mines

1592: Potosí reaches peak production

Most Powerful Lord. . . . In your Royal Name the Indians were ordered to be gathered into towns so that they could be taught the elements of the faith and to become experienced in civil life. And so we gathered in and populated the town of Píntag at your command; and at the same time our ancestors were assured by your royal certificate that the lands we had near Píntag would remain ours. . . . However, little by little, day after day, many Spaniards have been encroaching on these lands. . . . They have created so many farms and ranches that they now surround the whole town.

(Don Francisco Anaguampla and his fellow lords, 1580)

THUS DID THE NATIVE ELITE of a small Andean pueblo near Quito, Ecuador, address King Philip II of Spain in a formal letter of complaint now housed in a Spanish archive. Writing in 1580, nearly fifty years after the conquest of the Incas, they expressed their frustration not with Spanish colonialism itself but rather with what they perceived as its blatant mismanagement. Spanish ranchers and wheat farmers were not respecting their property, as had been explicitly promised, and Spanish cattle were eating their crops. What the villagers wanted was for the king to do his job: to order his representatives in the colonies to administer justice. Such complaints were by no means always redressed, but a surprising number were. As we have already seen, within a very short time, Spain's Native American subjects learned to exploit the colonial legal system to their advantage.

Despite the violence of early encounters, the Spanish and Portuguese did not wish to eliminate Native American populations. On the contrary, they viewed native peoples as the Americas' principal source of wealth. While trying to refute the claims of Bartolomé de Las Casas in 1612, the late-arriving Spanish conquistador Bernardo de Vargas Machuca put it this way: "...the Spaniard does not settle or inhabit deserted lands, however healthy and rich they may be in gold and silver; he inhabits and settles where he finds Indians, though they may be poor and sickly, for without Indians for tribute, one cannot enjoy the fruits of the land…" This vision, inspired by European feudalism, led Iberians to establish nearly all of their colonies on top of or alongside pre-existing native communities. Tribute in the form of agricultural surpluses and herd growth (and sometimes gold or silver from nearby mines) supported Iberian landlords, who also relied on surplus indigenous labor for everything from farm work to church construction. Although Brazil's early landlords tended to favor enslavement of Native Americans over such feudal-style arrangements, they too attached their societies to indigenous ones, at least until they could purchase sufficient African slaves.

In contrast, as we saw in the previous chapter, Native Americans did not willingly submit to foreign domination. Rebellions broke out in Hispaniola, Brazil, Panama, and Mexico. Andean peoples from New Granada to Chile struck back at the conquerors, sometimes retreating into deserts, rain forests, and inaccessible mountain ranges. The Portuguese in Brazil soon turned to slaving among the Tupi speakers and their less sedentary Gê-speaking neighbors as rebellious native peoples receded into harsher and more distant backlands. Yet although the Conquest can be seen as a process that took centuries (when viewed from the perspective of all the Americas), it was also a process that (viewed from the center or core colonies) shifted early on to the complex business of colonization and the negotiated imposition of colonial rule. At the heart of the old Mexica/Aztec and Inca empires, where populations were densest and agriculture most developed, the Spanish quickly established a variety of institutions of exploitation. Some resembled European serfdom; others were local innovations. Here, too, native peoples established their own agendas and often interpreted life under colonial rule in ways not imagined by their Spanish and Portuguese overlords. As long as indigenous languages and cultures survived, these starkly different views of the world persisted.

This chapter examines first how indigenous peoples at the colonial core were transformed into Spanish and Portuguese subjects as defined by their conquerors. We then look at how, within the bounds of colonialism, indigenous peoples carved out their own spaces and challenged or used the colonial regime to meet their own needs. Finally, the chapter takes a look at indigenous life on the colonial fringes, where some of the patterns of the core regions were sharply altered or simply did not apply.

What Was the "Republic of Indians"?

Spaniards divided the inhabitants of their colonies into two political categories, which they called the República de Españoles and the República de Indios. These were not republics in any sense of our understanding of the word, but rather referred to the fact that Spaniards and "Indians" governed themselves – albeit on different levels. At all levels beyond that of the village (from a valley of villages to the kingdoms of New Spain and Peru), political authority was in the hands of Spanish colonial administrators. In the new Spanish settlements, chartered as *villas* (towns) or *ciudades* (cities), government was in the hands of a town council, called a *cabildo*; the cabildo and local Spanish residents made up the República de Españoles in that town. African slaves and their descendants did not have their own *repúblicas* (with a few rare exceptions); they were instead attached subordinates of the República de Españoles, usually as slaves or employees but sometimes as free artisans or vendors (a topic to which we return in the next chapter).

Native American communities were semi-autonomous, but they remained subordinate pueblos ("villages" of widely varying size) in relation to neighboring Spanish *villas* and *ciudades*. Each native pueblo nevertheless elected representatives for its own cabildo, which functioned in some ways like the Spanish town council. On the surface, it looks as though the invading Spanish simply foisted this imported Iberian institution onto Native American communities, but thousands of documents, many of them written in native languages by indigenous scribes, reveal that beneath the veneer of similarity there flourished many variations of traditional governance by respected elders. Although the Spanish tried to intervene on some occasions, native communities generally favored election of senior male representatives drawn from pre-Conquest governing families. Not all Native Americans were happy with such political continuity, and occasionally upstart elites moved to the fore, arguing successfully that they had equal rights to leadership positions. Even so, local custom rather than Spanish dictates determined the numbers, titles, and terms of office of cabildo officers.

Every cabildo had a notary, an important and prestigious post, politically and culturally (see In Focus 8.1). Above the cabildo was the governor – sometimes called *gobernador*, sometimes given native titles of rule (e.g., *curaca* in Peru, *batab* in Yucatán), sometimes a cacique or dynastic lord descended from precolonial kings or rulers. In some places, such as in the Mixtec region of southern Mexico and parts of the northern Andes, *cacicas*, or elite women, ruled their communities (see In Focus 8.2).

At the local level, the República de Indios was thus made up of its governor and cabildo, its chartered pueblo status, and its residents. In sites where Spaniards had superimposed their cities on old native towns, two cabildos were formed, representing both *repúblicas*. In Mexico City, for example, there was both a Spanish cabildo and a Nahua cabildo, the latter to govern the native residents of Tenochtitlán (as Nahuas continued to call the city in the colonial period). It would be an exaggeration to call this genuine power sharing, but a similar arrangement appeared in the former Inca capital of Cuzco.

Figure 8.1. a. Page 1 of the Nahua Bible (MS 1692). Courtesy of the Schøyen Collection. **b.** Literate noblemen left behind tens of thousands of documents in colonial Mesoamerican languages. This example is a 1748 will written in Yucatec Maya. Photograph by Matthew Restall.

HEIRS TO THE HIEROGLYPHS

Every native cabildo (town council) in the Spanish colonies included a notary or scribe, a position of far greater importance in native cabildos than in Spanish town councils. Spaniards often commented on, and complained about, how litigious the Indians were and how well their cabildos engaged the colonial legal system. Native notaries in the Andes wrote overwhelmingly in Spanish, but Mesoamerican notaries wrote mostly in their own languages – an alphabetic continuation of the deep-rooted tradition of hieroglyphic writing. The literate nobility left behind tens of thousands of documents, mostly wills and land records, written in dozens of languages between the early sixteenth and late nineteenth centuries. The examples above are in Nahuatl (an indigenous version of sermons by saints Paul and Sebastian written by two Nahuas in the 1530s or 1540s) and in Yucatec Maya (the last will and testament of a Maya woman named María Tec, written down by her village notary in 1748).

In legal and other documents, native peoples referred to themselves as belonging not to the abstract República de Indios, but rather to the indigenous place name of their home community, which usually had a saint's name attached as a prefix. Indigenous terms for community also persisted. In Mesoamerica, for example, the Nahua municipal community was the *altepetl*, the Mixtec one was the *ñuu*, and the Yucatec Maya equivalent was the *cah*. Andeans in the Quechua-speaking regions mostly used the term *ayllu*. These terms applied to the smallest village as much as to the most impressive town or city, and they encompassed not just the cluster of homes centered on the local church but also the lands pertaining to the place, its people, and its history – that is, a deeply rooted sense of identity and belonging.

At the level of *altepetl* and *cah*, old traditions of micropatriotism persisted through the colonial centuries. Highly localized clothing styles, speech patterns, and religious affiliations, usually through the Catholic cult of saints,

IN FOCUS 8.2

Figure 8.2. a. The cacica of a native village outside Bogotá. Photograph by Mercedes Lopez. **b.** La Casa de la Cacica, Teposcolula. Photograph by Kevin Terraciano.

THE CACICA

In the image on the left, the *cacica*, or female chief, of a native village outside Bogotá is memorialized in a fresco painted on the wall of the local church. The privilege of being painted for posterity, combined with the depiction of her as piously praying, holding a rosary, and wrapped in a mantle of office, all reflect her high status in the community. Her elaborately patterned garment shows how indigenous craftsmanship was still highly valued and proudly displayed long after the Spanish Conquest.

The northern Andes was not the only region of Spanish America where noblewomen from old dynasties wielded local power. Among the Mixtecs of Oaxaca, in southern Mexico, *cacicas* ruled and laid claim to privileges of nobility. One such woman, doña Catalina de Peralta, was (despite her Spanish-sounding name) the Mixtec heiress to the rulership of the town of Yucundaa (called Teposcolula by Nahuas and Spaniards) in the 1560s. She presented ancient painted manuscripts and early colonial wills to prove her case, and in 1569, she took ritual possession of the palace (still called La Casa de la Cacica today, and shown in the image on the right). The ritual, described in the written record of the proceedings, featured both Spanish practices (symbolic door slamming and stone throwing) and traditional Mixtec ones (the noblewoman and her husband sitting on reed mats to mark their assumption of rulership).

distinguished one community from another. Indigenous foodways persisted virtually everywhere, though with the addition of certain introduced items, including barley, sugar, plantains, and meat and cheese derived from European domestic animals. A major point of contention with the Spanish was in the realm of religion, where Christianity was adopted and adapted in local and often unorthodox ways; this led, as we will see, to disagreements that often turned violent.

Not all communities managed to survive colonial impositions or maintain continuity of rule. A considerable number of native communities disappeared entirely, as a result of the early colonial population decline, combined with Spanish attempts to concentrate surviving villagers into central settlements (the flawed and largely unsuccessful policy of *congregación*, or "congregation"). Peru's Viceroy Toledo forced the remnants of some 900 precolonial Andean villages in what is today Bolivia into forty-four "congregated" pueblos. Many uprooted Andeans drifted back to their old homes and lands, just as thousands of Mayas did in the wake of congregación efforts in seventeenth-century Yucatán; but much of the damage done to local life was irreversible. Other places were profoundly altered by developments such as changes in the local economy, by the settlement in the area of outsiders (e.g., mixed-race migrants or natives from elsewhere), or by the village's location on one of the colonial trunk lines (the arteries of trade and communication, detailed further in Chapter 12).

Disruptions could be severe, yet in many core regions the colonial middle was a time of relative calm and stability – cultural, economic, and political. This equilibrium in parts of Mesoamerica and the Andes owed much to the actions and mediations of the local native elite. Spaniards sought out indigenous leaders who, in exchange for certain labor and tax exemptions, would act as intermediaries. This became increasingly important with the phasing out of the encomienda. As the encomienda disappeared in core areas, the crown began to collect indigenous surplus production in the form of tribute, first in products of the land, then in cash. Local headmen (and occasionally headwomen) were responsible for collecting tribute twice a year and for assembling workers for labor drafts. In some cases, village leaders protected their subjects from Spanish exploitation, and in other cases, they profited from it. Although most indigenous communities held together for many centuries despite these multiple exactions, strains between villagers and their leaders often had reached breaking point by the eighteenth century. By then a significant class gap had grown.

Native elite leaders were thus crucial on two opposing fronts: they were charged with guaranteeing both community survival and Spanish survival. Spanish colonialism essentially hinged on them, and they knew it. The colonial system permitted – and depended on – the persistence of native elites in three ways: (1) the institutionalization of village identity and corporate integrity, in the form of the República de Indios and cabildo government, as described earlier; (2) the redirection of ancient tribute systems in Mesoamerica and the Andes, so that tribute – in the form of labor, goods, and eventually primarily cash – became the essential material link between the crown and its native subjects; and (3) the need for intermediaries to govern native pueblos and mediate the tribute relationship between natives and the crown. Spaniards saw class differences, or socioeconomic hierarchy, as part of the natural order of things, with the maintenance of noble lineages as a sign of a civilized society. They therefore never really questioned the confirmation of local status and position by native elites. Only in the late-colonial period did native elites find their position under siege.

Land and Labor

Near the end of the seventeenth century, inhabitants of the Mexican village of Sula, a Nahuatl-speaking *altepetl* not far from Mexico City, decided to write down their local history. In one episode, Mexica (Aztec) forces – led by a Spanish woman – descended upon Sula bent on conquest. Fortunately, two brothers stepped forth to defend Sula with weapons that included the ability to turn into quail-serpents and the deft wielding of colonial-type land titles.

Sula's story exemplifies how native communities pragmatically adopted select elements of Spanish colonialism while still maintaining their own cultural traditions plus a highly localized or micropatriotic identity. From the Sula perspective, Mexico was divided less between Spaniards and Nahuas than it was between locals and outsiders (be they Spaniards or fellow Nahuas from Tenochtitlán-Mexico City). The telescoping of Mexica and Spanish conquests of the area reflected the fact that narrative chronology mattered less than Sula's historical ability to defend its territory, for the tale also illustrates the importance of land ownership to community identity. This folk history was written down as part of a land dispute between Sula and a Spanish estate owner, and the local cabildo was thus concerned with demonstrating that it had title to the lands – a title that was both ancient and verifiable within the colonial legal system.

Spanish monarchs were officially committed to defending indigenous lands as legally inalienable community property, although as the opening quote from 1580s Ecuador demonstrates, predatory Spaniards were quick to advance their own claims. A major source of friction was livestock, particularly large grazing animals such as cattle. Since there had not been any such animals in the Americas with the exception of llamas and alpacas (which preferred to graze in very high grasslands of the Andes), Native Americans were not accustomed to fencing off their farms and gardens. Once introduced to the fertile highlands of the Americas, Spanish cattle followed their noses straight into indigenous maize and bean fields, causing trouble and in some cases full-blown subsistence crises. Rogue livestock were but one of many challenges faced by indigenous villagers, many of whom still cling today to their colonial landholdings (commonly called ejidos).

The general trend throughout the colonial period was for Spanish landlords to encroach piecemeal on community lands and private plots held by native farmers. Sometimes Spanish estate owners used violence, threats, legal loopholes, debt traps, and other tricks to expand their holdings, but it is important to emphasize that most such transfers appear to have been legal sales and that this was very much a gradual development. Spanish colonial rule was openly exploitative, but its basis, as Vargas Machuca pointed out in his rebuttal of Las Casas, was the extraction of native people's surplus products and labor, not the acquisition of their lands. In regions with dense indigenous populations, in particular, it was generally seen as counterproductive for colonists to destroy native villages or seize the land that sustained native villagers. Like a giant parasite, the República de Españoles relied on the healthy survival of the República de Indios.

As we have seen, the Spanish first attempted to control indigenous labor with the encomienda. This institution, in its experimental Caribbean phase, was a compromise between outright enslavement of native islanders and a system that might have given indigenous subjects the option not to work in Hispaniola's goldfields. On the mainland, Spanish officials and conquistadors doled out encomiendas, or semifeudal "entrusteeships" of indigenous villagers, to prominent settlers. Most recipients had done military service, but a few encomiendas were granted to descendants of the Inca and Mexica royal families. Encomienda holders were promised indigenous surpluses in the form of foodstuffs, cloth, and other products, which they could then sell or trade on the open market. *Encomenderos* also had charge of surplus adult male labor, which they applied to ranching, mining, textile production, and other enterprises. In exchange, the *encomendero* was required to look after his subjects' physical and spiritual wellbeing, providing them with a priest for Catholic instruction and with arms should they need protection from marauding neighbors. The standard encomienda contract also stipulated that villagers not be moved from their traditional landholdings, the base for their subsistence. We see remnants of this agreement in the opening quote to this chapter from Ecuador.

The encomienda, though not slavery, sometimes came close to it, especially in the early sixteenth century and in places where crown oversight was minimal. The rules seemed made to be broken, and in many corners of Spanish America, native peoples were bought, sold, and rented, moved from their homelands, and otherwise abused. They might as well have been literally enslaved, as tended to happen in Portuguese Brazil. After the Spanish crown attempted to legislate the encomienda out of existence in 1542, at Las Casas's insistence, it began to disappear from core regions of Mexico and the Andes. Where it survived, and was even revived, was in unstable frontier districts, mostly jungle lowlands and deserts, and poorer provinces such as Yucatán. Here the crown kept the institution alive as an incentive for status-hungry late arrivals and descendants of the conquistadors.

The encomienda was first phased out in central Mexico, but colonists did not lose all access to surplus indigenous labor. In need of workers for lake drainage, mining, and other projects, crown officials devised a draft system called the *repartimiento*, or "allotment." Under this system, all nonnoble native men between the ages of eighteen and fifty were subject to labor service in the agricultural off-season. The law required that *repartimiento* laborers be paid and not abused, but as with the encomienda the rules were often observed in the breach. It was *repartimiento* draftees who helped staff many of Mexico's first silver mines, which were mostly located far from major population centers. Key among the early mining districts were Zacatecas and Guanajuato, many days' journey from Mexico City. Some mines, such as those of Taxco and Pachuca, were closer by, but still involved long-term absence from subsistence plots. By 1600, population decline had become so severe due to disease and displacement that *repartimiento* workers became scarce. A large number were also committed to the huge public works project of draining Lake Texcoco. By this time, some mine owners had accumulated enough capital or credit to purchase enslaved Africans as replacements, but wage labor also began to appear. Not all Spanish mine owners could afford slaves, and a small but significant number of surviving indigenous workers stayed on in the mining towns and gained enough skill to hire out as salaried professionals.

A somewhat different pattern emerged in Spanish South America, where the encomienda was replaced by an institution known as the *mita*. The *mita*, derived from the Inca *mit'a*, or "turn," system, resembled the Mexican *repartimiento* in that adult indigenous men were drafted to work for extended periods in numerous private and public projects (see In Focus 8.3). Of greatest importance to the Spanish crown were the silver mines of Potosí, staffed with nearly 10,000 *mita* laborers drawn from hundreds of miles away by 1575. Native Andean *mitayos*, as they were known, were required to travel to Potosí for one out of every seven years, usually with wives and children in tow. Many were killed, maimed, or sickened by lung disease, and between stints of underground work most were forced to staff Potosí's dozens of water-powered refineries, which ran all night and pumped mercury and lead into the air and water. As a stimulant, and as partial compensation for their work, native miners were given coca leaves to chew; by the 1570s, coca production was virtually monopolized by Spanish landlords based in Cuzco. Some 90 percent of their product went to Potosí (see In Focus 8.4). *Mitayos* also staffed the deadly mercury mines of Huancavelica, Peru, where many developed severe nervous disorders. Hundreds more were killed in cave-ins. Mine *mitas* were also developed far away to the north, in the districts of Quito and New Granada, where they had similarly negative effects. The Andean *mita*, like Mexico's *repartimiento*, sped the process of indigenous population decline while also providing money and credit for the purchase of African slaves. Unlike in Mexico, however, few slaves were put to work in Andean silver mines. Most Africans were instead made to staff vineyards, ranches, and lowland cane plantations, and to serve in households and artisan shops. More like Mexico, in depleting the labor pool while giving some workers access to new skills, the Andean *mita* also inadvertently gave rise to wage labor.

IN FOCUS 8.3

CANAVPOVR·PECHER·LESPERLES

Figure 8.3. Canoe for Pearl-Fishing (Margarita, circa 1570). Histoire naturelle des Indes: "Drake Manuscript". Credit: The Pierpont Morgan Library, New York. Bequest; Clara S. Peck; 1983. MA 3900, fol. 57r.

FORCED LABOR AND FRAGILE ECOSYSTEMS: CARIBBEAN PEARLS, COLOMBIAN GOLD, AND ARGENTINE CATTLE

Native American men, women, and children were drafted into many types of service under Spanish and Portuguese rule, but most able-bodied men were made to produce some cash crop or mineral for export. In Spanish South America, the silver mines of Potosí absorbed a vast portion of the central Andean labor force. Mines as far afield as northern Colombia and central Chile did likewise, often copying the Potosí *mita*, or "turn," system. But there were many other extractive activities that relied on native labor, among them pearl fishing along the Caribbean coast, alluvial gold mining in Colombia and Ecuador, and cattle roundups in the grasslands of Argentina and the surrounding Río de la Plata district.

In the midst of Columbus's last voyages, pearls were discovered along Venezuela's Caribbean coast, mostly in the vicinity of Margarita Island. Spaniards who had missed out on the gold bonanza of Hispaniola flocked to the region, establishing a town, complete with carved stone buildings, called New Cádiz on the island of Cubagua. Because indigenous slavery had not yet been outlawed, many coastal Caribs and other native peoples were simply kidnapped and forced to dive for pearl-bearing oysters. Like the slave trade in West Africa, such violence proved unsustainable, so a system of *rescate*, or "ransoming," soon emerged. Coastal chieftains who allied with the Spanish agreed to exchange war captives taken in skirmishes with neighbors for trade goods, including metal points and knives. Some ordered their own subjects to fish for pearls to trade. New discoveries were eventually made near Riohacha, on Colombia's Guajira Peninsula, and the Spanish thus extended their settlements all along this mostly desert coast.

Although the Spanish seemed unaware of the possibility, the Caribbean's pearl beds, like the Indian populations who worked them, were not an unlimited resource. Overexploitation of both workers and oyster beds led to a rapid bust in the pearl economy. New Cádiz was abandoned by 1540. By the late sixteenth century, the Caribbean pearl industry was partially revived, but most of the diving was done by enslaved Africans (as in the image above). Here a crew of black divers were painted in action by a late-sixteenth-century French visitor to the Caribbean.

New Granada, or modern Colombia, was home to the El Dorado legend, and this mostly wet and rugged region's riches in gold proved to be substantial. As in the silver mines of Mexico and Peru, Native American workers were in demand from the start. For some, the work was not entirely new, as the region boasted the most elaborate gold work of the pre-Columbian Americas. What differed was the greatly increased demand for gold under Spanish rule. *Encomenderos* demanded tributes in gold dust and forced their charges to build elaborate canals and earthworks to bring water to remote mineral deposits. The result, as in the case of the pearl beds of the Caribbean, was a combined environmental and human disaster. After an extraordinary bonanza that witnessed the exploitation of mines from Panama to south-ernmost Ecuador, both the deposits and native workers played out. Also like the pearl beds, only with the introduction of African slaves was the industry revived. It would again boom in the Chocó region in the eighteenth century.

A different example of how native workers were exploited in a marginal export sector comes from the temperate pampas, or grasslands, of the Río de la Plata. Here, cattle introduced by the Spanish in the early sixteenth century ran feral and proliferated (like runaway slaves, they were referred to as *cima-rrones*). Spanish merchants based in Buenos Aires, Montevideo, and other port towns hoped to tap into this cheap source of meat, hides, and tallow for export to Europe and the mining districts of the Peruvian highlands. Because most of the indigenous inhabitants of the pampas were as fierce as the Mapuche of Chile, however, the Spanish tended to rely on Guaraní cowboys recruited from the Jesuit missions of neighboring Paraguay, along with a small number of African slaves. These were the original gauchos, and they soon established a culture all their own. After gold was discovered in the Brazilian district of Minas Gerais, several months' journey to the north, Portuguese settlers established similar ranches in what is today Rio Grande do Sul and Uruguay, again using a mix of semicaptive Guaraní and enslaved African workers. Unlike the pearls and gold of northern South America, the cattle of the pampas did not run out. They did, however, radically alter the grasslands environment just as profoundly as they affected native lifeways.

Frontier Life

As life within the limits of the old Mesoamerican and Andean empires settled into a kind of uneasy equilibrium, a more dynamic, often violent pattern of life emerged on the Spanish colonial frontier. Brazil's backlands, as we will see, were even more dynamic and violent in the middle period. In places where native settlements were smaller and more scattered, the Spanish repeated Conquest-era settlement and exploitation patterns, often provoking conflict with nonsedentary peoples and then "punishing" them in retalia-tion. Settlers even revived the encomienda when possible, in some regions using it as a bridge to African slavery. As seen in In Focus 8.2, this pattern predominated in the goldfields of New Granada, for example, and in the cacao groves of Venezuela. A separate frontier model, characterized by widely dispersed strings of missions and forts, appeared in places with fewer obvious resources, such as the Amazon basin and the U.S. Southwest. Spanish priests,

Figure 8.4. Native horticulturists tending their garden: "Chew this coca, sister." From The Guaman Poma manuscript (GKS 2232 4°) at the Royal Library, Copenhagen, Denmark.

COCA AND COMMUNITY IN THE COLONIAL ANDES

Native American stimulants, such as tobacco and coca, continued to play important social and economic roles in indigenous life long after conquest. What changed, however, were everyday use and exchange patterns. In pre-Columbian times, these stimulants, along with alcoholic beverages and a wide range of hallucinogens, were generally reserved for chiefly or shamanic use. After the Conquest, however – and with the development of numerous, remote mining camps and thriving urban markets – the items became popularized, consumed by average indigenous workers hoping to stave off hunger or escape the harsh realities of colonial rule.

In parts of Peru and Bolivia, some Spanish *encomenderos* even became wealthy because of their investment in coca farms that supplied the markets of Potosí, Cuzco, and other cities with substantial native populations. Some smaller-scale native growers and dealers – such as the Andean *coquero* (coca dealer) of about 1600 pictured here – also prospered. Meanwhile, native market women in the Andes and Mexico alike became the major suppliers of cheap alcohol in urban areas, selling *chicha* (corn beer), pulque (fermented from maguey sap), and later distilled liquor (all discussed further in Chapter 12). Spanish authorities were quick to denounce both native stimulants and their sellers as immoral, but they proved unable to staunch either. The crown eventually saw a profit in indigenous drugs and drinks, as well as their utility as a labor enhancer – opting for taxation over suppression. In 1569, for example, Phillip II decreed coca production to be legal, taxable, and protected by the crown.

soldiers, and settlers exploited indigenous workers in the forts and missions, but native villagers sometimes voluntarily exchanged services and food for protection against nonsedentary raiders. An extra cost of congregation, as in so many places, was the increased risk of deadly disease. Despite their isolation and non-tropical locations, epidemics repeatedly ravaged the missions of Florida, Texas, California, and southern Arizona.

Settler-native relations followed a different path in less isolated regions such as Paraguay, which was home to many thousands of sedentary Guaraní and also smaller numbers of nonsedentary, often bellicose Guaycuruans. In and around the future capital of Asunción, Spanish settlers created a hybrid institution called the *encomienda-mitaya*. Large numbers of Guaraní men engaged in rotational farming, timbering, and livestock raising tasks, but there was nothing like the punishing mine *mita* of Potosí or the encomienda-staffed gold diggings of Hispaniola. The Guaraní so outnumbered the Spanish that they virtually absorbed them through intermarriage, and Guaraní quickly displaced Spanish as Paraguay's lingua franca. The language was further standardized by Franciscan and Jesuit priests, who established dozens of missions on the upper Paraguay and Paraná rivers after 1600. The Franciscans faltered, but the Jesuit missions survived and prospered thanks to income from sales of a local tea called yerba maté (the latter word referring to the gourd in which the tea was consumed). The missions sent yerba maté to bustling colonial markets such as Potosí, where even enslaved Africans working in the prison-like mint were drinking it by the 1620s. More elite buyers were soon found as far away as Bogotá, in New Granada. The tea, unlike American chocolate, never seems to have appealed to European or Middle Eastern consumers, but it found enough of an outlet in colonial South America to make the Jesuits the richest and most powerful religious order in the Southern Cone. Their missions, mostly clustered on either side of the Paraná River below Iguazú Falls, developed a complex Catholic Guaraní culture that defined itself in part by contrast with the neighboring Guaycuruans, who, rather like North America's Commanches, adopted Spanish horses to prey on vulnerable settlements and livestock herds. Other predators on Guaraní mission-dwellers, particularly in the early seventeenth century, included slave-raiding *bandeirantes* from São Paulo.

The *bandeirantes* were in part spurred to commit such raids because Brazil, unlike Spanish America, continued to rely on Native American slavery. Repeated prohibitions going back to the sixteenth century simply were not enforced, and the demand for labor on the thriving sugar plantations of Brazil's northeast coast was constant. For enterprising plantation and mill owners, native slavery served as the bridge to African slavery, which eventually predominated, but elsewhere in Brazil, for example in and around São Paulo, indigenous slaves continued to do almost every kind of manual task throughout the middle period, from running cattle to domestic service.

São Paulo was not atypical; widespread enslavement of Native Americans also persisted in the Amazon, or Maranhão.

In a way, Brazil's backlands mirrored the hinterland of Atlantic Africa during the colonial middle, as both witnessed the development of complex slave-trading networks stretching deep into the interior. What differed was the *bandeirantes'* tendency to use slave raiding as a means to territorial expansion. Roaming over enormous distances in the seventeenth century, mostly claiming to search for legendary gold, silver, and gemstone mines, they were largely responsible for extending Portuguese control beyond the limits of Tordesillas. The *bandeirantes*, many of them men of part-indigenous heritage from the São Paulo region of the southern interior (hence their more common name in colonial times, Paulistas), were something like a cross between backwoodsmen, entrepreneurs, and conquistadors. When Portugal's Spanish, Habsburg king (Philip II of Portugal, Philip III of Spain) once again outlawed native slavery in 1611, the Paulistas lobbied local authorities for a compromise: an encomienda-like system called *administração* (administration), which treated native servants as slaves in all but name. They continued to be traded, left to heirs in wills, and even given as parts of dowries. *Bandeirante* slavers continued to roam Brazil's backcountry well into the eighteenth century, when their activities were suppressed by order of the Marquês de Pombal.

* * *

Although harsher in some regions than others, forced indigenous labor regimes were standard throughout Latin America in colonial times. Whether through slavery, the quasi-serfdom of the encomienda, draft labor, or debt traps, Iberians sought to control Native Americans' labor power and, in one way or another, live from it. The mining zones were in many ways harshest, yet they offered the unintended possibility of native entrance into the cash economy through the underground trade in high-grade ore and gold dust, as well as through the emergence of wage labor. There more than anywhere, labor was scarce and some form of money near at hand. Those natives who survived quickly adapted and carved out a space of their own. Many indigenous women who accompanied their drafted husbands became small-scale merchants, evading sales taxes and upsetting town authorities and rich shopkeepers who proved powerless to stop them.

The sugar plantations offered none of the opportunities of the larger mining towns, and most proved so unhealthy for native workers that the Spanish mandated exemption from sugar production. Only Africans, they said, could tolerate such demanding tasks. More significant than the labor itself, of course, was the disease environment that cane plantations inevitably fostered. As we will see in the next chapter, enslaved Africans and their descendants would everywhere take up this burden. Many more natives in both Brazil and Spanish America were exploited in more prosaic roles, as cowboys, farmers, canoe paddlers, fishermen, porters, and construction workers. In the Valley of Mexico, a massive drainage project consumed the lives of thousands of indigenous men. Some indigenous work projects remain visible today. Like the great pyramids and temples of the ancient world, nearly all the great churches of Spanish America – the region's most tangible and often admired colonial heritage – were built by native carpenters, stonemasons, plasterers, and painters. Some were even architects.

SUGGESTIONS FOR FURTHER READING

This chapter is designed in part to go with the documents presented in *Mesoamerican Voices*, edited by Matthew Restall, Lisa Sousa, and Kevin Terraciano (2005). Instructors could assign the whole book to be read in conjunction with the chapter here, or they could leave students to make connections of theme and topic between our general comments and the case studies vividly offered by the sources in *Mesoamerican Voices* (e.g., document 4.8 is the written record of the ritual of palace possession mentioned in In Focus 8.2). There is no comparable corpus of Andean documents, but Guaman Poma's great commentary is available as *Letter to a King: A Peruvian Chief's Account of Life under the Incas and under Spanish Rule*, translated by Christopher Dilke (1978). The full original text has also been made available by the Danish Royal Library (http://www.kb.dk/elib/mss/poma/).

Also relevant are chapters 1–3, 8, and 11 of *Colonial Lives: Documents on Latin American History, 1550–1850*, edited by Richard Boyer and Geoffrey Spurling (2000).

For students writing research papers, there are many relevant monographs that study native communities and experiences in particular regions of Latin America. Among these are Kevin Terraciano, *The Mixtecs of Colonial Oaxaca: Nudzahui History, Sixteenth through Eighteenth Centuries* (2002); Matthew Restall, *The Maya World: Yucatec Culture and Society, 1550–1850* (1997); Kenneth J. Andrien, *Andean Worlds: Indigenous History, Culture, and Consciousness under Spanish Rule, 1532–1825* (2001); Peter J. Bakewell, *Miners of the Red Mountain: Indian Labor in Potosí, 1545–1650* (1984); Noble David Cook, *People of the Volcano: Andean Counterpoint in the Colca Valley of Peru* (2008); Barbara Ganson, *The Guaraní under Spanish Rule in the Río de la Plata* (2003); and Alida Metcalf, *Go-Betweens and the Colonization of Brazil, 1500–1600* (2005).

GLOSSARY

Cacique [kah-SEE-kay]: Arawak (Taino) word for ruler, adopted by Spaniards to refer to hereditary lords throughout the Americas (female equivalent, *Cacica* [kah-SEE-kah])

Altepetl [al-te-PET], **Ñuu** [NEW], and **Cah** [KAH]: examples of Mesoamerican terms for the city-state or municipal community (in Nahuatl, Mixtec, and Yucatec Maya, respectively)

Gaucho [GOW-cho]: cowboy of the pampas or grasslands of Argentina, Uruguay, and southernmost Brazil

Guaraní [gwa-ra-NEE]: indigenous people of Paraguay and neighboring territories who came under control of Jesuit missions over the course of the colonial period

Mita [ME-ta]: based on *mit'a*, literally "turn" in Quechua, the Inca language, but used by the Spanish to draft male workers from all over the Andean highlands to participate in mining, road construction, and many other types of projects

Potosí [pot-oh-SEE]: a city in south-central Bolivia founded in 1545 and home of the richest silver deposits in history

Huancavelica [wan-cah-VEL-ee-kah]: a city in highland Peru founded in 1564 and home of the Americas' largest mercury deposits.

9

Black Communities

They are embarked on a vessel, often not even a [large] carrack, 400 or 500 of them, such that the smell alone is enough to kill the majority, and indeed many die, so many that it is a miracle if only twenty percent are lost. And so that no one may think I exaggerate, only four months ago two shipping merchants took away for New Spain from Cape Verde a vessel filled with 500 [captives] and after only one night they had 120 dead, because they had packed them in like pigs, and even worse, all of them covered [in the hold]; they were killed by their own respiration and stench, which was enough to corrupt a hundred airs and take all their lives, and it would have been a just punishment from God if right along with them had died those beastly men who took them as cargo; and they did not cease in this business, since before reaching Mexico almost 300 had died.

(From *Suma de tratos y contratos*, 1569)

THUS DID TOMÁS DE MERCADO, a Spanish Dominican priest, describe in 1569 what is today known as the Middle Passage (see In Focus 9.1). Mercado was born in Seville around 1530 and was among the first students to attend the University of Mexico, founded in 1552. When he returned to Seville in the 1560s, he wrote a treatise for merchants inspired by the writings of his fellow Dominican and crusader for Native American rights, Bartolomé de las Casas. The manual, *Suma de Tratos y Contratos* (roughly *Treatise on Trade and Contracts*) was intended to bring Spain's burgeoning overseas commerce in line with Catholic doctrine, which treated lending money at interest, or usury, as a sin. After offering his observations on the growing trade in enslaved sub-Saharan Africans, at the time monopolized by the Portuguese, Mercado concluded that, although slavery itself was justified by Spanish law, the slave trade as practiced in western Africa in his day was so corrupt and full of abuses – most notably the mass kidnapping and sale of innocent

TIMELINE

1510–1519: rapid expansion of the sugar economy on Hispaniola, fueling early slave trade

1550–1640: first gold cycle in New Granada

1537: approximate start of the expansion of African slavery in the sugar fields of Brazil

1571: maroons of Panama aid Elizabethan corsair Sir Francis Drake

1580–1640: Portuguese hold asiento, or monopoly contract, to supply Spanish America with African slaves

1599: treaty between maroons of Esmeraldas, Ecuador, and the Spanish crown

1600–94: maroon complex of Palmares flourishes in the Brazilian interior

1630–1654: the Dutch occupy much of northeastern Brazil, from the mouth of the Amazon to Pernambuco

1680: expansion of slavery into Colombia's gold-rich Chocó region

1693: discovery of gold in Minas Gerais, Brazil

1726: discovery of diamonds in Minas Gerais

IN FOCUS 9.1

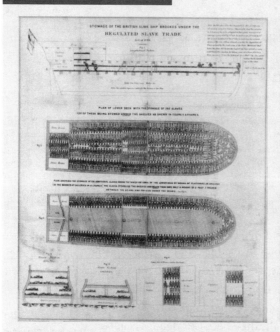

Figure 9.1. a. "Stowage of the British slave ship Brookes under the regulated slave trade act of 1788." Etching. Illustration showing deck plans and cross sections of British slave ship Brookes. Reproduction Number: LC-USZ62-44000. Image courtesy of the Rare Book division of the Library of Congress. **b.** M.Chambon, "marche d'esclaves" (slave market); Le Commerce de l'Amerique par Marseille (Avignon,1764), vol. 2, plate XI, facing p. 400. Courtesy of the John Carter Brown Library at Brown University.

THE MIDDLE PASSAGE

The Middle Passage, an oddly benign-sounding term, refers to the horrific, months-long voyage across the Atlantic suffered by more than 11 million enslaved Africans between the fifteenth and nineteenth centuries. The uncertainty of the voyage was clearly terrifying, and we know from various testimonies that some Africans awaiting shipment in Angola believed they were being taken to distant slaughter-houses, later to be eaten by white cannibals. (The image on the right, a 1764 French engraving, depicts the fear and anxiety that accompanied transportation to the slave ship off the African coast.) Most early Portuguese slave ships were small and tight, and sailors expected so many of their chained passengers to die they called them "floating tombs." Knowing how deadly the Middle Passage was, Portuguese Catholic priests established ministries in several slaving ports and fortresses, where they baptized tens of thousands of branded captives, many of whom died even before boarding a vessel. Barracks, dungeons, and other holding areas all along the Atlantic African coast were but a precursor of the horrors to come.

   When northern Europeans took over much of the transatlantic slave trade in the seventeenth century, the emphasis on religion, however cynical it may seem today, all but disappeared. Dutch, English, French, and Danish slavers treated enslaved Africans like livestock, not as humans with souls to be saved. The slaves' health and welfare were thus handled as commercial concerns, not moral or ethical ones. Most slaves received miniscule rations of gruel made from manioc, maize, millet, or rice, sometimes flavored with small amounts of salt meat or fish. Fresh fruits and vegetables are not mentioned in slavers' account books. Exercise on deck, usually in the form of dancing, was sometimes demanded, often followed by a shower of seawater. Captives were separated by gender in the hold, but clothing was minimal. Many men were left entirely naked to increase their sense of humiliation in hopes of suppressing revolt.

Despite northern European attempts to improve some basic sanitary conditions on board, great numbers of African captives continued to die during the one- to three-month Middle Passage. Documents suggest that overall between 10 and 20 percent of enslaved passengers died on their way to the Americas. These percentages are stunning enough, but we also know that the slaves chosen for shipment were considered healthiest, so this is yet further evidence of the inhumanity of this traffic. Many more slaves died in the barracks and dungeons of Atlantic Africa, and once in the Americas, yet another considerable percentage died of diseases contracted on board, of dysentery, or of malnutrition. In American slave ports such as Cartagena de Indias, nursing slaves back from the brink of death for resale was a thriving small business by 1600. Some of the enslaved killed themselves in desperation during the Middle Passage, and a few attacked and killed crewmembers. Harsh discipline and constant shackling were effective barriers to resistance, however, and when coupled with short rations and ethnic mixing, successful slave mutinies were extremely rare.

Whereas Spanish theologians and others loudly debated the question of Native American enslavement from the time of Columbus forward, no Europeans seem to have protested the horrors of the Middle Passage in a serious way prior to the late eighteenth century. In part, this was because it could no longer be ignored; more and more prominent families, and even whole cities, had become deeply invested by the first decades of the eighteenth century. It was after about 1750 that the slave trade reached its highest volume, however, and when slave ships routinely carried four hundred or more captives at a time. Both Enlightenment and radical religious thinkers, though not quick to denounce slavery itself, began to ponder the ethics of the slave trade, and the Middle Passage at last became a showcase 'Western contradiction' and focus of debate. (The image on the left, a detail from the plans of the English slave ship *Brookes*, shows how "tight packing" was designed to squeeze on board as many slaves as possible.) England, by far the largest shipper of enslaved Africans in the eighteenth century, also became the center of the abolitionist cause. Quakers and other religiously motivated critics called upon survivors of the Middle Passage such as Olaudah Equiano, who testified before Parliament. Despite much opposition from Caribbean planters and prominent investors in the slave trade, England outlawed the traffic by decree in 1808. As Europe's greatest naval power, the British felt uniquely capable of enforcing such a sweeping international policy, and it became a pillar of a new imperialist rationale. Even so, several million captives suffered the Middle Passage into the 1850s, when Cuba and Brazil finally agreed to stop the inhuman trade.

villagers instead of war captives – that any Spaniard with a conscience ought never to buy or sell an African slave.

Mass Slaves, Auxiliary Slaves

Few Spaniards took Tomás de Mercado's advice. After Native Americans, black Africans and their descendants made up the second largest group of exploited peoples in colonial Latin America. For their part, the Portuguese never even thought to justify their actions beyond claiming that they were saving African souls by introducing them to Christianity. African slavery, as we have seen, was a fully developed institution in the Mediterranean and East Atlantic before Columbus's first transatlantic voyage, and it quickly took root throughout Latin America in early colonial times.

Although it was Spaniards, not Portuguese, who carved out colonies throughout much of the Americas in the sixteenth century, the Portuguese continued to dominate the slave trade well into the seventeenth century – aided by the effective union (through royal marriages plus an invasion of Lisbon by Philip II) of Spain and Portugal from 1580 to 1640. In fact, we can divide the era of the slave trade to the Americas into two halves: the Portuguese half, from 1492 to 1640, and the English half, from 1640 to the nineteenth century. During the latter decades of the Portuguese period, some seven thousand to eight thousand slaves were brought across the Atlantic every year; by 1640, some quarter million Africans had been forced to come to Spanish America and a similar number to Brazil.

It was not only the English who took up slave trading in the middle-colonial period – the Dutch and French played major roles, Portuguese and Spanish ships continued to transport slaves, and almost every European power was involved to some degree – but the English dominated the slave trade in later centuries, bringing far more slaves to American colonies than even the Portuguese did.

The only brake on African slavery was that it was expensive, and thus it proved profitable only in zones of intense exploitation of exportable resources, or where slaves could be trained in a lucrative skill, such as carpentry. African slaves in the Americas fell into two broad categories – mass slaves and auxiliary slaves. Most slaves were mass slaves forced to labor on sugar plantations or in gold mines, but many were auxiliary slaves, incorporated into the service sector and often acting as intermediaries between Spaniards and native workers.

Mass slavery on plantations, ranches, and in mines created what some historians call "slave societies," whereas auxiliary slavery created "societies with slaves" – the latter included colonial cities, especially ports and regional capitals. In a slave society, the master-slave relationship was the model for all social relations, slaveholders were exclusively the ruling class, most workers (if not most people) were slaves, and slave revolts and maroon communities were common. In a society with slaves, economic and social relations did not revolve around slavery, individual slaveholders owned small numbers of slaves, slaves were a minority of workers, free people of color typically outnumbered slaves, manumission was possible (if not encouraged), and slave revolts and maroon communities were rare or nonexistent.

With a few exceptions – such as Mexico City in the early seventeenth century and Popayán (today in southern Colombia) in the late seventeenth century – Spanish America contained societies with slaves. They had fought as black conquistadors in the invasion campaigns, and in the early colonies, they had served as guards and porters, cooks and laundresses, grooms and majordomos, often overseeing large households and ranches whose main workforce was indigenous. The relationship between native peoples and those of African descent was complex and crucial to the development of colonial societies. Generally speaking, auxiliary slaves and African-descended free servants lived and worked in middling roles, supervising native laborers for Spaniards or in other ways bridging Spanish and native communities. Urban Africans tended to find at least as much affinity with Hispanic society as with native society, but they also persisted in many African beliefs and practices. Many urban Africans and their descendants were accused of practicing their own religions in secret. A small number were prosecuted by the Inquisition for practicing Islam, but many more were indicted, tried, and punished for alleged witchcraft.

Some auxiliary Africans adapted readily to indigenous cultures. Slaves in overseeing roles, for example, had to learn indigenous languages, share food ways, and live in the countryside, which made them more knowledgeable in many cases than their European masters of indigenous ways and concerns. Slaves in positions of relative power could command a degree of respect from native subjects, and considerable trust from their masters, but documents suggest this varied a great deal. Some indigenous workers resented African overseers, and occasionally murdered them or rose up against them. In work-houses such as textile factories, bakeries, and mints, African and indigenous laborers seem to have shared in the suffering, sometimes breaking out together or sharing rations of maize beer supplied by indigenous women. In time, more and more enslaved and free-colored men married native women, which helped turn indigenous communities into Afro-indigenous ones.

In contrast to most of Spanish America, Brazil became a slave society in the late sixteenth century and remained such for three centuries. In the fields and mills, Africans gradually replaced enslaved indigenous workers, who were referred to as *negros da terra*, or "blacks of the land" – which suggests that both Africans and Native Americans were imagined by the European outsiders to be "natural slaves." Despite this seeming equality, or fusion of perceptions, Portuguese planters preferred African laborers whenever they could afford them. Africans were seen as more cultured than most native Brazilians, more open to Christian conversion, and most of all, more likely to survive the rigors of plantation or mine life. As Africans replaced indigenous slaves, however, the potential for revolt grew.

Portuguese masters attempted to pre-empt rebellion by dividing slaves among themselves, creating distinctions and ranks that helped prevent solidarity. One method of division was to treat newly arrived slaves as uncultured beasts, to be ridiculed and made to perform the dirtiest and most physically demanding tasks. Incorporation into Brazilian slave society was thus a traumatic affair for many newcomers. Acculturated slaves were given

Part Three. The Colonial Middle

certain higher-level tasks and greater physical freedom, and those born in the colonies even more so, including overseeing responsibilities. Rewards in the form of extra food rations or better clothing made individuals even more likely to look out for themselves or their loved ones than to find common ground in shared oppression. Slaves born of African women and Portuguese masters were often assigned to supervisory or skilled artisan roles, and their affinity with Africans and with blackness was further diminished by the creation of religious brotherhoods, militia regiments, and other roles and institutions reserved specifically for those classified as mulattoes. Enslaved natives and their occasionally mixed offspring were similarly divided by color and culture, encouraged to despise those below and admire those above.

Whether in slave societies or societies with slaves, displaced Africans and their descendants established vibrant and durable communities, and created new, blended cultures. Iberian law encouraged marriage and baptism among slaves, and this profoundly affected the nature of slave regimes throughout Latin America. Family and godparent ties served as the base of virtually all black communities. Religious brotherhoods (which included women among their members) were also encouraged, thus creating networks of social assistance in an otherwise unforgiving and racist environment.

Slaves in early Latin America were considered a form of capital beyond their direct labor power. They were a source of both rents and credit, and they were even mortgaged, yet they were also legally recognized as human beings with souls to be saved and bodies that could be redeemed through self-purchase. Under Spanish and Portuguese law, slaves had the right to initiate a legal process called a *coartación* (or *coartação*), in which two appraisers (one chosen by the master and one by the slave) examined the slave before a magistrate; a price was set, the slave made a down payment, and thus began the process of self-purchase. Rural slave owners were less likely to observe these requirements than urban ones, but access to freedom through self-purchase – or the purchase of children, spouses, and other loved ones – was far more common in the Iberian colonies than in those held by northern Europeans. Paradoxically, greater access to freedom appears to have helped make Iberian slave systems more durable. It was not uncommon for free people of color to purchase slaves themselves, renting them out for income while also allowing them to save towards their own redemption.

Access to freedom and incorporation into the Catholic fold were thus core features of the slave system in Latin America. As a result, free coloreds soon became significant actors in the colonial world, many as property owners, freelance miners, ranch managers, and small-scale merchants – many of them were women. Freedom could be had in other ways, too. Where slavery was harshest, as in the sugar plantations and gold mines, slaves ran away in significant numbers to form "maroon" communities, alternatives to the colonial system that nevertheless tended to be parasitical on it.

Black communities in Latin America were diverse from the beginning. As the colonial middle wore on, high levels of mixing, usually outside marriage through rape, casual union, or concubinage, swelled black communities with free coloreds. In sugar plantation colonies like Brazil and slave-trade centers like Cartagena (on the Caribbean coast of present-day Colombia), the steady importation of new slaves kept black communities primarily African in makeup; but in most corners of Spanish America, free coloreds outnumbered black slaves by the mid-seventeenth century. Thus, although increasing numbers of African slaves were imported in the colonial middle, it is important to remember that the free-colored presence slowly extended into every region of Latin America.

Sugar and Slaves, Gold and Diamonds

Enslaved Africans did not end up evenly spread throughout the Americas. Most were taken to the Caribbean islands (a reasonable estimate is 4.7 million) and to Brazil (4.2 million) (see Map 9.1). Sugar plantations dominated the economies of Portuguese Brazil and of the English, French, and other European colonies in the Caribbean; it was thus in those places that the greatest demand for slave labor developed in response to soaring overseas consumer demand for sugar. Another half million Africans ended up in British North America, many to work on the tobacco, rice, and later cotton plantations that developed there in the eighteenth and nineteenth centuries. British North America was unique in that the enslaved population grew naturally, with substantial encouragement from slave owners, whereas the tropical colonies relied on constant imports, mostly of young men. Thus, the majority of Africans brought to the Americas had the misfortune of being mass slaves, mostly plantation workers, and the largest portion was absorbed into the Brazilian plantation system.

But Spanish America was also a highly significant destination, as it received more than three times the number of Africans sent to the future United States. The first Spanish American plantations were established on Hispaniola shortly after Columbus's time, and the model soon spread to Mexico, Peru, and other mainland districts. By 1519, sugar mills and plantations were found all over the island of Hispaniola, some staffed by as many as three hundred African slaves. Plantations on Cuba and Puerto Rico soon followed. On the mainland, none other than Hernando Cortés invested a substantial portion of the wealth he accumulated through conquest in a large sugar plantation staffed by African slaves. Similar plantations and mills, most of them staffed and run by black Africans, could soon be found from Venezuela to coastal Peru. For the Spanish, like their Portuguese neighbors, African slavery and sugar plantations seemed a natural combination. The pattern was soon expanded in Brazil and later, after about 1640, in the non-Spanish Caribbean (see Map 9.2).

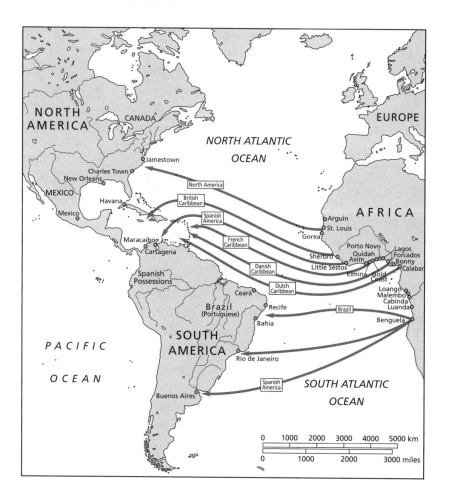

Map 9.1
The Transatlantic
Slave Trade

In the early years, black community formation was slow and difficult. African slaves were often relatively few in number, mostly male, born in many unrelated and distant parts of western Africa, and isolated by the nature of their work. Still, Africans soon blended traditional cultural practices, languages, and beliefs with those thrust on them by the Spanish and Portuguese. Sexual relations with both Europeans and Native Americans quickly led to the appearance of mixed-heritage children whose status was legally ambiguous. The result – often noted within one or two generations of arrival – was a hybrid culture, more often than not influenced by a heavy dose of Native American practices, lifeways (including cuisine, house construction methods, and religious ideas), and languages. Particularly in the early years, many African men found mates among Native American women, in some cases guaranteeing freedom from slavery to their children. Uncomfortable with the idea of a new population that could not easily be enslaved, charged tribute, or drafted to serve like those defined as "pure Indians," the Spanish legally forbade (but never managed to prevent) such unions.

Map 9.2
Sugar in the Americas

Where groups of slaves living on one plantation reached the hundreds, as happened in several Spanish American regions as early as the sixteenth century, local identities and mostly endogamous, or intracommunity, marriage patterns prevailed. Unlike their counterparts in Brazil and the non-Iberian Caribbean, many Spanish American plantation owners encouraged family formation, and hence natural reproduction, among their slaves. African women, in other words, were avidly sought by Spanish buyers. Families made slave communities stronger, but encouraging slaves to reproduce had the adverse consequence of allowing owners to exploit the considerable labor power of women and children. In some places, women and children were made to perform highly dangerous tasks, such as well digging and diving for sunken cargo. Family and fictive kinship ties, established through the Catholic practice of godparentage, or baptismal sponsorship, soon interweaved to create a tough and durable social fabric, one that served to mitigate somewhat the worst abuses of planters. In areas where plantations bordered substantial indigenous communities, as in parts of Ecuador, Peru, and Central America, ties of godparentage linked enslaved Africans and their descendants with Native Americans.

The plantation regime in Brazil was generally harsher, with many slaves literally worked to death within a few years of their arrival on American shores. Cutting sugarcane was backbreaking work, and many of the tasks in the sugar mill were dangerous; all in all, Brazilian sugar plantations were lethal destinations for literally millions of African slaves (see In Focus 9.2). Opportunities for forging family life were restricted by working conditions and the emphasis planters placed on what they considered men's work; African women were proportionally very few in Brazil, throughout the nearly three and a half centuries of the slave trade, which further stimulated the transatlantic trade to supply more young men.

Nevertheless, despite the gender imbalance among Afro-Brazilian slaves, there is evidence of early and significant community formation in all of Brazil's sugar zones, especially in Pernambuco and Bahia. Plantation slaves were expected to grow their own food between cane planting and harvest cycles, and some managed to produce a surplus that they then marketed in exchange for clothing and other material comforts that rendered slave life less demeaning. Others managed to trade items like tobacco and fish caught on feast days for cash, which was then used to purchase freedom for oneself or for loved ones. As in Spanish America, religious brotherhoods (*irmandades*) in Brazil often played the role of savings and loan institutions, holding money safely until the needed sum was accumulated. Brazil's black brotherhoods became especially prominent in the mining districts opened by the early eighteenth century.

The other type of work that proved profitable enough to support a labor form as costly as African slavery was mining. As we have seen, most laborers in the silver mines of Peru and Mexico were indigenous draftees and wage earners. In part since underground work could be crippling or deadly, only the wealthiest mine owners and refiners in these regions purchased Africans for such tasks as cutting and hauling ore. More commonly, enslaved African men were made to work in refineries and mints, where they could gain skills but also be closely watched. The famous mint of Potosí relied almost entirely on the labor and skill of enslaved Africans from its founding in 1575. The same was true of the mints of Lima, Mexico City, and Bogotá. Mint conditions were generally prison-like, and the work quite taxing and continuous.

Figure 9.2. **a.** Image from Willem Piso / Historia natvralis Brasiliae. Leiden University Library, 1407 B 3. **b.** Image from Willem Piso/ Historia natvralis Brasiliae. Leiden University Library, 1407 B 3.

THE SWEET AND THE BITTER

A ubiquitous ingredient and condiment today, sugar was once a prized and exotic commodity. When first brought west to the Mediterranean by Muslim traders and colonists over 1,200 years ago, cane sugar was considered a medicine or spice. This slowly changed, and by the fourteenth century Muslims and Christians around the Spanish city of Valencia were processing considerable amounts of sugarcane. Cutting and pressing cane were tasks initially done by mixed gangs of slaves and free workers.

Cutting the cane stalks was punishing business. Sugarcane is woody, which makes juice extraction a technical challenge. For sugar making to be profitable, specialists were required to design and build massive and complex mill machines. Animals such as oxen were used for power, but waterwheels were always preferred for their greater efficiency. As access to water was sometimes limited, and sugar mills were prohibitively expensive, mill ownership remained a dream of most sugarcane growers. For their part, mill workers, particularly the slave women who usually fed canes through the rollers, faced loss of limbs and sometimes death. Mills ran throughout the night, leaving many workers exhausted and accident prone. Early documents from Brazil mention hatchets kept next to mill rollers for emergency amputations. (The images here are from an early seventeenth-century Dutch account of Brazil.)

Making crystal sugar from sugarcane juice was also complex and difficult. Laborers stoked fires through the night to boil the fresh-squeezed juice, which they reduced to a syrup in copper vats. Clay molds were prepared by teams of women, who took them to crystalizing tables to cool. Here, clay was used to whiten the resulting brown sugar, which formed a conical loaf. The whitened loaves were packaged and crated by another group of workers, then rafted or taken by oxcart to port for shipment to Europe by yet more slaves. Sugar making was a highly skilled process, and its many steps led to considerable specialization among the enslaved workforce. At the same time it was labor-intensive, monotonous, and physically dangerous, leading some historians to consider it a foreshadowing of modern industry.

IN FOCUS 9.2

THE SWEET AND THE BITTER, *continued*

The rise of sugar as a product that more and more people craved, one that made European elites on both sides of the Atlantic rich and powerful, also sealed the fate of millions of Africans. Without sugar, the Atlantic slave trade would have looked very different, and it might have barely existed at all.

Some mining town slaves enjoyed greater than usual access to self-purchase or the purchase of loved ones, given the relatively high availability of silver coin. A few of the most skilled slaves probably enjoyed somewhat higher status than indigenous temporary workers. Even so, slave prices were generally highest in mining towns, which made self-purchase a long-term affair, and enslavement remained a badge of dishonor.

Enslaved Africans and their descendants were far more prominent in gold mining, which was mostly an above-ground affair in colonial times, whether in Spanish America or Brazil. African miners were already panning for gold alongside native Americans on Hispaniola in Columbus's time, and the pattern was soon repeated all over the mainland, from Mexico to Chile. Gold mining and slavery were particularly interconnected in New Granada (present-day Colombia), where whole provinces were transformed by African forced migration. Colombia's Chocó, on the Pacific coast, remains almost entirely populated by descendants of enslaved African miners. Here and elsewhere in New Granada, Spanish mine owners shifted quickly from indigenous encomienda to African slave labor. The speedy shift was made possible by gold's extreme value in relation to all other commodities, including silver.

This rapid creation of black mining communities was aided by other factors, and it would have a number of important, long-term effects. Many of New Granada's richest gold deposits were located in the hot lowlands, a fact that severely limited Spanish settlement. It thus became common for absentee owners to remain in distant, highland towns, while the mines themselves were operated almost entirely by enslaved Africans and their descendants, headed by trusted "captains." Most slave captains and "counter-captains" were African-born men who reported periodically to Spanish over-seers who, like the slaves' owners, tried to avoid long-term residence in the mines. The captains were responsible for handing off an amount of gold dust each month or two based on a joint assessment of each mine's likely productivity. In such circumstances, enslaved Africans and their descendants had virtually no contact with Spaniards throughout most of their lives. Blended African cultural forms, including, for example, drum and marimba music with call-and-response singing, were standard all along Colombia's Pacific coast. Slaves also had ready access to gold, which made self-purchase far more likely than on any plantation. By the later colonial period, large numbers of free black gold panners scoured New Granada's many rivers in search of subsistence. Among slaves, work stoppages in exchange for better rations and other concessions became increasingly common. Given the many dangers of life in such a demanding, rain-forest environment, African *curanderos*, or healers, emerged as a special, elite class among slaves. As in some Brazilian and Caribbean plantation zones, Colombia's Pacific coast gold district soon became a "neo-Africa."

Brazil's vast gold mines, discovered about 1695, also became "neo-African" enclaves based on mass slavery. What made Brazil's mines different from those of New Granada was the overwhelming predominance of men, a pattern repeated in the diamond diggings discovered nearby in the 1720s. The massive influx of men was aided by Brazil's relative proximity to Africa, and by Portugal's long involvement in the transatlantic slave trade. These factors, plus gold's high exchange value, made slaves cheaper, and as in the case of sugar a century earlier, made quick profit a larger concern than reproducing the labor force locally. High numbers of enslaved men in the backcountry made for an unruly society in the first decades after discovery. Rebellions were frequent, as was flight and illegal trade in diamonds and gold dust. Indigenous populations were small in Brazil's mining districts, and almost no Portuguese women migrated to them in the early years. African women were first to arrive, and many were made to work as prostitutes or were kept as concubines of Portuguese men. As tough as conditions were on Brazil's mining frontier, both enslaved men and women found avenues to freedom and social advancement far beyond what would have been possible in the plantation zones or anywhere else in the colonies. In one spectacular example, the enslaved woman Francisca, or "Chica," da Silva became one of the wealthiest women in Brazil. The diamond diggings were practically her personal fiefdom in the later eighteenth century.

Urban Communities

The other major concentration of Africans and their descendants in colonial Latin America was in cities. Mining towns, as we have seen, were noted for the presence of slaves, but more substantial black communities developed in port cities and regional capitals. Common practices in these "societies with slaves" were slave rental and self-hire. Slave owners frequently rented their male and female slaves (sometimes their only capital) to others for various jobs or even long-term projects, or as temporary nursemaids and cooks. An inherited slave was often a widow's or a spinster's only source of income. According to law, on Sundays and feast days, slaves were not to be forced to work, so many were allowed to hire themselves out, for a peso or two a day, to buy extra clothing or food or to set aside as savings toward self-purchase.

Slaves were thus often mobile and able to interact with one another outside the homes and convents where they lived.

The factors that forged and defined an urban black community varied greatly, depending on the size of the city and the percentage of slave and free-colored residents. Usually most, if not all, of the following were relevant: (1) occupation and working life (e.g., the shoemakers in a town being predominantly black, or African women working together in the market); (2) kinship and family life (community as a network of households); (3) the balance of enslaved and free people of African descent (a slave minority tended to assimilate into a larger free community); (4) the presence and nature of interaction with a substantial native or mestizo community (a smaller community of predominantly black men might become, through marriage to nonblack women, part of the larger mixed-race community); (5) ethnic or racial classification (e.g., in larger black communities, African-born men and women tended to maintain ties – including marriage – to those from the same linguistic area in Africa); and (6) religion (black urban communities tended to be Christian ones, with formal religious institutions such as brotherhoods helping create a sense of connection; but in late colonial Brazil there were exceptions, such as where substantial numbers of black Muslims lived in one city or town).

Port cities such as Acapulco, Buenos Aires, Cartagena, Lima, Panama, Rio de Janeiro, Santo Domingo, and Veracruz relied almost entirely on slaves for construction work, transport, and warehousing. Nearly all the imposing stone forts seen today in these cities were built by enslaved African men. In Havana and Guayaquil, black slaves cut timber and built the ships of the line. In southern Brazil, slaves hunted and processed whales to supply European demand for their oil. As in the goldfields of western Colombia, African resistance to certain lowland tropical diseases, most importantly malaria, allowed for a relative expansion of the black population in otherwise deadly, or at least unhealthy, ports. As a result, African and African-descended majorities were common in nearly all of Latin America's port cities and towns by the early seventeenth century (see In Focus 9.3).

In some places, this was true even where tropical diseases were not a major concern. Lima, for example, was practically an African enclave by 1640 and was home to the Americas' only black saint, the former slave Martín de Porres. Enslaved black women served many of Spanish America's thousands of cloistered nuns, meanwhile, and one such servant, Úrsula de Jesús of Lima, became an esteemed beata, or holy woman, herself. Her written visions frequently refer to the hardships faced by black women in a status-obsessed and racist colonial city. Slavery penetrated almost every urban elite household in Spanish America, and the mix of tension and intimacy created by this situation was constantly discussed by priests and city councilors. Many mixed children were born out of wedlock, some to be freed and others

IN FOCUS 9.3

Figure 9.3. *Watson and the Shark*, 1778, John Singleton Copley, Oil on canvas, Accession number: 89.481. Photograph © 2011 Museum of Fine Arts, Boston.

DIEGO THE DEVIL AND THE BLACK JACKS

The Middle Passage was not the only seafaring experience of Africans and their descendants in the Americas. Beginning in the sixteenth century, shipyards, docks, and ships at sea became centers of slave and freemen activity – and thus ports and ships became places where black communities developed. Examples include Havana – one of the Caribbean's busiest ports and full of black slaves, sailors, and dockworkers – and Cartagena, a major slave-trade port on the Caribbean coast. A third example is the Gulf of Mexico port of Campeche, which was half the size of Cartagena but contained the largest concentration of people of African descent in the colony of Yucatán. Campeche was not the province's capital, but it was its main gateway to the outside world, and therefore Africans arrived in Portuguese and English slave-trading ships, were sold there on the auction block, and worked in Spanish urban households. At the same time, free Afro-Yucatecans lived and worked in the town and the Maya villages that surrounded it as dockworkers, fishermen, domestic servants, corn farmers, and militia soldiers – some of whom fought, and died, to save Campeche from pirates in the seventeenth century.

Blacks and mulattoes not only defended Spanish ports from pirates; some were themselves pirates. The number of sailors of African descent grew steadily during the middle-colonial period, and by the eighteenth century, as many as one-fifth of the men aboard European whalers and merchant vessels in the Atlantic world were black slaves or free men of African descent. Such men, who historians refer to

IN FOCUS 9.3

DIEGO THE DEVIL AND THE BLACK JACKS, *continued*

as black jacks (*jack* was English slang for sailor) and Atlantic creoles, constituted a kind of vast black community at sea. The attraction of the sea, and especially piracy, for black sailors was the possibility of escape from a restricted, prejudiced work environment on land. Yet black sailors were often ill treated and assigned to lesser jobs, such as cabin boy, cook, or musician. On pirate ships, however, survival skills were more important than skin color, and the annals of piracy are full of legendary captains of African descent. For example, in the seventeenth-century Caribbean, there were at least three black pirates who went by the name of Diego the Mulatto or Diego Lucifer the Mulatto – a name that inspired such fear that it seems to have been adopted for that very reason by Afro-Spanish pirate captains. The first was a former Havana slave who escaped abusive masters in that port city to join a pirate crew, soon rising to captain and terrorizing the Gulf coast in the 1630s. The second conducted a similar rampage along the coast of Yucatán in the 1640s, sacking Campeche in 1642 and prompting a royal edict authorizing "every possible remedy to be taken to capture the mulatto pirate." This second Diego Lucifer evaded capture, but a third was seized and executed by Spaniards in 1673, after he had fled slavery in Havana and plagued Spanish shipping in the Caribbean for years.

The image here (a 1778 John Singleton Copley painting titled *Watson and the Shark*) is based on a real-life rescue in the sea off Havana; the port is in the background, and a black sailor is prominently featured in the middle of the rescue boat.

kept in captivity. As noted by indigenous writers from the colonial middle, such as Guaman Poma de Ayala and Diego Chimalpahin, people of African descent were very much a part of urban life, usually in closer contact with the República de Españoles than the more rural República de Indios.

One way to gauge the importance of the African presence in Spanish America's colonial cities is to look at musical and religious traditions, some of which have survived in altered form. Almost every black brotherhood staged colorful and elaborate parades to honor their patron saint or as part of a larger, lenten or nativity festival. African rhythms and words infused the so-called *negrillo*, a Baroque musical style and poetic form based on traditional Spanish religious themes. At such festivals, Spanish observers found African drumming both entertaining and unsettling, with its complex rhythms inciting even the most pious Christians to feel as though they were sinning. A wide variety of African instruments, among them banjos and marimbas, joined Spanish and indigenous ones to make up a new range of ensembles. When these instruments and rhythms were blended, out came something new: the roots of modern Latin American music, from samba to merengue.

Brazil's cities were generally slower to develop, but all relied from an early date on the labors of enslaved Africans and their descendants. Salvador, the colonial capital from 1549 to 1763, developed perhaps the deepest and most complex Afro-Brazilian urban culture, but Rio de Janeiro was not far behind.

By the end of the colonial period, Rio had the largest enslaved black population of any city in the Atlantic world. Slavery was so ingrained in everyday life in Rio, and indeed much of Brazil, that freed slaves often considered slave ownership a natural avenue to social and economic gain. The mining towns of the interior, such as Vila Rica and Diamantina (Tejuco), were similarly African in character from the start. Brazil's most famous colonial architect and sculptor, Francisco Antonio Lisboa, known popularly as Aleijadinho, was the son of a Portuguese immigrant and an enslaved African woman. Afro-Brazilian religious traditions such as candomblé and musical styles like the samba emerged from these urban, colonial environments.

Fugitive and Rural Communities

The form of slave resistance most feared by Europeans besides mass murder was mass flight. From the very beginning of slavery in the Americas, the enslaved ran away, sometimes forming rebel settlements known in English as "maroon towns" (derived from the Spanish term for runaway: *cimarrón*). Even in Columbus's day, Africans fled Hispaniola's plantations and mines for the freedom of the hills, sometimes joining with native peoples and even the odd European fugitive. Many more enslaved Africans made a run for freedom in Panama, where huge numbers of "maroons" under one King Bayano threatened Spanish control of the Isthmus and even sided with English pirates such as Francis Drake in the early 1570s. Other maroon communities appeared throughout the Andes and Mesoamerica, usually within raiding distance of Spanish farms, ranches, and towns.

An illustrative example of maroon community formation in the early colonial period comes from the heavily forested province of Esmeraldas, on the Pacific coast of present-day Ecuador. There in the 1540s and 1550s, a number of slave ships on their way from Panama to Lima were wrecked on this rugged and rainy coast, allowing surviving slaves to flee into the forest. Near the mouths of the Esmeraldas and Santiago rivers they established a string of free communities, allying with some local indigenous peoples and fighting against others. Spanish authorities in the highland capital of Quito, meanwhile, sponsored numerous attempted conquests, often substantial military missions headed by local elites who hoped to reenslave the maroons and force them to mine for gold and emeralds. One after another, the expeditions failed, leading Quito officials to sign treaties with the maroons by the last decade of the sixteenth century.

To the great consternation of the Spanish, the maroons had entertained the English corsair Richard Hawkins in 1594. The reasons for the failed conquests were several, but key among them was the astute leadership of maroon chieftain Alonso de Yllescas. According to surviving testimonies, Yllescas was born in the Cape Verde district of West Africa but had spent much of his youth as a slave in a merchant household in Seville. He was thus keenly aware of both Spanish motives and weaknesses, and he managed to play an astute cat-and-mouse game with a series of failed conquistadors, missionaries, and officials. When any of these competing outsiders got too close, Yllescas and his maroons simply faded into the forest. In addition to intermarrying with local Indians, Yllescas and another maroon leader, Francisco de Arobe, accepted a small number of Spaniards unhappy with their own society. They, too, joined in the fight for autonomy. Like many indigenous peoples who managed to remain autonomous long after the first wave of conquest, the Esmeraldas maroons blended accommodation and resistance in a way that consistently confounded Spanish authorities. Ironically, crown authorities ended up treating the maroons not as runaway slaves but as locally rooted Indians. They were exempted from tribute and draft labor in exchange for agreeing not to ally with pirates.

In Mexico around the turn of the seventeenth century, several maroon groups became so strong that district authorities were forced to cede them legal autonomy. In exchange for promising not to aid foreign intruders, or to raid plantations for more fugitives, the maroons were granted autonomy and peace. Maroons in the hills near the port of Veracruz, led by King Yanga and his chief general, Francisco Angola, defied the Spaniards for decades – forcing them in 1619 to a treaty that granted the community official pueblo status as San Lorenzo de los Negros, with Yanga as governor. Yanga's goal was not revolutionary; he aimed simply to win for his people the right to tend their crops and cattle and to nurture their families, in peace. In return, they built a church, paid taxes, and pledged to defend the colony in time of war. Maroons in New Granada were still more numerous, given that region's many gold mines, plantations, and other slave-based activities. One community in the hilly interior beyond Cartagena, San Basilio, remained outside Spanish domination for so long that its inhabitants developed a separate dialect and festival culture still evident today.

Far and away the largest runaway community of all was the *quilombo* of Palmares, which flourished throughout the seventeenth century in the Brazilian backlands of Pernambuco. Aided in part by the Dutch occupation of Pernambuco between 1630 and 1654, Palmares became a confederation of maroon settlements, or *mocambos*, that by the 1680s totaled some ten or twenty thousand inhabitants. Like the maroons of Orizaba, Mexico, and eastern Panama in the sixteenth century, those of Palmares respected a monarch. After the Dutch were expelled from Pernambuco, Portuguese planters sought to regain control over Palmares by negotiating with King Ganga Zumba. Once it became clear that the Portuguese were trying to divide Palmares in order to conquer it, a more militaristic leader, Zumbi, assumed leadership. Despite some successful battles, hardened *bandeirantes* led by the Paulista Domingos Jorge Velho ultimately destroyed Palmares

IN FOCUS 9.4

JOGAR CAPOËRA
ou danse de la guerre.

Figure 9.4. Capoeira Dance, Brazil, 1830s, from Johann Moritz Rugendas, Voyage Pittoresque dans le Bresil; Image Reference NW0171, as shown on www.slaveryimages.org, sponsored by the Virginia Foundation for the Humanities and the University of Virginia Library.

THE DANCE OF WAR

Aspects of African cultures survived in the Americas in interesting ways. Some West African martial arts, or traditional fighting techniques, evolved into forms of entertainment – albeit violent and potentially lethal ones. Under the watchful eye of plantation owners or urban officials, violent sport was controlled or curtailed. But off the plantation, on the beach, in rural villages, or at night, Afro-Brazilians enjoyed the ritual fighting of capoeira (the Tupi word for "bush," or "scrub forest"). This was a blend of acrobatic dance and aggressive play of apparently Angolan origins, often accompanied by drums and other instruments. Capoeira was mostly practiced in the context of feast days and other special occasions. The painting here – a French reprint of an 1835 work by Johann Moritz Rugendas titled *Capoeira or the Dance of War* – illustrates the playful nature of an art whose intention was generally not to shed blood. But on some occasions, the two male opponents mimicked the cockfight by attaching blades to their ankles, and capoeira was considered threatening enough by Brazilian authorities to be restricted in the eighteenth and nineteenth centuries, and then outlawed completely in 1892. Legalized in 1937, capoeira has since become a formalized martial art and a Brazilian national sport.

by 1694. Some residents managed to scatter and regroup in smaller numbers farther inland. New maroon communities quickly formed around the gold and diamond diggings of southern Brazil, but none grew as large – or lasted as long – as Palmares.

Some fugitive slaves managed to blend into remote villages in the countryside, but this was nearly impossible in most cities, even relatively large ones. Colonial officials were always on the lookout for runaways, and harboring fugitives was harshly punished. Slaves routinely escaped the Potosí mint works, for example, but despite the city's large population, virtually no one would harbor them. Their other option, fleeing into the high and barren Andes, was even bleaker. In another example, slaves who escaped masters in Yucatán and Belize and tried to melt into the Afro-Maya population of Bacalar (the Spanish port town near the Yucatec-Belize frontier) lasted only a matter of weeks before being detained by the local authorities.

However, out in the countryside, one seldom ran across ranking Europeans of any kind. Indigenous communities in such regions routinely absorbed black migrants, some of them maroons, but also free men of color. Black men married into local societies and took on most of the cultural traits of their hosts, including language, dress, diet, and religion. Examples abound from Guatemala and the Yucatán, where Africans became effectively Mayas, as well as Mexico's Veracruz region, where they became Totonacs. By the eighteenth century, the Maya *cah* (municipal community) was in many ways the Afro-Maya *cah*. In other areas, such as the coasts of Colombia and Venezuela, and the Costa Chica (on the Pacific coast of southern Mexico), Afro-indigenous towns sprang up around military outposts, tobacco farms, and cacao (chocolate) groves, some of them ultimately more African than Native American in character.

* * *

Despite constant attempts by priests, planters, and crown officials to control and monitor free and enslaved people of African descent, everywhere in colonial Latin America they carved out their own spaces and built their own communities. On the plantation, slaves created family and religious kinship networks that formed a bulwark of dignity and group pride against an otherwise demeaning and harsh existence. In the gold mines, slaves found access to freedom in some of the Americas' harshest physical environments, negotiating constantly for more autonomy vis-à-vis the master class. In cities, people of African descent asserted themselves in numerous ways, through group tasks, public events, and active participation in the market economy.

Most black slaves and free people of color also became devout Catholics, contributing to religious celebrations; developing their own confraternities and saint cults; and forging unique, regional interpretations of Christianity – in other words, generally complicating Latin America's Spiritual Conquest (the topic of the next chapter). Even where blacks and their mixed-race descendants were a small minority, the documents suggest they were never a silent one. Colonial Latin American life virtually always had an African flavor.

SUGGESTIONS FOR FURTHER READING

As possible supplemental texts to this chapter, we recommend any of the following volumes in the University of New Mexico Press's *Diálogos* series: Matthew Restall, ed., *Beyond Black and Red: African-Native Relations in Colonial Latin America* (2005); Jane Landers, ed., *Slaves, Subjects, and Subversives: Blacks in Colonial Latin America* (2006); and Ben Vinson III and Matthew Restall, eds., *Black Mexico* (2009). An excellent alternative is Herbert S. Klein and Ben Vinson III, *African Slavery in Latin America and the Caribbean*, rev. ed. (New York: Oxford University Press, 2006).

On the early slave trade, see John Thornton, *Africa and Africans in the Making of the Atlantic World*, 2d ed. (2000). On the topic of sugar and slavery in the American colonies, we recommend Sidney W. Mintz, *Sweetness and Power* (1985). On the early sugar plantation, see the many fine essays in Stuart Schwartz, ed., *Tropical Babylons: Sugar and the Making of the Atlantic World, 1450–1680* (2005). We also recommend *Captive Passage: The Transatlantic Slave Trade and the Making of the Americas*, which focuses more on the British colonies than the Iberian ones but is superbly illustrated. For rich, gendered views of slave life in Brazil's gold- and diamond-mining districts, see Kathleen Higgins, *Licentious Liberty in a Brazilian Gold-Mining Region* (1999), and Júnia Ferreira Furtado, *Chica da Silva: A Brazilian Slave of the Eighteenth Century* (2008).

The best study of black sailors is W. Jeffrey Bolster, *Black Jacks: African American Seamen in the Age of Sail* (1997), although note that it focuses mostly on black sailors in the English-speaking Atlantic. Monographs on various aspects of the African experience in Latin America include Colin Palmer, *Slaves of the White God: Blacks in Mexico, 1570–1650* (1976); Herman L. Bennett, *Africans in Colonial Mexico: Absolutism, Christianity, and Afro-Creole Consciousness, 1570–1640* (2003); Laura A. Lewis, *Hall of Mirrors: Power, Witchcraft, and Caste in Colonial Mexico* (2003); Matthew Restall, *The Black Middle: Africans, Mayas, and Spaniards in Colonial Yucatan* (2009); Frederick Bowser, *The African Slave in Colonial Peru, 1524–1650* (1974); and James H. Sweet, *Recreating Africa: Culture, Kinship, and Religion in the African-Portuguese World, 1441–1770* (2003).

An example of the *coartación* proceedings mentioned herein is chapter 20 in Richard Boyer and Geoffrey Spurling, *Colonial Lives: Documents on Latin American History, 1550–1850* (2000); also of some relevance here are chapters 6, 9, 11, 13, 17, 19, 21, and 22 of that book.

GLOSSARY

Capoeira [kah-poh-AIR-ah]: Brazilian fighting art of Angolan origin

Cimarrón: Spanish term for runaway slaves, or "maroons"

Coartación [koh-ar-tah-see-ON]: legal action of self-purchase initiated by a slave in the Spanish Empire (the Portuguese term was *Coartação* [koh-ar-tahs-YOAN])

Criollo/crioulo: "creole" in Spanish and Portuguese, respectively, an adjective meaning "locally born"; applied to both humans and animals

Irmandade [ear-man-DAH-zhee]: Portuguese term for religious brotherhoods, many of which were formed by enslaved and free men of African descent (the Spanish term was *cofradía*)

Negrillo [neg-REE-yoh]: musical fusion of African rhythms, Afro-Spanish lyrics, and traditional Spanish themes

Palenque: literally "palisade," the Spanish term for runaway slave communities

Quilombo: Portuguese term (of Angolan origin) for runaway slave communities (also common was the term *mocambo*)

La V. M. Maria de Jesus de Agreda Predicando
à los Chichimecos del Nuebo mexico. *Antt.º de Cozio f.*

10

■ ■

The Religious Renaissance

TIMELINE

1478: Spanish Inquisition founded; spreads to Portugal in 1547; formally established in Spanish America in 1569–1571; informally operating before then and in Brazil throughout colonial period

1524: the first twelve Franciscan friars arrive in Mexico

1536: Don Carlos Ometochtzin, Nahua ruler of Texcoco, burned at the stake

1560s: Taki Onqoy rebellion in Peru; violent campaign against idolatry among the Mayas of Yucatan, led by Diego de Landa

1569, 1570, and 1610: founding of Inquisition headquarters in Lima, Mexico City, and Cartagena

1571: founding of a separate inquisitorial body, sometimes called the Indian Inquisition, to police native peoples

1610s–1750s: growth of missions in North America, Paraguay, and Amazonia

The Indians venerate Christ only in word, they venerate Him as long as the priest or judge urges, they venerate Him, in short, only in the appearance of Christianity. They do not venerate Him from deep inside, they do not give true worship nor hold the faith in their hearts as is truly required.

(Jesuit priest José de Acosta on native Andeans, 1588)

IN 1606, the Andean cacica Catalina Tuza, heiress of a paramount chiefdom near modern Pasto, Colombia, was on her deathbed. She began the dictation of her last will and testament with a demonstration of her knowledge of the Catholic faith – "In the name of the Holy Trinity, the Father, Son, and Holy Spirit, three persons and only one true God in whom I truly believe as a faithful Christian" – and went on to request a splendid church burial and to arrange for various payments and donations to friars and religious organizations. Most notably, she ordered the auction of roughly half her assets, including considerable real estate, livestock, jewelry, and fine clothing, to erect a chapel in her family's namesake village of Tuza (today San Gabriel, Ecuador). A portion of the money raised in the sell-off was to pay for a Spanish priest to visit the chapel periodically to say masses for her and her parents' departed souls. The costs of these conspicuous devotions ran into the thousands of pesos.

This story, repeated with minor variations throughout colonial Latin America in the colonial middle, illustrates several key aspects of what historians often call the Spiritual Conquest – the Iberian effort to convert Native Americans to Christianity. Iberian clergy displayed no tolerance at all for the persistence of indigenous, pagan religious beliefs and practices, and testaments such as Catalina Tuza's would seem to confirm that Catholic Christianity was firmly entrenched in native communities by the turn of the seventeenth century. Was this really true? In Catalina Tuza's case, we have no way of testing the sincerity of her faith, but in reading between the lines of her will, we find that she was using a Spanish legal document loaded with religious significance to name a subsequent female heir – technically an illegal, pre-Hispanic procedure. Embracing the trappings, if not all of the content, of the invaders' religion was politically wise.

The persistence and pervasiveness of Roman Catholicism is one of the most obvious legacies of the colonial period in Latin America. Yet just below an apparently homogeneous surface, a wide variety of local beliefs and practices developed and flourished – many of them not approved by church officials. Indeed, the nature of Latin American Catholicism has been contested since the beginning of colonial times. Many of the most persistent of these disputes originated in the years following the Spanish invasion. At the time the Catholic Church was itself embattled in Europe – sharply challenged by Protestants, internal critics, and the powerful Islamic empire of the Ottomans. In the Americas, the missionary friars who entered Mexico in the 1520s, and other regions of Mesoamerica and the Andes in the decades that followed, were full of optimism. The same was true of the Jesuits who first landed in Brazil in 1549. They conducted mass baptisms of hundreds, occasionally thousands, of native converts, convinced that they were rapidly routing the devil – whom they believed was the architect of native religions. However, that optimism faded quickly, leading to harsher approaches to conversion and a generalized suspicion of indigenous backsliding and outright heresy, or total rejection of Catholic doctrine. As we will see, people of African and Jewish descent were also singled out and persecuted.

However, one result of these efforts was an extensive body of writings – mainly by Franciscan priests, at first optimistic, later more stoic – on Native American religion and the challenges of the Spiritual Conquest. At the same time, native rulers brought up as Christians often embraced the faith; like Catalina Tuza, they contributed to the building of elaborate local churches and to the growth of local saint cults and religious brotherhoods (or *cofradías*, called *irmandades* in Brazil). In the colonial middle period, a general turn to piety spurred the foundation and expansion not only of lay brotherhoods sponsored by Iberian settlers, native peoples, and African slaves but also of more rigorous and exclusive male and female monastic orders. The Jesuit order, created in 1534 by the Basque soldier Ignatius of Loyola, was another institution that sought to aggressively defend, spread, and to some extent modernize Roman Catholicism. For a time, the Jesuits monopolized the mission field in Brazil. In this chapter, we have dubbed the sum of all these developments – from Franciscan literature in Mexico to Afro-Peruvian *cofradías* – colonial Latin America's religious renaissance.

The Spiritual Conquest

Don Carlos Ometochtzin was a Christian convert. He was also the native ruler of Texcoco, an important Nahua *altepetl* (city-state) that sat on the edge of Lake Texcoco and had been one of the three city-states that made up the so-called Triple Alliance that had underpinned the Aztec Empire. In the wake of that empire's collapse, the Franciscans placed great emphasis on the conversion of native lords and nobles, reasoning that their subjects would thereby more readily follow their leaders into the new faith. It was therefore momentous – and shocking to almost everyone in colonial Mexico – when don Carlos was arrested in 1539 by the Spanish Inquisition.

Don Carlos Ometochtzin was charged with bigamy, idolatry, and apostasy, meaning that he was accused of clinging to his pre-Conquest or pagan religion. Particularly damning from the Franciscan viewpoint was the fact that don Carlos had secretly kept, and worshipped, a large collection of images of the old gods (or idols, as Spaniards classified them). The Texcocan ruler's fate was also sealed when evidence surfaced of his seditious attitude towards the new colonial regime. Referring to the Franciscans, don Carlos allegedly complained,

"Who are these people who bother us and perturb us and live among us and try to rule us? . . . This is our land and our way of life and our possession. The rule of it belongs to us and will remain with us. Who comes here to subjugate us? Who are these people who are not our relatives nor of our blood nor equal to us?"

Such statements convinced both the bishop and the viceroy that don Carlos was not the loyal convert he had once appeared to be. He was tried by Inquisition officials and, five months after his initial arrest, sentenced in the Plaza Mayor of Mexico City and burned at the stake outside the city walls the next day. The execution of this supposed model of the Christian native ruler – who turned out to be a hidden pagan – sent ripples throughout the Spanish provinces in the Americas. In the words of church historian John F. Schwaller, "the friars were chastened in the appreciation of how quickly the conversion would take."

Early confidence faded, but the church's resolve to root out paganism and idolatry hardened. The Franciscans were soon joined by Dominicans and Augustinians. By 1560, there were more than eight hundred friars in Mesoamerica alone. Because Spaniards invaded the Andes later than they did Mesoamerica, and then fought among themselves for a decade, the Spiritual Conquest in Spanish Peru was more protracted than it was in Mesoamerica. Still, by 1580, there were friars at work in almost every corner of what had once been the Inca Empire, plus the Muisca highlands and other parts of New Granada.

Meanwhile, popular protests in Mexico over the public burning of the Nahua ruler don Carlos Ometochtzin contributed to a prolonged debate over Inquisition methods, including discussion over possibly removing Native Americans from Inquisition jurisdiction. In 1562, Diego de Landa, the head of the Franciscans in Yucatan, tortured more than four thousand Mayas during

Map 10.1
The Religious Orders
in New Spain

a summer-long campaign against idolatry; hundreds died under torment or committed suicide. When detailed reports on Landa's campaign reached Spain, the debate moved more quickly. Although Landa himself escaped condemnation and was appointed Yucatan's bishop, a new and separate body, often referred to as the Indian Inquisition, took over responsibility in 1571 for the religious policing of native Christians in the New World.

The creation of the Indian Inquisition, however, did not mean that coercion and violence were abandoned as methods of conversion. The death penalty was no longer to be used on native idolaters, but torture was approved as an investigative tool from the sixteenth through the eighteenth centuries, as were various types of corporal punishment. Priests whose livelihood revolved around the indoctrination of indigenous parishioners reacted to this prohibition of inquisitorial interference by adopting many of the Holy Office's functions – and even torture mechanisms – themselves.

The result – from northern Mexico to southern Peru – was an inconsistent, yet occasionally violent, application of Inquisition-style investigations into charges of idolatry. In virtually all indigenous cultures, the Spanish concept of *idolatry* was meaningless. Stones, graven images, and other material manifestations of the sacred were omnipresent. From the native perspective, these were hardly distinct from Baroque Catholic images, which were widely understood to be sanctified representations and even containers of holiness.

But Spanish priests did make sharp distinctions between native and Catholic approaches to the material world, and in seventeenth-century Peru, a full-blown indigenous conspiracy to revert to the old faith was feared. To root out what became known as the Taki Onqoy rebellion, Andean villagers were called in to testify against their neighbors. Those named were tortured, exiled, and otherwise punished. Although consistent with the temper of the times, Peru's so-called Extirpation of Idolatries, which flared up in the hinterland of Lima several times in the seventeenth century, was mostly the pet project of a small number of ambitious priests and bishops.

In Yucatan, too, there were sporadic campaigns of extirpation throughout the middle-colonial period. As in Peru, these campaigns were dependent on the zeal of particular senior priests. Unlike Andeans, the Mayas had maintained a vibrant writing tradition before the Spanish Conquest, and thus extirpators in Yucatan focused as much on codices or hieroglyphic books as they did on idols. Although Diego de Landa had publicly burned a large number of codices in his campaign of 1562, priests continued to find and destroy Maya books for more than a century after this. As a result, only a handful of pre-Conquest codices survive today. One of them, dubbed the Madrid Codex, was likely found by don Pedro Sánchez de Aguilar during his anti-idolatry campaign of 1603–1608 in northeastern Yucatan and brought back to Spain by the ambitious priest in 1619. In another irony, Peruvian "idolatry extirpators" produced the critically important "Huarochirí Manuscript," a gold mine of ethnographic and mythological detail written by an indigenous scribe in Quechua shortly after 1600.

In Yucatan, Peru, and elsewhere, extirpation campaigns claimed to emphasize the positive messages of Christian teaching and indoctrination. But these aspects of church efforts were often overshadowed by the violent methods of coercion, correction, and punishment. Public executions were

IN FOCUS 10.1

Figure 10.1. Woodcut of Sor María preaching in New Mexico, by Antonio de Castro, originally used for 1730 Mexican edition of 'Benavides' Memorial of 1634'. Courtesy of Catholic Archives of Texas, Austin.

WORSHIPPING CHRIST AND SERVING THE GODS

Sor María de Jesús de Agreda was abbess of the Franciscan Conceptionist nuns in the Spanish town of Agreda from 1627 to 1665. Although she never left Spain in her life, she believed that she could leave her body and circumnavigate the globe in a trancelike state, thereby appearing and preaching to native peoples in northern Mexico. Her claims were taken seriously by some, such as Padre Alonso de Benavides, director of the Franciscan missions in New Mexico in the 1620s, who claimed that various native groups, as far north as the Jumanos of northern Texas, were overawed by the sacred beauty of María de Agreda's supernatural appearances in her blue mantle. (The image here – the frontispiece to the 1631 *Letter of Fray Alonso de Benavides to the Friars of New Mexico* – depicts María de Agreda preaching to the Chichimecs of New Mexico.)

José de Acosta was a Jesuit priest who served for many years in Peru as a theology professor and missionary. Among his many writings was the guide *How to Provide for the Salvation of the Indians*, composed in the 1570s and published in 1588. In the guide, he compared the native Andeans or "Indians" to the Samaritans of the Old Testament, who had converted while continuing to worship their old gods. The Indians, complained Acosta, "give worship to Christ and they serve their gods, they revere the Lord and they do not revere Him" (more of the passage is quoted at the beginning of this chapter).

How, then, did native peoples really respond to campaigns to convert them to Christianity? Did they at first resist openly, like certain Mayas and Caribs? Did they pretend to convert while secretly maintaining old traditions, as don Carlos Ometochtzin was accused of doing before he was burned at the stake and as Acosta believed Andeans did? Were they eventually convinced by the efforts of friars and miraculous appearances like that of Sor María de Agreda in the image here?

The answer is all of the above. Native responses were complex and varied. The insistence by priests in colonial times that conversions were either sincere or false, or perhaps a mixture of the two that resulted in syncretic or hybrid local forms of Christianity, simplified the fact that native peoples responded to and accommodated Christianity on several levels. One was that of the universal level of the Catholic Church as an institution, Christianity as an official religion, and its cornerstone beliefs. Another was the local level of the patron saints and deities that protected – and were in turn nurtured by – native communities. The third level was the most private, the realm of healing and interpersonal magic (a topic we turn to in Chapter 11). At none of these levels was the process of accommodation completed during early colonial times; the Spiritual Conquest, like the military conquest and imposition of Spanish colonial rule, was a protracted process of negotiation that lasted the whole colonial period.

relatively rare, but many natives, including esteemed elders, healers, and midwives, suffered torture, humiliation, and exile. The efficacy of these methods – the degree to which they resulted in a profound embrace of the Christian faith by native peoples – was the subject of much debate by priests in colonial Latin America and continues to be debated by historians. Many indigenous religious practices simply went underground, but much sacred knowledge was undoubtedly lost (see In Focus 10.1).

Either way, it is becoming increasingly clear that native people engaged with Christianity in creative and multiple ways, adjusting its theology and practices to local cultures. By the end of the colonial middle, the Spiritual Conquest had resulted in something different from the simple spread of Christianity across the Americas or the laying of foundations for a Latin American Catholicism (or national Catholicisms, with their various patron saints); it had led to the creation of scores, perhaps hundreds, of distinct local forms of Christianity, each one reflecting the African and/or Native American culture of its creators. As with the military conquest and colonization, native and African participants soon laid claim both to the process and the outcome, thus making Christianity their own.

Books and Buildings

One of the friars involved in the trial of don Carlos Ometochtzin was Bernardino de Sahagún. He concluded from the trial, and from his experiences preaching to Nahua villagers in New Spain, that Spanish missionaries and priests needed to be better informed. Only by studying, recording, and truly understanding native religion and culture could Spaniards hope to fully convert native peoples. Sahagún became one of the leading figures in the literary manifestation of the religious renaissance in New Spain.

Beginning in the mid-sixteenth century, Sahagún – along with other Franciscans, with Dominicans, Augustinians, and later on Jesuits – produced a great series of written guides. These included grammars and dictionaries of native languages; detailed accounts of native religions; and conversion tools such as confessional manuals, catechisms, and sermons in native languages. Similar efforts were made in the Andes and Brazil, although by far the most was written in and on Mesoamerica. These methods were a renaissance of Christian ideas in ways that the friars did not always intend, for they turned conversion into a conversation – a two-way exchange of concepts and practices that forced Christianity to adapt to local native ways of thinking and doing things.

Thus, while Mesoamericans found it harder and harder to produce traditional literary works, and saw hieroglyphic and pictographic books burned or marginalized, they contributed to many church-sponsored books as informants, ghostwriters, and artists. At the same time, new genres of books developed, written in native languages but alphabetically. Among these were the primordial titles (or *títulos*). These were land titles that were turned into community histories by native scribes throughout Mesoamerica, drawing on since-lost codices and local oral traditions. Pre-Conquest and pre-Christian literary roots are even more in evidence in the Books of Chilam Balam (or Books of the Jaguar Priest). These Maya-language manuscripts were maintained in dozens of villages across Yucatan by local scribes throughout the colonial period. The books recorded a wide variety of information – from local history to calendrical knowledge and herbal cures – often presented in the form of riddles and fables. Both primordial titles and Chilam Balam books reflected the impact of the Spiritual Conquest, as the arrival of Christianity was more often presented in matter-of-fact or positive ways than in critical ones. In both examples, native authors sought to reconcile traditional knowledge with Christianity and to adapt old ways of recording knowledge to new technologies and political realities.

The Franciscans and other friars thus significantly altered the cultural landscape with their vigorous literary activities. But they also made a physical impact on the landscape by tapping into native traditions of monumental architecture and encouraging the construction of church buildings. New churches were typically built on the same site as pre-Christian temples, often using the same foundations, pyramidal platforms, and many of the same stones. By the end of the sixteenth century, hundreds of churches had been constructed in Mesoamerican parishes. Friars sometimes had to begin with modest structures of wood or adobe (see In Focus 10.2). But the pride that Mesoamerican towns had invested in local pyramids and temples was soon transferred to churches, producing oversized and highly varied church buildings throughout Mesoamerica. Church construction in Peru was slower but equally extensive by the middle of the colonial period, as suggested by Catalina Tuza's chapel.

IN FOCUS 10.2

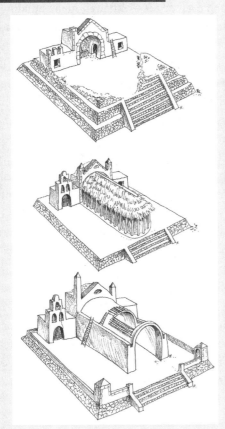

Figure 10.2. **a.** The three drawings above depict the evolution of the prototypical early church built in late-sixteenth-century Yucatan. Drawing by Matthew Restall. **b.** Yucatec church. Photograph by Matthew Restall. **c.** Yucatec church. Photograph by Matthew Restall.

FROM VILLAGE PYRAMIDS TO PARISH CHURCHES

The three drawings here depict the evolution of the prototypical early church built by Mayas under Franciscan supervision in late-sixteenth-century Yucatan. For many centuries, Mayas had built temples on top of pyramids or pyramidal platforms. During the Spiritual Conquest, Franciscans and Mayas agreed that the new Christian temples would be built on these same platforms. The earliest of these buildings took the form of open chapels. In the second stage, a thatched-roof extension provided shade from the hot Yucatec sun, in the same architectural style used by Mayas to build houses for thousands of years. Finally, that extension was converted into a pole, masonry, and plaster nave. This happened in most parishes in the colony by the end of the sixteenth century, as the local elite soon transferred onto the new church building the dynastic pride and municipal status that had earlier been invested in pyramid and temple. The photographs here are of churches in Maya villages, two of the many early colonial churches that have survived in Yucatan.

In cities throughout the colonies, the transition from old temples to new churches was more spectacular and even faster – although many buildings were expanded and rebuilt for decades, if not centuries. One of the more beautiful Inca temples in Cuzco, the Coricancha, served as the base for the less elegant church of Santo Domingo. The stately Franciscan church in Quito was begun with reworked Inca stones in 1534. An impressive cathedral was begun in Mexico City in 1563; immediately adjacent to the ruins of the great pyramid and temples of the Aztecs, it was continually expanded into the eighteenth century. The most opulent churches of Brazil were concentrated in the northeast sugar zone, in Bahia and Pernambuco, until the discovery of gold and diamonds in Minas Gerais around 1700. By contrast with Spanish America, no Brazilian churches, as far as we know, were built on indigenous sacred sites.

The dominant architectural style of Ibero-American church buildings throughout the seventeenth century was the Baroque, which featured highly detailed exteriors and elaborate interiors centered on gold-drenched altarpieces. The style extended from Mexico City and Lima all the way to modest parish churches in Venezuela and Yucatan, where, although parishioners might not be able to afford much in the way of gold decorations, exteriors were brightly and distinctively painted. Even relatively modest cities such as Arequipa, Peru, and Tunja, Colombia, boasted an impressive collection of Baroque stone churches, hospitals, and convents by the mid-1600s.

The Inquisition in America

In the so-called Baroque period – our colonial middle – Iberians developed a number of institutions to defend, enforce, and spread the Catholic faith. Officially, nothing else was tolerated. The Spiritual Conquest was led by friars from various religious orders and taken up by friars and secular clergy under the auspices of the Indian Inquisition, or Extirpation of Idolatries. But the regular Inquisition – the *Santo Oficio* or Holy Office – remained arguably the most important religious institution in the colonies, with far-reaching political and social influence. Inquisition officers were charged with rooting out heresy, policing public morality, and preventing the spread of allegedly dangerous books. Even swearing fell under their purview.

True believers, like gemstones, were difficult to judge. Everyone had their opinions, and all Baroque Catholics, regardless of wealth, education, sex, or color, were deemed fallible sinners. In ascertaining the depth of an individual's faith, church leaders thus chose to emphasize visible evidence of belief, such as ritual practices and daily comportment, rather than an ability to articulate doctrine. Heretics and apostates were identified by their deviant practices. Such practices included bigamy, homosexuality, failure to attend mass, improper observance of feasts, use of blasphemous language, and hiring witches to cast love-magic spells. It was believed that unless they were caught, punished, reformed, or rooted out, followers of unorthodox practices and beliefs would "infect" the larger body of believers. This stern view, which amounted to a sort of religious nationalism (especially against Protestant "heretics" from France, England, and Holland), was heavily reinforced by the Habsburg monarchs. The pious example was set by Philip II, and it spread to Portugal and Brazil during the 1580–1640 union of the crowns. In Baroque times, church and state were essentially two sides of the same coin.

The Inquisition in the New World had thus evolved somewhat from its medieval European roots. First established in Italy, the Holy Office was imported to Spain in 1478 under Ferdinand and Isabella. As Columbus sailed to the Americas, the fledgling Spanish Inquisition set about persecuting, and sometimes executing, the peninsula's remaining Jews and Muslims. When the Inquisition was established in Portugal in 1536, it touched off another wave of anti-Semitic hysteria and mass emigration. Following the Council of Trent, Inquisition offices were established in Lima (1569), Mexico City (1570), and Cartagena de Indias (1610) (see Map 10.2). No permanent office was ever established in Brazil, although periodic visits by Portuguese inquisitors in the late sixteenth and early seventeenth centuries led to some startling discoveries and gruesome punishments.

There is still debate as to whether the Inquisition was a medieval survival or a modern innovation; either way, it was a fairly efficient promoter of conformity in the places where it was most powerful. Few wished to fall into its clutches. Its own records suggest that even in Lima, Mexico City, and Cartagena, where the Holy Office was headquartered, heretics never seemed to be in short supply. As in its earliest campaigns in Spain, the Inquisition in Baroque Spanish America continued to focus on rooting out alleged practitioners of Judaism. "Hidden Jews," usually so-called New Christians, or forced converts and their descendants of Portuguese or Andalusian descent, were most avidly sought and most harshly punished. A series of terror-inspiring autos de fé, or public humiliations and executions of alleged Jews and other nonconformists, took place in Mexico City and Lima between 1639 and 1651. This wave of persecution, the deadliest in colonial Latin American history, coincided with the rebellion of Portugal against Spanish rule, and with the unhappy settlement of a long conflict with the Dutch.

There were thus marked waves of tolerance and intolerance, coinciding with the political and military calms and crises experienced in Spain and Portugal. Campaigns against other crimes were also subject to trends, with inquisitors periodically turning their attention to the "problems" of bigamy, blasphemy, homosexuality, witchcraft, and those Protestant pirates unlucky enough to fall into Spanish hands. Bigamy – or "the crime of double marriage" – was not uncommon because divorce in the modern sense did not exist, forcing irreconcilable couples to seek their own solutions.

Map 10.2
The Inquisition and
the Mission

Manuel Bolio's tale of bigamy is typical in many respects. A former African slave, Manuel ended up in the 1750s as a free resident of Yucatan's provincial capital of Mérida, where he married a Maya woman named Josepha Chan. But when their newborn baby died, their marriage fell apart, and Manuel moved down to work in Bacalar (near the frontier between Yucatan and Belize). At first Manuel continued to visit Josepha in Mérida, but eventually they separated permanently, and he crossed the Caribbean to Cartagena, where he married a local black woman. Upon her death, he went to a local priest and asked to be married again; this time, questions were asked, the priest wrote letters to priests in Mérida, and Manuel was arrested and tried as a bigamist. He was convicted and probably returned to slavery.

Whatever the crime, the Inquisition relied on voluntary denunciations and carefully gathered witness testimonies. An individual under investigation was arrested but not presented with any charge. Instead, defendants were calmly asked whether they had anything to confess. Under this subtle and insidious form of pressure, and faced with an apparently open-ended inquiry, many defendants gave Inquisition authorities more information than they were after. Others knew precisely what was expected of them, and what the consequences of confession or denunciations of others might be, so they clammed up. Inquisitors then decided whether to apply a variety of torture mechanisms to lubricate the process, including the rack, simulated drowning (or water boarding), and cords tightened around various fleshy and bony parts of the body. A physician was usually on hand to attend to any unexpected bleeding or broken bones. Torture in the course of interrogation was standard throughout Europe in the Baroque era, but the Inquisition's highly methodical and documented application of it set it apart – and made it infamous.

It is difficult to know if or how much ordinary Baroque Catholics in Spanish and Portuguese America feared the Inquisition, but its ability to ruin lives and tear apart friends and family was certainly known. In addition to the focus on alleged Jews, Inquisition records indicate an inordinate tendency to punish people of African descent for alleged deviancy. African and African-descended women were frequently tried in all of the Inquisition's Spanish American and Portuguese tribunals, usually for witchcraft. Many men of African heritage, often long-distance mule drivers and others of limited status and means, were charged with bigamy – as Manuel Bolio's story illustrates. This tendency to focus on the so-called New Christian and Afro-American minority populations has led some historians to view the Inquisition as an institutional precursor to the modern terror mechanisms employed by fascist states. However we may wish to categorize it today, the Inquisition's long, Baroque shadow certainly appears to have reinforced the notion of an embattled Iberian Catholicism. To belong socially in Baroque Latin America was to participate, actively or passively, in making scapegoats of potential traitors. The auto de fé, according to several middle-colonial memoirists, was a popular form of entertainment.

Baroque Catholicism

Much of the stimulus for the Catholic renaissance in both Iberia and the colonies derived from the edicts of the Council of Trent, a series of meetings among cardinals, theologians, and other church officials in northern Italy that lasted from 1545 to 1563. In what amounted to a conservative defense of medieval Catholicism, the edicts reemphasized the central importance of the sacraments, most importantly marriage, the celibacy of the priesthood, and the existence of purgatory. The various local cults of Mary and the saints were also reinforced, along with the central role of relics, or holy objects, and their importance in sustaining pilgrimage sites. Most scandalous for

Protestants, indulgences, or payments to the church in exchange for a guarantee of a shortened stay in purgatory, were not only retained but also expanded. The *cacica* Catalina Tuza appears to have been aware of this, and to have "invested" accordingly.

What this meant for the Spanish and Portuguese, blessed (or burdened) as they were with the world's most lucrative overseas empires, was a self-ascribed responsibility to defend and spread Catholicism worldwide, in Europe, the colonies, and beyond. As believers in the core regions of Spanish and Portuguese settlement hunkered down and devoted more of their time and income to church-related activities, missionaries set out to transform more and more distant frontiers. This was the age of the church militant. We have seen how this manifested in the core colonies in Mesoamerica and the Andes, and to some degree along the shores of Brazil; we will shortly turn to the topic of missionary activity in the colonial hinterlands and on the frontiers.

The Baroque period was also marked by exponential growth in the power and social influence of religiously devout Catholic women, particularly those who entered convents. The women of the Habsburg and (after 1640) Braganza courts set the tone for one form of solemn, matriarchal piety by founding and funding whole new reclusive female orders. At the same time, lone, visionary figures like Teresa of Ávila created another. Elite women in Baroque Iberia were not simply followers of priests' and other men's orders; they were builders of the faith in their own right, and more radically, exponents of its deepest mysteries. Women of the lower classes, meanwhile, were arguably the greatest torchbearers and reproducers of the faith – its strongest demographic base.

In the colonies, this trend toward female religious exuberance was far more notable in Spanish America than in Brazil. Convents, initially created to house the orphaned mestiza daughters of the conquistadors, ballooned into virtual cities within cities after 1600. Regional capitals had at least half a dozen of them by the later seventeenth century, each technically overseen by male priests and religious orders. There were different convents, and states of profession, for all classes and tastes. Women from the lowest social classes, like Úrsula de Jesús, the freed slave and visionary of Lima, could only become lay sisters, not nuns. Latin America's only female saint, Rose of Lima, was also a beata. Widowed elite women sometimes entered convents in a similar role (having sacrificed their precious chastity to the vile but necessary tasks of marriage and child rearing). They were often accompanied in their reclusion by indigenous or enslaved African house servants, who toiled away in the convent's kitchens and washrooms much as before. Suffering inside the convent walls, in other words, was not limited to those who, like the anorexic St. Rose, dedicated themselves to enlightenment through mortification. Few nuns were able to convince themselves that, like Sor María de

Agreda, they could leave their bodies and preach to "the Indians" in Mexico (see In Focus 10.1).

Because nuns entered convents as symbolic "brides of Christ," they tended to bring dowries with them, sometimes substantial sums of money. Without a spendthrift husband to fritter away the funds on cockfights or reckless business ventures, nuns' dowries were pooled and managed in various ways. Abbesses and wealthy widows sometimes directed the funds, but most were invested conservatively by male priests. Some convents owned rural haciendas, urban rental properties, and even gold mines, all of them administered by salaried men. Convents also loaned cash to large landowners at a church-mandated rate of 5 percent a year in exchange for a lien on some piece of property. Many such borrowers, never able to repay the principal, paid interest on these loans (called *censos*) for multiple generations, leaving the convents in effect owners of the pledged estates. Convents served, like other church institutions, as colonial banks. With the steady addition of new sisters, they were increasingly wealthy ones.

The period of the colonial middle corresponded with two major historical trends: the decline of Iberian political power in Europe, and the so-called Counter-Reformation of the Catholic Church. The result, both in Iberia and in the colonies, was the emergence of what the Spanish historian José Maravall has called a "Baroque culture of crisis." A general turn to religious reflection, self-punishment, and increased church building was notable throughout Spanish and Portuguese America. The proliferation of convents was but one of many manifestations of the trend. Baroque ideas, practices, and institutions would subside only following the slow penetration of Enlightenment thinking in the middle of the eighteenth century. With the Baroque period's heightened sensitivity to public displays of faith came an interest in identifying alleged unbelievers who might "pollute" the faithful corps. Finally, the church militant went also to the untamed fringes, to "reduce" semisedentary and nonsedentary native peoples to both church and state authority. Unbelievers could be found on every front.

The Mission

One way to maintain the optimism of the early years of Spiritual Conquest, then, was to carry the Gospel to new peoples beyond the conquest frontier. Both Spanish and Portuguese authorities sponsored members of the regular religious orders, primarily Franciscans and Jesuits, to open new mission fields in the rugged backcountry. The main areas of expansion in the Baroque era were northern Mexico and Amazonia. In those regions, missionaries penetrated deeply, although their attempts at conversion were no more satisfying than they had been in the old colonial core. After a series of dramatic martyrdoms, the missionaries settled in for a long stay.

Because native groups in colonial hinterlands such as Amazonia were semisedentary or nonsedentary, the missionaries' insistence that new converts settle in concentrated settlements or mission towns was highly disruptive to traditional lifestyles. During the seventeenth century, the Franciscans established hundreds of missions across the far Mexican north and what is now the southern United States – from the Chesapeake to Georgia and Florida, and from Texas to New Mexico and Arizona. Almost none resulted in a permanent settlement, and the most successful of them, among the Pueblo peoples of New Mexico, erupted in a violent revolt in 1680.

In Amazonia, Spanish and Portuguese Jesuits vied for control of hundreds of nonsedentary and semisedentary peoples while also competing with slave raiders and other unscrupulous colonists. The great Portuguese Jesuit Antônio Vieira (1608–97) preached fiery sermons denouncing the practice of Indian slavery in the Amazon in the late-seventeenth century, but he was investigated by the Inquisition and in the end his words had little effect. Spanish Jesuits from Quito, meanwhile, established a chain of missions extending deep into the Amazon province of Mainas, which would later be claimed as part of Brazil. Spanish Jesuits based in Paraguay similarly expanded their missions, ultimately encompassing huge swaths of Bolivia, Argentina, Uruguay, and Brazil. Conflicts with settlers over access to indigenous workers became increasingly serious as the missions grew wealthy through sales of cattle and yerba maté. The Jesuits, according to some colonists, were not running missions but rather tax-free, labor-subsidized businesses. Whatever the truth, it appears that most indigenous peoples who accepted the Jesuit (or Franciscan) yoke preferred mission life to the potential hazards of enslavement or debt peonage.

* * *

Historians would love to know more about daily life among mission residents and other frontier dwellers, partly because so little is known about such communities compared to the cities and towns that grew rapidly throughout the colonies in the middle period. It is to that topic – the nature of life and work in the colonial city, town, mining camp, and countryside – that we now turn.

SUGGESTIONS FOR FURTHER READING

Wills similar to that of Catalina Tuza can be found in Matthew Restall, Lisa Sousa, and Kevin Terraciano, *Mesoamerican Voices: Native-Language Writings from Colonial Mexico, Oaxaca, Yucatan, and Guatemala* (2005); other documents in the volume are also relevant here, most notably those in chapter 8 (pp. 174–201).

The writings of José de Acosta, quoted in In Focus 10.1, are quoted in more detail in Chapter 19 in *Colonial Latin America: A Documentary History*, edited by Kenneth Mills, William B. Taylor, and Sandra Lauderdale Graham (2002); other chapters are also relevant here, most obviously 7–9, 13–14, 26–27, and 29–36. The volume's emphasis on religious matters makes it an excellent accompaniment to this chapter. On convents, see Asunción Lavrin's masterful *Brides of Christ: Convent Life in Colonial Mexico* (2009).

Also of relevance are several chapters in Restall's *Maya Conquistador* (1998), specifically chapters 7 (which presents examples of the Chilam Balam literature mentioned earlier), 8 (on a Christianized Maya nobleman), and 9 (on Landa's anti-idolatry campaign of 1562 and Yucatec Maya responses to it).

For advanced undergraduates, we recommend Nicholas Griffiths and Fernando Cervantes, eds., *Spiritual Encounters: Interactions between Christianity and Native Religions in Colonial America* (1999), and Kenneth Mills, *Idolatry and Its Enemies* (1998). On missions, see Steven Hackel, *Children of Coyote* (2004), Barbara Ganson, *The Guaraní under Spanish Rule in the Río de la Plata* (2003), and Cynthia Radding, *Landscapes of Power and Identity* (2007).

GLOSSARY

Spiritual Conquest: a blanket term for all Spanish and Portuguese efforts to convert Native Americans to Christianity

Cofradía [koh-frah-DEE-ah]: religious brotherhood or confraternity, whose members were usually restricted to one ethnic or racial group and whose officers maintained a treasury and the cult of a patron saint

Apostasy [ah-POSS-tah-see]: in the context of colonial Latin America, the renunciation of Christianity by a convert and the return to pagan religion

Huarochirí [wah-roh-chee-REE]: a region of highland Peru not far from Lima that was subjected to Inquisition-like investigations beginning just before 1600

Extirpation of Idolatry: campaign to uproot and destroy native religious beliefs and practices (including the worship of pre-Christian images or "idols")

Beata [bay-AT-ah]: a woman who has devoted herself to a life of piety and chastity but has not taken the full vows of a nun

Aldeia [al-DAY-ah]: village (Portuguese); mission settlements in colonial Brazil

11

Defining Deviancy

TIMELINE

1545–1563: Council of Trent redefines deviancy in the Roman Catholic world

1640s: main campaign of torture, execution, and property confiscation against New Christians, accused of covert Judaism, in Spanish America

1590s–1690s: century of greatest Inquisition interest in witchcraft in Spanish America, more or less coinciding with the witch craze in Europe and North America

Do you know how I can stop a certain man from visiting a certain woman and coming to see me instead?

> (Spanish woman asking her Maya servant to perform love-magic, Yucatán, 1626)

MARIA MALDONADO was a lonely widow in mid-seventeenth-century Mérida. A Spanish woman from an elite family, descended from the conquistadors of the province of Yucatán, Maldonado maintained a household with a black slave and various native Maya and free Afro-Yucatecan servants. Another Spanish woman, Maria Casanova, also lived in the household as a companion who helped run the household. Among the various tasks Casanova did for Maldonado was to go out and fetch witches – that is, practitioners of love-magic, who were brought to the house and employed to cast spells to help Maldonado attract the affections of men. Among these witches was Michaela Montejo, a free mulatta who lived in one of Mérida's predominantly Maya neighborhoods and who was one of the city's better-known witches – investigated repeatedly by the Inquisition in the 1660s and 1670s. Two others were Ana, a mulatta, and Ursula, a free black woman, both of whom provided the Spanish widow with enchanted flowers (local blossoms whose spell would magically influence a man's emotions if placed near him). Casanova claimed that she also brought various Maya witches to Maldonado's house – claims she made when, following a falling-out with Maldonado, she twice went to Inquisition officials to denounce her old friend.

Maria Maldonado's efforts to improve her love life in colonial Mérida were no more desperate or abnormal than a woman today using the personal columns in a newspaper or Web site. But in theory, there were not supposed to be love-magic professionals or other witches in the Iberian colonies in the Americas. Nor were Spaniards supposed to be interacting with people of native or African descent in ways other than sanctioned labor relationships.

Nor were widows supposed to be pursuing relationships with men, unless both were single and the relationship was a sexless prelude to marriage. There were laws on the books of church and state against witchcraft, against extramarital sex, and against people of African descent living in native communities. The Inquisition existed in large part to police such illegal activities. How could it be, then, that throughout the colonies there were Spanish women like Maria Maldonado hiring mulattas like Michaela Montejo to bring romance to their lives?

One may imagine that in the colonial middle, when torture was standard practice and the Baroque Catholic church seemed all-powerful, that few individuals, much less organized groups, might have questioned authority. Certainly, conformity was the aim of both church and state in the Iberian colonies. But on close examination, it appears that neither Spain nor Portugal – nor, for that matter, the missionary orders or the Inquisition – were anywhere near as powerful or all-knowing as some observers have claimed. There was much room, in other words, for alternative beliefs and behaviors – what officialdom regarded as deviancy. That said, if one did get caught, the consequences could be dire.

This chapter builds on the previous chapter's discussion of the Inquisition to look at larger issues of orthodoxy (conforming to norms of belief and behavior) and deviancy (behaving differently from the norm) in colonial society. After examining how colonial officials attempted to establish orthodoxy – and how they defined deviant behavior – we focus on three categories of deviancy: heresy and witchcraft, bigamy and forbidden sex, and bending the rules of identity. We end by briefly examining workplace discipline along with crime and punishment in the somewhat more conventional sense, summarizing the way in which colonial authorities used public punishments to dissuade crimes against person and state.

Orthodoxy and Deviancy

In the middle period, deviancy was defined according to cumbersome sets of secular and religious rules, most notably the Compiled Laws of the Indies (or Philippine Code, as these laws were called in Brazil) and the Edicts of the Council of Trent. The Laws of the Indies covered everything from flag design to the size and shape of mining claims. They also contained a number of criminal statutes. Some laws derived from Greek and Roman precedent; others had grown out of Spanish or Portuguese, and later American colonial, experience. Laws regarding slavery derived mostly from late medieval experience, in the wake of the Reconquest, whereas those regarding native peoples grew out of the colonial one.

The Edicts of the Council of Trent (1545–1563), or the Tridentine Code, strongly reiterated the importance of eliminating heresy in all forms. They also mandated prosecution and punishment of baptized Catholics allegedly engaged in superstitious practices such as witchcraft, fortune-telling, and astrology. These popular tendencies proved far more difficult to monitor and punish than heresy. Finally, the edicts reinforced the church's focus on core life-stage rituals called sacraments, especially marriage. Codifying marriage meant codifying sex. Sex outside marriage was strictly forbidden by church elders, and sex within it sharply circumscribed. In essence, sex was defined as an inherently sinful and filthy act that happened to be essential for human reproduction.

Defining deviancy in a far-flung, multicultural world like that of colonial Latin America was a daunting task. Effective communication of rules and edicts was stymied by vast distances, interruptions in the fleet system, gaping language barriers, and wildly varying levels of religious and civic literacy and acculturation. Fornication, for example, or premarital sex was technically both a sin and a crime in Baroque times. Yet even among cloistered, closely monitored Spanish nuns, it happened with alarming frequency. Men, and most notably priests, seemed intent on penetrating convent walls. But the laws and edicts kept coming, and some individuals appear to have been singled out for public trials and exemplary punishment. It seems that in their frustration, state and church authorities sometimes resorted to terror to induce conformity. As in countries where capital punishment is still practiced, gauging how well people learned the lessons of state terror was difficult.

The forms of criminal deviancy in the colonial middle would be relatively familiar to modern observers, with crimes ranging from petty theft or plagiarism to rape and murder. Some misdeeds not often taken up by criminal courts today but of great concern to colonists included slander, or public name-calling meant to besmirch another's honor. Honor claims were often settled outside the courts by men of high rank in the form of duels. Resulting deaths and injuries were then often taken to court and presented as willful murders or attempted ones. Colonial Latin America's courts were always busy thanks to a culture that promoted litigiousness as a standard form of social interaction and status assertion. The colonial legal system also differed from modern ones (at least in terms of the letter, if not the execution, of sentences) in that identical crimes were punished differently according to the rank of the offender. Whether in Havana or Rio de Janeiro, a slave convicted of theft, for example, might be punished with fifty lashes on the public pillory, whereas the son of a wealthy landowner convicted of the same deed might expect to pay a fine of fifty pesos. There could be even starker differences in sentencing, as we will see here.

Far removed from today's legal guarantees of religious freedom, the early-modern Iberian states sought to sharply control the beliefs and practices of subject peoples. Patrolling this more subjective realm of deviancy, as we saw in the previous chapter, was the Holy Office of the Inquisition. In indigenous communities, a range of parish priests and members of regular orders like the Franciscans and Jesuits policed belief and behavior, although as few priests lived in native communities for any length of time, attention to native activities was intermittent. Whether in a native village or in a Spanish city, officials viewed heresy – the rejection of orthodox Catholicism in favor of some other religion or sect of Christianity – as most threatening. Use of magic or witchcraft to achieve some specific, short-term goal (usually one not admissible by prayer) was somewhat less challenging to the core faith but still highly punishable. Priests were always concerned with the sexual behavior of parishioners, indigenous and otherwise (and if the documents are to be believed, priests were almost as consistently accused of sexual transgressions themselves). Idolatry, as we have seen, was considered the peculiar vice of Native Americans virtually everywhere in the Spanish colonies. The Portuguese in Brazil, notably, seemed less interested in labeling native religious deviancy as idolatry. The church's view of heresy, idolatry, backsliding, witchcraft, and other "thought crimes" would shift according to place and time, but the intensity of punishments was most profound in the colonial middle.

Heresy and Witchcraft

Roman Catholic authorities in the middle period conceived of the Church as an embattled body of believers, threatened both from without and within. Thus militant Catholics were quick to label not only Protestant corsairs such as Francis Drake or Piet Heyn but also Iberian Jews and Muslim "heretics." Heresy was thought to be like a cancer, a disease that could sicken the body of believers if not cut out and destroyed. In this way of thinking, so-called heretics were not worrisome because of their ability to persuade good Catholics to think differently, but because their mere presence was thought to be a kind of pollution, or corruption, which if allowed to continue would impede the salvation of the faithful. Although they were inconsistent, Church authorities aimed to root out all alleged heretics from New Spain to Pernambuco. They usually offered the accused a chance to repent and join the Roman Catholic fold – or face exile or death.

How were heretics identified? In most cases, it was by denunciation to the Inquisition. Neighbors reported on anyone performing unusual rituals such as lighting candles or fasting outside Catholic feast days, or even for not eating pork. Other frequently denounced behaviors included invocation of spirits or even the devil for divining purposes, plus all manner of shamanistic practices, including use of hallucinogens. These latter were usually labeled "witchcraft" rather than heresy, and were not as harshly punished. When the cases are examined in aggregate, the main victims of this anxious intolerance of "unbelief" or errant religious practices were Jews, enslaved women of African descent, and Native American shamans.

Whether in Iberia or the American colonies, inquisitors gave special attention to exposing and punishing heretics. A small number of foreign Protestants, most of them captured pirates, were tried and executed by the Inquisitions of Mexico, Lima, and Cartagena in the sixteenth and seventeenth centuries. But it was New Christians, many of them Portuguese, who bore the brunt of inquisitorial fury in the middle period. Merchant families were especially targeted for practicing the "Law of Moses," although records show that awareness of alleged heretical beliefs or practices among the accused varied tremendously. Some of those jailed thought themselves to be good Catholics, and regularly attended mass, whereas others openly defied inquisitors and proclaimed themselves practicing Jews, even willing martyrs for their faith. The persecution of New Christians crested in the years around 1640, when dozens of families were jailed, tortured, killed, and deprived of their estates. Why the Inquisition largely backed away from such "witch-hunt" type prosecutions in subsequent years is the subject of intense debate among historians.

If true, unrepentant heretics were rare in colonial Latin America, witches were not. Hundreds were tried and convicted across the whole colonial period, with a notable spike in the middle that corresponded to larger, "Atlantic world" anxieties over witchcraft. Even so, unlike in northern Europe and in English colonies such as Massachusetts at this time where many women died as a result of witch crazes, witches in the Iberian world were virtually never "rounded up" en masse, much less executed. Most were able to reconcile with the Church following public humiliation, flogging, or exile – or some combination of the three.

Why were alleged witches treated so differently from so-called heretics? In general, Iberian Church authorities considered witchcraft – or the employment of potions, powders, spells, and herbs to control, help, or harm others – a superstitious practice, associated with ignorance rather than with willful defiance of Catholic doctrine. Only when witches explicitly invoked the devil were they treading on deadly ground. A few men were tried for witchcraft in the middle period, including some of part-indigenous or African background, but the vast majority were women, often of principally African ancestry. Known as *brujas* or *hechizeras* in Spanish America, and *feiticeiras* or *curandeiras* in Brazil, witches were almost as often treated as charlatans as they were true "corrupters" of the faithful body of believers. Many were locally esteemed healers and midwives who supplemented their incomes by concocting love potions, but a few also specialized in deadly spells, or "black magic."

Even when considered a serious menace to society – as happened with a Portuguese woman of color named Maria Barbosa accused of sorcery in Bahia,

Brazil, in 1610 – punishment ultimately consisted only of public penance. Of greater concern to town authorities was Barbosa's reputation as a prostitute and procuress. The fact that women of color were most often accused of witchcraft in colonial Latin America lent credence to the patriarchal and Eurocentric Church view that such persons were fakes who had simply managed to exploit the emotional weaknesses and gullibility of their neighbors. Paradoxically, perhaps, almost no one doubted that witchcraft was real in the sense that all spells were taken seriously and purposely "broken" by investigating authorities or the accused witches themselves.

Who sought the services of witches? Inquisition documents frequently mention women, some of them from colonial high society, paying for spells that would guarantee the fidelity of their mates – or help them acquire new affections, as in the Maldonado case that began this chapter. Both men and women contracted witches to see into the future or to find lost things or loved ones, too. Angry or disaffected individuals used witches to help them exact revenge through sickening or deadly spells and even poisons. Elites routinely feared, sometimes correctly, that their slaves or servants were using witchcraft against them, usually as payback for excessive demands or mistreatment. Many masters accused slaves of giving them the "evil eye," planting so-called disease bundles around their houses, or simply poisoning their food. Witches may have been disparaged by Church authorities for their low social rank, but they were certainly feared by colonial subjects of all classes. Whatever we may make of the accusations and persecution, Inquisition and other records hint at the existence of a thriving hidden world of beliefs not sanctioned by the Roman Catholic Church.

Forbidden Love

Enforcing the Edicts of Trent took the Inquisition into colonists' bedrooms. Sexual behavior, like fasting and other daily ritual activity, was closely tied to salvation. After Trent, Church fathers had to hand a longer and more precise list of sexual sins to consult, including fornication, masturbation, adultery, polygamy, sodomy, incest, and bestiality. The only allowable form of sexual intercourse was between married male-and-female partners, and even this was to be carried out only for purposes of procreation, "without lust," and in the so-called missionary position. According to this mindset, sexual desire was something "devilish" to be willfully repressed, and should it find outlet in masturbation, oral sex, or involve other "mistaken" orifices one was committing sodomy and risked wasting the sacred "seed."

Inquisition documents and much other evidence suggest that ordinary people in the colonies did not universally accept these narrow rules of "safe" sex. Native Andeans, for example, continued to practice "trial marriage" despite priests' claims that it was sinful fornication. Muleskinners, sailors, and other long-distance travelers routinely kept multiple households, often marrying multiple times to the great consternation of Church authorities. Many of those tried for bigamy or polygamy were free men of color who saw no sin in their actions as long as they could properly support their multiple wives and children. At the elite level, priests and nuns broke the rules of chastity with seeming regularity, and many women complained of being sexually harassed, and even accosted in the confessional. The Inquisition did try and convict a significant number of people for alleged sex crimes, including rogue priests, but it is difficult to say how much this affected people's heartfelt beliefs about sex as sin. Even bestiality, regarded as a grave sin "against nature," was sometimes rationalized when the participants were youthful or ignorant. (Notably, few women were convicted of sex crimes; see In Focus 11.1.)

Sodomy convictions from the middle period suggest that what would today be called homosexual acts provoked more complex and even ambivalent responses than might be expected given their illegality. In 1630, the Lima courts ordered an Aragonese merchant accused of sodomy and bestiality to be burned alive, along with his dog; his alleged black lover was publicly whipped. Not long after, a mestizo and mulatto convicted of being lovers were similarly executed in Callao, the port that served Lima (whose inhabitants flocked to watch the burning). To the south, in Charcas (in modern Bolivia), a Spanish official named Damián de Morales was arrested in 1611 for attempting to seduce an African slave named Antón; although the slave's testimony was persuasively explicit, Morales was not convicted of a crime and a judge suggested that the man who brought the original accusation solve his dispute with Morales by sword (i.e., by the sort of honorable duel mentioned earlier) rather than slander. Other cases suggest that although the Inquisition was willing to pursue alleged sodomites and see them publicly humiliated and punished, it rarely treated elite suspects with the rigor seen in the case of the Aragonese merchant. Lower-class lovers were usually the ones who suffered.

Significantly, none of these cases came from Mexico, where sodomy prosecutions (and executions in general) were far less common throughout the colonial period than they were in middle-colonial Peru and Bolivia. Furthermore, these cases imply that at least some men in Mexico could maintain same-sex relationships as long as they remained discreet. If this reading of the evidence is correct, homosexuality in colonial Mexico was a luxurious risk that men of position of status could perhaps afford to take. We know less about alleged sodomy in Brazil since the Portuguese Inquisition only briefly visited the colony, but the few cases prosecuted seem to follow the Mexican pattern: elite offenders had less to worry about than their social inferiors. Sexual behavior among Portuguese colonists and their multicolored servants in Brazil fairly stunned inquisitors with its variety, and they left describing the colony as lying squarely within the "tropic of sins."

Figure 11.1. Engraving made by Fauchery from Pacheco's 1630 portrait of "Lieutenant Miss Catalina de Erauso". Used with permission of Biblioteca Nacional, Madrid.

THE NUN CONQUISTADOR(A)

One of the few women to receive Inquisition attention for sexual deviancy was the famed globetrotting cross-dresser Catalina de Erauso (c. 1585–1650) (shown here in a contemporary portrait). According to her own memoir, Erauso entered a convent in Spain's Basque country as a young teenager and was about to take vows. Having second thoughts, she cut her hair, dressed as a pageboy, and escaped to Seville. Dressed now as a man, Erauso boarded a ship to the Indies and eventually reached Peru. In rough-and-tumble cities such as Potosí, she routinely got into fights, often over women, made friends with fellow Basques involved in their own scuffles, and otherwise lived the picaresque life. She was even briefly captured by Dutch pirates off the coast of Peru in 1615. When discovered to be a woman, Erauso was turned over to Inquisition authorities, who proved far more interested in her chastity than in her mode of dress. Once it was determined that Erauso had remained a virgin despite her wild, masculine exploits, she won a special papal dispensation to go on wearing men's clothing. She ended her well-known career as a mule driver and petty merchant in Mexico.

Working Discipline

Sex, whether defined by the church as orthodox or deviant, was among the few pleasures that the working masses could afford. Most people had neither money nor time for the kinds of entertainments enjoyed by the elite (see Chapter 12). This meant that the elite did their best to maintain this inequality; the popular classes were driven hard, for little pay, with church and state to enforce discipline in the workplace.

Elite demands were manifold, and they came on top of the already considerable requirements of subsistence farming, household maintenance, food preparation, and child rearing. Workers in the colonial mines, refineries, and sugarcane mills faced the most rigorous schedules, often working night and day for long stretches depending on the availability of water or the ripeness of the cane. A typical workday on a sugar plantation or in a textile mill was twelve hours long, six days a week. Some enslaved African gold miners in lowland New Granada worked at night by torch and moonlight in knee-deep water, and workers in silver and sugar mills also commonly labored around the clock. Women, particularly enslaved African women – and some children – worked alongside men in these near-industrial, and often very dangerous environments. Indigenous workers on haciendas and in public works projects were also commonly abused, and many were killed or maimed by accidents.

Wages were typically just sufficient to fend off starvation, as long as sickness or injury did not prevent work. In the mid- to late-colonial Valley of Mexico, workers on rural estates were paid two reales (a quarter peso) a day, the same wage that Afro-Yucatecan militiamen received. Although this was barely enough to sustain a small family, others fared much worse: late-colonial road construction workers in Yucatán got one real a day; and laborers in the Ecuadorian countryside, like Mayas forced to perform personal service under the rotational *tanda* system, got a mere half a real a day, sometimes in addition to basic lodging and food.

Not surprisingly, such extreme conditions provoked periodic worker rebellions and mass flight. But most colonial workers did not rise up or run away, because punishments for recalcitrant workers were often violent and severe. Floggings, time in the stocks, head shaving, and other forms of public humiliation – even permanently crippling torture – are amply documented in both slave and indigenous work regimes throughout the colonies and across the period. Most of the punishments were not carried out by European masters themselves but rather by their majordomos and overseers, many of them free or enslaved men of color.

In addition to threatening violence, a system of incentives also kept workers working in the Spanish and Portuguese colonies. Incentives varied widely, but in most intense work situations, a clear task hierarchy was laid out. Trusted native and African "captains," "countercaptains," and other such officers were put in charge of overseeing work gangs and assuring higher-ranking majordomos that they would meet daily or weekly production quotas. Such captains, and even lower-level workers, were eligible for gifts and promotions to less demanding tasks in exchange for superlative performance. In slave regimes, newly arrived Africans were often clustered in the heaviest tasks, whereas creoles, or locally born, slaves and mulattoes were placed in charge of lighter, more technical tasks. Although this was still forced labor, the system of incentives and task specialization prefigured in some ways industrial production.

Other factors that squelched rebellion and flight included family and community pressures and a complex legal tradition. Violent uprisings led to violent reprisals, and these hurt everyone. As we have seen, the Spanish and Portuguese generally encouraged family and community formation among both indigenous and enslaved workers in the Baroque period. Black slaves, free coloreds, and Native Americans were full members of the Catholic Church, and as such they required all sacraments. The Spanish and Portuguese, being relatively few in number in relation to their workers, rightly believed that natives and Africans would be less likely to rise up in rebellion if their basic social subsistence needs were met. This entailed forced acceptance of Catholicism, of course, but it also led to a measure of autonomy that was less common in contemporary northern European colonial contexts. Such accommodation went beyond custom to be inscribed in colonial law, which was widely discussed. Workers, including slaves, could thus appeal to church and civil authorities to force masters to adhere to the law.

Crime and Punishment

The threat of gruesome public punishments kept most mills, mines, and haciendas busy but seemed not to deter thieves, confidence artists, murderers, and other criminals – at least the vast bundles of records from the middle period suggest as much. Jails were found in every colonial city, and in many towns, but none was designed for long-term imprisonment. True prisons and penitentiaries were not yet invented, so convicts were simply held in rudimentary jails until they could be punished, usually by flogging, exile, or execution. Criminal exiles were routinely sent to frontier military outposts along the Caribbean coast or served time rowing galleys. This kind of exile, which exposed people to malaria and other tropical diseases, often amounted to a death sentence.

The Portuguese had a different tradition, with exiles going back to the earliest years of overseas expansion. They dropped convicts off in remote parts of Africa and Brazil, for example, in hopes that they would marry into local families and aid later trading expeditions. If they failed or were killed, the loss to the homeland was negligible; if they succeeded, they could both benefit the realm and redeem themselves. Hardened Brazilian criminals did face exile in Angola, however, and the Chilean "Mapuche Front" served a similar function for deviant Andeans. Innocence was not assumed, and in fact detention implied guilt. Thus, judicial processes often moved quickly toward the extraction of confessions, frequently involving torture. As with the Inquisition, the rules of torture were explicit, and generally followed. Suspects could expect seven "rounds" on the rack, or squeezed by

IN FOCUS 11.2

Figure 11.2. Cartagena Inquisition rack. Photograph by Kris Lane.

THE RACK

The most common colonial-era torture device was known as the *burro*, or "rack," here displayed in the Inquisition museum in Cartagena, Colombia. The suspect or victim was laid on the burro's table face up, his or her wrists and upper arms tied to one end, ankles and thighs to the other (the objective was to inflict pain both by stretching joints and squeezing large muscles). Inquisitors then asked questions, while assistants, usually native servants or African slaves, turned the large handles. As each ratchet clicked, the pain mounted, and the interrogation continued. Victims were repeatedly ordered to "tell the truth." A notary recorded the entire business, including the number of times the rack was turned and the cries of pain and agonized facial expressions made by the victim. It was not uncommon for victims to end the sequence of torture *vueltas*, or "rounds," permanently disabled.

tourniquets, then another five to seven rounds of water-boarding, a kind of simulated drowning procedure in which jars of water were poured into the prone victim's mouth. Scribes were expected to jot down everything said in these sessions, and surviving documents frequently include lines saying "Ay, ay, ay!" (see In Focus 11.2). To add insult to injury, suspects were required to swear that all injuries sustained during torture, including eyeballs popping out and dislocated limbs, were their fault and not their torturers'.

Torture was not considered punishment, but rather a means to identifying guilty parties. Punishments tended to be gruesome, and far more painful than torture. Anyone convicted of murder, rebellion, or treason could expect to be torn apart by horses, with their salvaged body parts displayed along roads and in town squares as warnings to all (see In Focus 14.5 in Chapter 14). Public executions by hanging or garrote (strangling against a post) were more common, and anyone from a horse thief to a rapist might face such an end. Vigilantism was strongly discouraged by regional audiencias, which reserved the right to hear capital appeals, but rushed executions were not unknown. Public whipping, a partly naked ride through town in a cart or on a donkey, and other forms of humiliation were frequent, but those tended to be applied to only Indians, African slaves, and others regarded by elites as members of the "vile plebe." Two hundred lashes was a standard sentence for petty theft. People of means paid for their crimes largely in the form of fines. Brazilian *pelourinhos*, or public pillories, greeted all visitors to the center of town, and reminded everyone of the punishing power of royal justice.

Public executions vied with bullfights and religious processions as the biggest colonial spectator events, but it is worth noting that among those jailed by the Inquisition, only about 1 percent to 5 percent were executed. More deadly by far was jail, where poor sanitation, malnutrition, and exposure killed an alarming number of those waiting on appeals. Death from torture wounds and public whipping was also common, a reminder that even without the public spectacle conviction for almost any crime could bring about a premature end. On the flip side, jails were frequently insecure, the colonial world was vast, and many criminals managed to break free and live for many years on the lam, reinventing themselves in each new town they entered.

Bending Identity

Just as the inhabitants of colonial societies were supposed to believe certain things as loyal Catholic Christians, and behave in certain ways based on their gender, so were they supposed to understand their place in society based on their ethnoracial or socioracial status. Modern concepts of race did not exist until the very end of the colonial period. Instead, Spaniards emphasized the differences between types (*géneros*) of people and used notions of ethnicity and class to create two related socioracial concepts. These concepts were (1) a person's *calidad*, or socioracial "qualities" (ancestry, skin color and physical features, occupation, wealth, degree of Hispanization, public reputation and honor), which determined (2) his or her *casta* identity (e.g., *negra libre*, "free black woman"; *mestizo*, "man of mixed Spanish-native parentage"). Because these concepts incorporated racial elements, and because there were dozens of *casta* categories by 1700, it was long assumed that Spaniards had developed a rigid and racist "caste system" in their colonies.

In fact, the system was hardly systematic at all, as all the determinants of *calidad* were plastic or changeable – wealth and honor could be won and lost; occupation changed; ancestry rewritten; and although skin color was immutable, its perception by others could be altered. *Casta* identity, in other words, could be bent, and as the historian María Elena Martínez has put it, "genealogical fictions" were a colonial commonplace.

The political and economic hierarchy was likewise different in practice from in theory. As outlined earlier, Spaniards saw people in the colonies as ideally fitting into two "republics," consisting of Spaniards and "Indians" – with Africans denied their own "republic" and instead attached, but subordinate, to Spaniards. Theoretically, because in mid- and late-colonial times only Africans (not natives) could be slaves, the social hierarchy placed Spaniards at the top, followed by mestizos and "Indians," with free coloreds and then Africans at the bottom. However, political and economic reality placed people of African descent above natives. Free mulattoes acquired political bargaining power through militia service, and some passed sufficiently as Spaniards to enter the priesthood or hold political office. Black slaves and free-colored employees acted as intermediaries between Spanish *encomenderos*, estate owners, and businessmen, on the one hand, and native community leaders and workers, on the other hand.

This is not to say that colonial Latin America was a racial democracy; on the contrary, it was rife with ethnocentrism, color prejudice, and discrimination of all kinds. But the fact that identities and behavioral norms could be bent and stretched meant that individuals could improve their status and use the legal system to protect it – even if such efforts served only to reinforce social prejudices. For example, Lázaro del Canto went from being a slave in mid-seventeenth-century Yucatán to a free mulatto militiaman to a property owner and officer with a royal pension and heroic record of service against English buccaneers – a career that earned him the right in his old age in the 1680s to be called Captain Lázaro del Canto, with no *casta* label attached. Likewise, women of African descent often insisted, sometimes successfully, that they be described in legal records not as *mulata* or *parda* (literally "brown" but often used to mean "mulatto") but as *morisca* or *castiza* (terms that implied more Spanish than non-Spanish ancestry). Beatriz de Padilla, a woman accused of murder in middle-colonial Guadalajara, admitted in court that her mother was a mulatta but claimed that, as her father was a Spaniard, she should be labeled *morisca*. One late-colonial Sunday morning, outside the church in San Juan Teotihuacán (near the famous pyramids of that name north of Mexico City), Josefa Cadena was knocked to the ground and called "a black whore"; Josefa's husband sued the elite Spanish woman who had attacked his wife, less because she had been physically assaulted and more because she was a *castiza*, and the insult had "offended her fidelity and her *calidad*."

How could Catalina de Erauso (see In Focus 11.1) get away with living as a man, even after she became notorious throughout the Spanish world as a transvestite? How could Dr. González retain positions of authority even after his homosexuality became widely known? How could Lázaro del Canto pass from being a slave to a non-*casta*? These cases are better understood within the larger question of identity – rather than just within the narrower questions of gender, sexuality, and socioracial categories. Under certain circumstances, it was possible to bend the definitions and restrictions of identity. As a virgin and a conquistador(a), Erauso proved herself loyal to church and state, winning and retaining some honor, and thereby the right to live discretely as she chose. For those who sought lovers of the same sex, sexual identities and norms of behavior might prove elastic if a man was wealthy and well connected. An exemplary career of service as a militia officer might allow a man to shed his earlier identity as a mulatto and be treated in some ways as a Spaniard.

In the second century of colonial occupation, the Spanish and Portuguese attempted to promulgate and enforce a host of secular and religious laws in the Americas. Given the communication difficulties typical of the times, they were surprisingly effective. By the end of the colonial middle, Spanish subjects living in places as distant from one another (and from Madrid) as Arizona, Puerto Rico, and Bolivia had the same basic understanding of state and church laws and regulations. To judge from their litigiousness and intense devotion to Baroque Catholicism, Brazilians from Amazonia to Santa Catarina were equally astute and indoctrinated. This tendency to conform to the laws of the realm was nevertheless counterbalanced by a similar human tendency to rebel or persist in more localized or tried-and-true beliefs and practices.

*   *   *

With righteousness so narrowly defined, deviancy was understandably common in the colonies, particularly at the more petty levels and among the barely educated rural masses. Even with a general idea of right and wrong in mind, one could not help but stray. Spectacular punishments of alleged heretics and hard-core criminals were rare but undoubtedly memorable – a marker of the outer limits of secular and religious behavior. On a more day-to-day level, one had to be careful around priests and magistrates, and even more so one's personal enemies; in an instant they could turn your life upside down. Most people probably learned to steer clear of authorities or enemies of any kind or to bow deeply in their presence.

The conscious avoidance of deviant behavior, the accidental slippage into deviancy, the deliberate embrace of unorthodoxy, the witnessing of the punishments meted out to a transgressor – these were all part of daily life in middle-colonial Latin America. To add further color to this picture, we turn in the following chapter to other aspects of daily life – from bullbaiting and card playing to eating and drinking.

SUGGESTIONS FOR FURTHER READING

The primary source readings that go especially well with this chapter are Catalina de Erauso's early seventeenth-century autobiography, published as *Lieutenant Nun: Memoir of a Basque Transvestite in the New World* (1996) and chapters 3, 6–7, 9–10, and 12–13 of *Colonial Lives: Documents on Latin American History, 1550–1850*, edited by Richard Boyer and Geoffrey Spurling (2000). See also William B. Taylor's classic *Drinking, Homicide, and Rebellion in Colonial Mexican Villages* (1979).

Students writing research papers might consider any of the following monographs: Richard Boyer, *Lives of the Bigamists* (1995); Fernando Cervantes, *The Devil in the New World*; Martha Few, *Women Who Live Evil Lives* (2003); Laura A. Lewis, *Hall of Mirrors: Power, Witchcraft, and Caste in Colonial Mexico* (2003); Laura de Mello e Sousa, *The Devil in the Land of the Holy Cross* (2003); Peter Sigal, ed., *Infamous Desire: Male Homosexuality in Colonial Latin America* (2004); Irene Silverblatt, *Modern Inquisitions: Peru and the Colonial Origins of the Civilized World* (2004); Gabriel Haslip-Viera, *Crime and Punishment in Late Colonial Mexico City, 1692–1810* (1999), María Elena Martínez, *Genealogical Fictions* (2009); and Javier Villa-Flores, *Dangerous Speech: Blasphemy in Colonial Mexico* (2005).

GLOSSARY

Bruja [BREW-hah] and **Hechizera** [etch-ees-ER-ah]: Spanish terms for "witch"

Burro [BOOH-roh]: the "rack," a torture device used by the Inquisition

Feiticeira [fay-tee-SAY-rah] and **Curandeira** [koo-rahn-DAY-rah]: Portuguese terms for witch

Pelourinho [pell-oo-REEN-yoo]: public pillory in Brazil

12

Daily Life in City and Country

TIMELINE

1533–1544: decade when most of the important Spanish American regional capitals were founded

1622 and 1628: Spanish lose part of the silver fleet in a hurricane, and then all of it to Dutch pirates led by Piet Heyn

1630: Dutch take Pernambuco, Brazil, from the Portuguese; hold it until 1654

1655: English take Jamaica from the Spanish

1697: French possession of the western end of Hispaniola is formally recognized by the Spanish as the colony of Saint-Domingue

1700–1725: founding of major mining towns in Brazil's south-central highlands

Saturday, the 28th of September of this year: eight men were sentenced in the chapel of the Inquisition for being married two, three, four, and five times; and others for other offenses they had committed. Of these eight, only three were flogged through the streets.

(Diary of Don Josephe de Mugaburu)

CAPTAIN DON JOSEPHE DE MUGABURU was a prominent Spaniard in Lima in the seventeenth century. As an officer in the viceroy's palace guard, stationed on the main plaza of the city, Mugaburu was witness to many of the public events and activities of his time. This was fortunate for future historians, for Mugaburu kept a diary. The last entries he made, before his death in November 1686, give us some sense of life in a major Latin American city.

The entry quoted in the epigraph was followed four days later by a description of the return of don Tomás Paravisino, general of the armada, or official fleet, which had left Lima's port of Callao the previous May. The general sailed "from Panama with many ships loaded with dry goods" – an event that inspired "much rejoicing for his arrival." A month later, to celebrate the king's birthday, "bulls were run in the plaza of Lima," following a procession by General Paravisino and other crown officials, who "rode around the plaza three times on the footboard of a carriage. It was a very happy afternoon."

The impression given by Mugaburu's diary is one of a bustling metropolis with a varied and dramatic public life. People of all ranks and races participated in public events, and the colonial authorities seemed ever present. Law and order, and official spectacle, seem to triumph over crisis and dissent. There were pirate threats and native rebellions, but the violence that took place in the city was typically the judicious violence of hangings and burnings at the stake. This impression raises some of the questions that we will examine in this chapter. For example, how ordered was daily life in city and town in the middle-colonial period? To what extent did people of different backgrounds interact? How did urban life compare with that of the countryside? Was the countryside as diverse and multiracial as the city, or did it remain completely indigenous? How different were the pursuits of the privileged classes from the lives of working men and women, and did they all share the same diet and suffer the same diseases?

We end the chapter with a brief coda on a different topic – that of piracy and imperial defense – that serves as a bridge to the chapters of Part Four.

The Dynamic City

Life in the colonial middle varied at least as much by place as it did by time. The Spanish American capitals of Lima and Mexico City, and even the mining metropolis of Potosí, were highly cosmopolitan by 1600 – such that even the most sophisticated snob was challenged to keep up with changes in fashion. Brazil's regional capitals of Salvador, Rio de Janeiro, and Vila Rica emerged somewhat later, but by the mid-eighteenth century, all three gave the great Spanish American cities a run for their money. Certain streets and neighborhoods were already famous for their craft specializations, others for their gambling and prostitution houses, and still others for their transient populations and mixed cultural flair. Whole city blocks were dedicated to female enclosure in the form of convents. Here, in the centers of colonial city life, were schools and universities, monumental churches and monasteries, courts of justice, palatial homes, and exclusive shops. In the capital, one rubbed elbows with the colonies' most powerful people. The capitals in particular – but the provincial cities, too – were labyrinths of intrigue.

For the Spanish especially, the colonial city was a kind of theater space for the display of civic and religious virtue. It was also a carefully orchestrated cluster of symbols of power, a planned monument to a particular vision of civilized life. If the countryside was uncouth, illiterate, pagan, and earthy, the city was (at least ideally) a paragon of rectilinear order, education, Catholic religious devotion, and refinement. Spaniards saw the city as a place of permanence, of stone, whereas the countryside was all thatch and mud, transient and dirty. The city was also a place of concentrated authority, of governmental, religious, and commercial power. Often walled at least on the coast, it was thought to be safe and was meant to demand, like the castles of medieval Spain, the respect of the less fortunate inhabitants of the countryside.

Early in the colonial period, the Spanish established a rigid, gridiron plan for their overseas cities (see In Focus 12.1). Whether built on a pre-Columbian capital or town site, or on virgin land abutting some creek or river, the Spanish city in America looked much the same in its layout, whether in Chile or New Mexico. At center was a square, open plaza fronted by a church, the town council building, a royal government palace, and assorted wholesale

Map 12.1
The Cities of Colonial Latin America

merchant shops. Wealthy and important people, the self-styled *españoles* of increasingly variable colors, lived in thick-walled, two-story houses as close to the plaza as possible – within the *traza*, or central grid of blocks. All cities also had rules that governed everything from the supply of water, meat, and grain to the sorts of garments market women were allowed to wear in public. Some cities established night patrols to snare citizens engaged in naughty after-hours behavior. Church and state were never separate in the Iberian world; urban moral order, like clean gutters or a properly located slaughter-house, was thought to be a reflection of godliness.

From the very start, the city was a place of great diversity, despite being dominated by elites, such as the *encomendero* class and their descendants, and later merchants and government officials. Indigenous, African, and mixed-race servants, salespeople, artisans, porters, and builders made up the

IN FOCUS 12.1

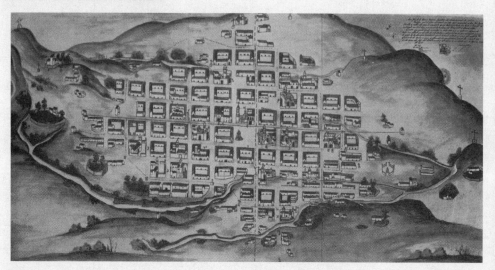

Figure 12.1. AGI, MP-BUENOS AIRES, 244 – Ciudad de la Plata, 1777. © Spain. Ministry of culture. Archivo General de Indias.

THE BEST-PLANNED CITIES

"Since the city was founded in our own time, there was opportunity to plan the whole thing from the start," wrote the royal chronicler Gonzalo Fernández de Oviedo in 1535, describing the capital of the island of Hispaniola. "Thus it was laid out with ruler and compass, with all the streets being carefully measured, and as a result, Santo Domingo is better planned than any city I have seen." Spaniards arrived in the Caribbean with early Renaissance ideas on city planning, loosely consisting of the notion that cities should be well ordered, with streets running in straight lines.

Conquistadors like Francisco de Montejo brought plans with them; along with his conqueror's license, Montejo had "a large sheet of paper upon which the city [plan] was drawn," a plan that was the basis for the plaza and eight blocks that was Mérida, Yucatan, in its early decades. There was a certain irony to Montejo choosing the name of Mérida; the crumbling pyramids of the Maya city of Tiho, on which Mérida was founded, reminded the Spaniard of the Roman ruins in Mérida, Spain. But Montejo sought to imitate neither Roman Mérida nor the jumble of the medieval Spanish city. His basic plan was adjusted to fit the layout of Tiho. Even that basic plan had partial Mesoamerican roots, as the crucial, under-recognized influence on sixteenth-century Spanish city planning was the Mexica capital of Tenochtitlán, whose central plaza and grid of canals and streets had so impressed Spaniards. Mérida was founded in 1542, during the crucial period of 1533–1544, when many of the most important Spanish American cities were established and planned. These included Bogotá, Buenos Aires, Cartagena (see In Focus 13.2), Lima, Quito, Santiago de Guatemala, and Sucre (founded as La Plata, or Chuquisaca, in 1538 and illustrated here). All were laid out on a grid, influenced by Tenochtitlán and other native cities, such as the Chimu capital of Chan Chan. These influences also crossed the ocean back to Spain, reflected in the new Spanish capital of Madrid (founded in 1561) and the new laws of 1573 requiring cities to be laid out with grids and central plazas. This idea of what a city should look like spread through the capitals of Europe, where it eventually became seen as an entirely Renaissance invention. In fact, its origins are as much Native American as European.

Founded by the Marqués de Campo Redondo in 1538, the city of La Plata (in today's Bolivia) became the regional capital or audiencia (high court) seat of Charcas in 1559, gaining a cathedral when Charcas became an archbishopric in 1609. As in all Spanish American cities, the important edifices of church and state, along with the residences of the local Spanish elite, were built on or adjacent to the central plaza. Lesser Spaniards and mixed-race residents lived further from the center, and native neighborhoods tended to be on the edge of the city – if not a short distance from it. Called various names in the colonial period, primarily La Plata and Charcas, in 1825, the city was renamed Sucre, after one of the leaders of the independence movement in South America. The bird's-eye view here was painted by Ildefonso Luján, the official painter for the viceroyalty, in 1777.

mass of urban dwellers. Their movements were constant, difficult to monitor, and in times of rebellion, profoundly subversive. Lower-class links with the countryside allowed wanted persons, male and female, to evade the law by slipping in or out of the city, from safe house to farm and back again. In most Spanish American cities, the urban lower classes tended to be predominantly indigenous in the middle period, although ports such as Cartagena and Lima had achieved African and African-descended majorities by the second quarter of the seventeenth century. Brazilian cities followed this latter pattern, such that by the later eighteenth century, Rio de Janeiro had the largest black population of any city outside Africa. Merchant-dominated cities such as Buenos Aires and Havana, which grew in importance mostly in the later eighteenth century, also had significant slave populations.

By modern standards, none of these cities were large. Even at their height in the middle period, the Spanish American metropolises of Lima, Potosí, and Mexico City barely topped one hundred thousand inhabitants. These numbers were nevertheless comparable to the populations of Europe's biggest cities of the time. More modest cities such as Guadalajara, Santiago de Guatemala, Bogotá, Quito, Cuzco, Arequipa, and Salvador da Bahia only topped fifty thousand inhabitants when their near hinterlands, a truly rural space, were included in the total. Cities such as Caracas, La Paz, Asunción, Santiago de Chile, and Mérida (Yucatan) were smaller still – more like large towns until the eighteenth century, when they rapidly gained in size and importance. Still other cities, such as Recife and Santo Domingo, faded from importance and shrunk in size, their age of splendor having passed.

Town and Country

Towns of a few hundred to perhaps a few thousand inhabitants proliferated in the hinterland of colonial Latin America's great cities. Some of these towns were centers of agricultural or livestock-raising enterprises in their own right. Others sprang up around trading and provisioning points or crossroads along the main mule or oxcart tracks that linked the colonies internally and externally. Still others began life as missionary or military frontier outposts. Whatever their initial reason for being founded, most towns were in essence miniature versions of the great cities, complete with town squares (in Spanish America) and centrally located pillories (in Brazil).

Towns that aspired to city status might be blessed with the royal assignation of *villa* or *vila*, a title that was more often a reflection of the status of certain residents than overall size. Villas were sometimes distinguished from other towns by their stone churches and other permanent buildings. Many, such as Ibarra, Ecuador, and the Vila Rica do Ouro Prêto, Brazil, grew into important regional capitals. Others grew and prospered because of their location along the trunk lines of the colonial economy – that is, the routes that brought in new settlers, African slaves, native workers, and imported goods while simultaneously bringing out export goods like Bolivian silver or wax from Yucatan. La Paz and Oruro (both in modern Bolivia) owed their growth to being on the trade routes that linked the Peruvian coast to silver-rich Potosí (South America's largest city in the middle period). Campeche, for example, remained a villa and was politically subordinate to Mérida, the capital and only official city in Yucatan, but the port town was just as important to the colony's economy. Puebla de los Ángeles benefited from its location on the Mexico City to Veracruz highway; Puebla was the size of Lima in late-colonial times, with cathedral bell towers deliberately built a tad taller than those of Mexico City.

Occupying a space somewhere between town and country were the many mining camps of the middle period. Mines tended to be located in rugged backcountry regions, often in places not otherwise amenable to urban development. Still, as the extraordinary case of Potosí demonstrates, mining camps could grow to enormous size and sophistication despite their geographical isolation. In part because of their general isolation from agricultural and manufacturing centers, mines in Spanish America – and later in Brazil – stimulated a quick linking of city and countryside. Some mining camps became mining towns, and some of these, like Guanajuato and São João del-Rei, became regional capitals. It could be said, in fact, that precious metals mining more than any other colonial activity spurred both colonial expansion and regional economic articulation. Most mining towns settled down and became more orderly with time, but all had a deserved reputation for crime, prostitution, filth, contraband trade, and corruption. The prospect of easy money, in short, drew a variety of hustlers, charlatans, and thieves.

In the vast Latin American backcountry, meanwhile, and even in the near hinterland of these large cities and towns, everyday life could seem – to well-traveled outsiders, at least – to be stuck in a pre-Columbian time warp. The majority of indigenous peoples carried on farming maize, potatoes, manioc, and other crops much as they had done for millennia. In the Andes, others

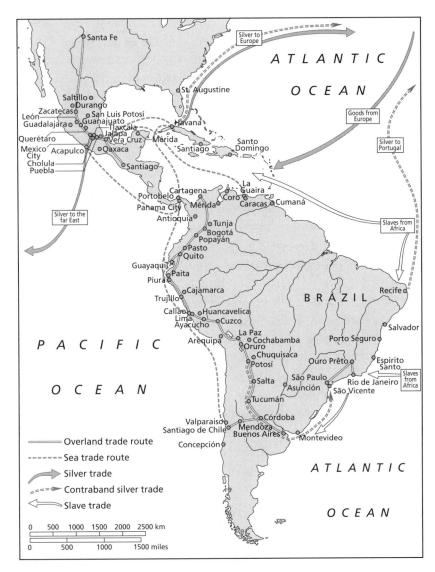

Map 12.2
The Trunk Lines

herded llamas and alpacas. Most paid tribute to imperial authorities twice a year in goods or cash. Many worshipped the old fertility gods, too, though sometimes behind the guise of Catholic saints. Most native peoples continued to live in self-governing villages. There the pace of life was slow, the year marked by the seasonal cycles of agriculture and the calendar of saints' days. The influence of the outside world was gradual, and the absorption of native villagers into the exploitative economic systems of the Atlantic world not yet so blatant and disruptive as to produce the kinds of village rebellions that were to mark the late eighteenth century. To be sure there were exceptions – in the 1660s, whole villages of Mayas fled into the unconquered forests from southwestern Yucatan to escape colonial demands, and in 1680, the Pueblo peoples of New Mexico rose up violently – but such exceptions tended to prove the rule of a relative middle-colonial rural stability.

Indigenous languages survived everywhere. European missionaries learned to preach in local tongues if they wished to be understood. If their language skills were inadequate, they ran the risk of being denounced as ineffectual by native parishioners, such as the late-sixteenth-century Maya village elders who complained to Yucatan's governor that the local priest "delivers the mass in a twisted fashion." Only in certain commercial enclaves, most of them urban, were native languages beginning to be displaced by Spanish and Portuguese in the seventeenth century. With their large and densely settled indigenous populations, the two core colonial regions of Mesoamerica and Upper Peru were perhaps most notable for the persistence and everyday character of native languages (and, more broadly, cultures). In those regions, even elite Spanish speakers tended to be raised by Nahuatl-, Maya-, or Quechua-speaking wet nurses and house servants. A similar "Indian" and often female cultural dominance prevailed around São Paulo and other parts of southern and interior Brazil. Rural life, considered by educated Spaniards and Portuguese as generally coarse and beneath contempt, was overwhelmingly associated with "Indianness."

Yet looks could be deceiving. In truth, native men and women in larger rural communities were often as cosmopolitan as their European overlords. Some traveled great distances to find employment, to avoid forced work stints in mines and other projects, to transport goods by sea and land, or to participate in the market. Some native noblemen even traveled to Spain to seek an audience with the king. In Spanish colonial cities, indigenous women soon became a fixture in the marketplace, constantly hustling alongside mestizas, mulattas, and other women of color to carve out a space for profit making against the wishes of male Spanish merchants and wholesalers.

Even the most elite Spaniards and Portuguese, meanwhile, often fell into the comfortable habit of navel gazing, becoming absorbed in the petty squabbles of their home parish or small town. Young men sometimes grew highly familiar with the nearby countryside, but their knowledge of distant capitals was often minimal. This was most true of creoles, or locally born, elites, both men and women. In the aftermath of conquest and initial settlement, horizons narrowed. In smaller rural settlements, men of all backgrounds tended to engage in the same agricultural pursuits. For example, a census of rural Yucatan in 1700 showed that corn farming was not just the preserve of Mayas; although Spaniards were more likely to own wealthy estates and cattle ranches, one in five Spaniards in the Yucatec countryside was a *milpero*, or corn farmer, compared to 40 percent of mestizos and mulattoes and 75 percent of Maya men. In other words, Spaniards, mulattoes, and Mayas were not equal in wealth, opportunity, and occupation – but, in the countryside, nor were they that far apart either.

Beyond the realm of tastes and travels, it is clear that town and country in colonial Latin America were more closely linked than has often been suggested. Cattle – introduced early into the colonies and outnumbering the declining native population by 1600 – were a major link between town and country. Every Spanish American and Brazilian city, town, and mining camp was tied to local livestock-raising ranches. These provided urban residents with steady supplies of meat, hides, tallow, and dairy products. Substantial numbers of raw cowhides were also exported to European markets. Only in highland Peru and Bolivia were native herd animals (llamas and alpacas) significant, mostly for indigenous use in transport and textile manufacture. Some ranchlands or pastures were carefully measured by surveyors and even divided by trenches and stone or adobe fences. This was especially true of agriculturally rich and densely populated highlands, where keeping grazing animals out of neighboring agricultural fields was a constant battle.

Far more often, ranches were extensive, vaguely delineated territories, as in the semiarid expanses of northern Mexico and northeastern Brazil. Some ranches extended for miles in all directions, and their shapes shifted over time according to inconstant rains, overgrazing, and other uncertainties. The only way to keep track of animals in the land of the open range was by branding and through periodic roundups, or rodeos. Ranchlands in the middle-colonial period were dominated by small numbers of men – most of them black, indigenous, or mixed-race – and wherever they worked, they developed distinctive cowboy cultures. The Mexican *charro*, Andean *chagra*, Venezuelan *llanero*, Brazilian *vaqueiro*, and Argentine *gaucho* were all products of the colonial ranch economy. These hard-bitten, hard-drinking, leather-clad men came periodically to the city with their herds. Their visits, marked by whoring, drinking binges, and violence, were not soon forgotten.

Connected to many of the ranches of backcountry Latin America were large agricultural estates built around the mass production of wheat, maize, sugar, and other foods. Some estates in Guatemala produced indigo dye, derived from plants that were sown and harvested several times a year (indigo was also produced in Mexico and later in Venezuela). The great estates, called haciendas in Spanish America and *fazendas* (or *engenhos*, in the case of sugar) in Brazil, tended to be owned by urban elites and church organizations, such as the Jesuit order. Formerly equated with feudal estates in medieval Europe, the colonial hacienda or plantation has more recently been described by economic historians in terms of its relative flexibility, dynamism, and market orientation. These were not simply self-sufficient New World fiefdoms, in other words, but sophisticated agricultural businesses.

Although economically dynamic in the main, the great estates of Latin America shared several social features with their feudal European antecedents. Whereas European landowners in the seventeenth and eighteenth centuries were turning increasingly toward free labor and an open land market aimed at driving out sharecroppers and other dependents, in Latin America, forced labor and other means of holding workers on site were widely practiced and generally growing in frequency. Haciendas and plantations depended overwhelmingly on the labor of neighboring native villagers and resident black slaves. When those labor systems were absent, estate owners tried to ensnare free workers, often peasants driven to desperation by drought or other contingencies, through advances of merchandise and other forms of indebtedness. The great estate was, for the most part, a place of bondage and discipline.

The great estates were of two basic types: (1) those oriented toward overseas export, such as the slave-staffed sugar *engenhos* of northeastern Brazil and the cacao, or chocolate, estates of Venezuela; and (2) those oriented toward internal, urban markets, such as the hundreds of wheat, maize, brandy, and cattle haciendas of the Spanish American interior. Ranchers on the islands of Cuba and Hispaniola helped supply the great annual fleets with salted meat and hides. In all cases, elite owners only rarely visited their landholdings, preferring instead to reside in what they regarded as the more civilized city. Overseers and majordomos – who tended to be Spaniards on the larger estates but more often mestizos, mulattoes, or blacks on the smaller ones – were left in charge of everyday production on both export and internal market-oriented estates. The archives contain numerous complaints by native or slave workers against majordomos. In some cases, their cruelties were repaid with violence.

Small farms – called *fincas*, *chacaras*, or *estancias* in Spanish America – were another feature of the middle-colonial rural landscape. Like the great estates, some were oriented toward urban markets and others toward transatlantic ones. In Brazil, some small landholders, called *lavradores de cana*, or "cane farmers," produced sugarcane for neighboring *senhores de engenho*, or mill lords. They paid the mill lords for use of the expensive machinery needed to squeeze and distill sugar in portions of cane or juice. Refined sugar was then traded to merchants for slaves, tools, and luxury commodities. Many cane farmers in the middle period hoped to accumulate slaves and money and someday to build a mill of their own; a few even realized such an ambition. As in Spanish America, some farmers in Brazil tapped into the export market by growing tobacco, a product that required little capital investment but that could yield some cash return. Eventually, tobacco would become a significant alternative to sugar for small farmers in Cuba, coastal Mexico, and New Granada.

Many other small farmers, among them poorer Europeans, mestizos, and various free people of color, grew a mix of subsistence crops and products for sale in urban markets. Tobacco was one of the few export crops that smallholders could produce, as it required little capital investment (although it was highly labor intensive). Because the owners of the great estates increasingly monopolized arable bottomlands through the process of *composición*, or official surveys, especially after about 1590, small farmers tended to get pushed into more hilly and marginal terrain. Some of this land was quite fertile, in fact, but it presented farmers with special challenges and risks. Higher lands were more subject to frost, and hilly ones to landslides following deforestation. Lands bordering forests were more subject to attacks by predators, both animal and human. Lands more distant from market centers meant an increase in transport costs. In general, the great estates expanded at the expense of small farmers in the middle period, leaving them the options of joining the hacienda or plantation workforce as sharecroppers or hired hands or of farming the increasingly distant margins, a more independent life, but one laden with risks. As indigenous populations rebounded in Spanish America and the number of Portuguese immigrants expanded rapidly in the early eighteenth century in Brazil, land pressures throughout Latin America grew in intensity. The trend would continue through the Independence period, with more and more violent consequences.

Pursuits of the Privileged

Wealthy Latin Americans may have been deeply devout Catholics, but their lives consisted of more than prayer and contemplation; they also constituted a genuine leisure class. No elite male worked with his hands unless dueling a social equal who had besmirched his honor or engaging in the conquest or defense of some frontier. In conscious imitation of the ancient Greeks and Romans, the work of colonial elites in both Spanish America and Brazil was concentrated in the realms of civil and religious governance. In part thanks to the roaming tendencies of elite men, elite women often were left to manage rural estates and urban households. With plenty of time on their hands as a result, elites sought diversion in various forms – from card games and music recitals to poetry and theater, from bullfights to massive fireworks displays. Even the Inquisition's autos de fé were viewed as a form of public entertainment; the floggings and hangings that don Josephe de Mugaburu witnessed in seventeenth-century Lima were events that brought the elite, as well as the plebeian classes, onto balconies, rooftops, and streets to enjoy the spectacle. Colonial life, in short, was not boring.

The century and a half of the colonial middle coincided with Spain's golden age of literature. Despite their isolation from the mother country, colonial elites proved avid consumers of this boom in secular literary production. Some of the great works of the period, especially poetic and historical ones, were written by elite colonists themselves, although most printing was done in Spain. The printing presses of Mexico City and Lima were mostly devoted to production of religious works, which were widely distributed in the colonies, including some in indigenous languages. Ships' manifests and sale records from the Baroque period show that wealthy urbanites from New Mexico to Chile were reading the picaresque novels of Miguel de Cervantes and Mateo Alemán within a year of their printing in Spain. Such works were sold in colonial cities, but it was not uncommon for elite Spaniards to make business trips to Spain – typically a two-year affair – and to return with a few of the latest publications. Spanish Americans also purchased and even staged the plays of Lope de Vega and Calderón de la Barca, and some colonial authors were inspired to write plays treating local themes. Others enjoyed the epic poetry of colonial authors Ercilla and Castellanos. The historical works of the mestizo writer Garcilaso "El Inca" de la Vega were also wildly popular.

Elite readers in the colonies were also avid consumers of the classics. Aristotle was considered the prime authority in many things, but Greek and Roman authors such as Herodotus, Thucydides, Cicero, and Marcus Aeneus Lucan were also widely available. The Inquisition maintained a list of prohibited books, the *Index Librorum Prohibitorum*, but surviving colonial libraries and other references show that allegedly forbidden works were not difficult to find. Most of these books were not expensive for elites, although an average title cost as much as a year's tribute for most Native Americans. Literacy outside elite circles was not widespread.

Elite colonial music, like much literature, was overwhelmingly religious. Some colonists purchased songbooks that included romantic and military ballads, but most music was intended to accompany religious services. Polyphonic choir music was common everywhere, accompanied by pipe organs and a variety of wind and string instruments. European choral and instrumental traditions were adopted by African, indigenous, and mixed-race musicians. New forms and rhythms soon emerged. The Guaraní of Paraguay produced a massive corpus of religious music to be sung in Guaraní and following Guaraní forms. Africans and their descendants developed an extraordinary range of blended musical styles that formed the base of most modern Latin American popular music – the complexity and variety of which reflects the centuries of cultural interaction among Iberians, Africans, and native peoples in the colonies. Elites often found these popular appropriations and transformations disdainful and even subversive, but there was ultimately no denying their power to entertain, particularly in the midst of religious festivals such as Carnival.

Don Josephe de Mugaburu noted that in 1686 the authorities in Lima chose to celebrate the king's birthday by running bulls in the city plaza. Such a decision symbolizes how popular bullbaiting was in Spanish America, beginning with its introduction from Spain in the sixteenth century. The bullfight, or *corrida de toros*, has been traced to the Roman gladiatorial tradition, and even today it remains a highly theatrical and occasionally deadly spectacle. Colonial bullfights were not as finely choreographed as modern ones, but the essential contest between man and beast was still at the core. Lancers on horseback and matadors with capes and swords were standard in some places, whereas in others the "fight" was a more informal, country affair oriented toward teasing and dodging the bulls amid much drinking and clowning. The latter was more often the scene in native villages in Mesoamerica, for example, where the community could not afford a fine fighting bull, and where the "fight" usually ended with an on-the-spot butchering and selling of the cuts of meat. Elsewhere, as in northern Mexico and the South American pampas, bullbaiting was subsumed within larger rodeo festivities, in which lassoing, horse breaking, and other cowboy skills were showcased.

The cockfight was even more popular than the bullfight. This was partly because it was easily appropriated by the popular classes, as raising fighting cocks was not an expensive hobby. Still, cockfights were staged at official times in the colonial period, and were administered by elites who held special licenses. In the same way that alcohol and playing cards were supposed to be sold only by licensed officials, the cockfight was considered a source of state revenue. The license holder purchased the right to stage cockfights for several years in a row from crown officials, then recouped his costs by gathering a portion of the wagers made by participants and spectators. Like the bullfight, the cockfight was as much a ritual of machismo as it was a bloody spectacle.

Diet and Disease

The sciences of medicine and nutrition were not well understood in colonial Latin America (as was true in most of the world at the time). The Columbian Exchange would eventually greatly enrich the variety of foods and medicines available to all colonial inhabitants. But for much of the period, the kinds of foods one ate and the types of cures one sought were highly restricted by cultural affinity and class. Traditional native medicinal practices were often suspect in the eyes of Spaniards, so while important exchanges of healing knowledge did occur, the process was slow. Enslaved Africans found their nutritional and medical needs closely watched because slaves were so valuable, but in the end their care was poorly handled. African foodways and medicinal practices brought to the Americas are only now starting to be appreciated by historians.

The creation of new regional cuisines in Latin America was thus a very gradual process. From their first contacts with the American tropics, Iberians were stunned by the variety of unfamiliar foods and herbs. Although elites found indigenous foods interesting, they were slow to appreciate most of them, especially the ordinary staples of maize and manioc, and wealthier Spaniards declined to eat what they regarded as "Indian food." For their part, they brought a wide variety of domestic animals, along with a significant number of food crops they hoped to transplant. They eventually found ecological niches for virtually everything they brought, including vine and olive cuttings. Just as Native Americans were often unimpressed with the foods – such as olives and wheat bread – that Spaniards considered essential to civilized living, so were Europeans slow to adopt New World foods. But in time foods such as the tomato, chili pepper, and potato were not only taken overseas but became essential ingredients of many world cuisines. Chocolate, vanilla, and other Mesoamerican luxury foods – and later the Andean stimulant coca – eventually took hold among Europeans (see In Focus 12.2).

Lowland indigenous peoples adopted imported food crops such as plantains and sugarcane, while natives everywhere avidly consumed pork, chicken, and other Old World domestic animals and their by-products. African slaves were generally given a high-calorie but nutrition-poor diet based on salted beef, plus a ration of starchy carbohydrate such as maize or plantains. Enslaved women did their own cooking. By raising a variety of mostly indigenous fruits, herbs, and vegetables, they added vitamins and minerals, as well as flavor, to the slave diet. In some places, African vegetables such as okra and even the imported luxury of cola nuts were consumed. Rice cultivation developed throughout Spanish America and Brazil from an early date, and it is likely that this labor-intensive food tradition blended Iberian and West African techniques of planting and preparation. As far as we know, the most common variety of rice grown in the colonies was the East Asian *Sativa* type.

Poor diet in the cities, combined with unhealthy sanitation practices and hygiene habits, nurtured disease and kept mortality rates high. Streets were open sewers, considered appropriate places to leave excrement and animal corpses (and sometimes even the bodies of dead slaves). Only the elite owned manufactured soap, although bathing among Europeans appears to have been infrequent. Until modern medicine began to emerge toward the end of the colonial period, physicians were not sufficiently knowledgeable or trained to do more good than harm. Even by the low medical standards of the day, many practitioners were quacks. Studying medicine lacked the prestige of theology or the law; most universities in Spanish America were religious institutions, and the relative weakness of the church in Brazil meant that colony had no universities at all. Surgery was even less prestigious, and many surgeons were just barbers who had acquired a certain skill with the saw and lancet. Barbers also doubled as dentists, as the remedy to all toothaches was extraction.

In the countryside, age-old indigenous medicine and habits of personal hygiene created more sanitary living conditions than those found in the city. Most Mesoamericans, for example, benefited from a deeply rooted tradition of herbal remedies, many of which they wrote down alphabetically after hieroglyphic books were burned and banned by Spanish priests. Franciscans noted, with some bemusement, how often Mayas bathed, and how the women prided themselves on their clean hair and clothes. Other indigenous peoples, along with many enslaved Africans, bathed with aromatic and cleansing herbs in streams and rivers.

IN FOCUS 12.2

EXTRACTING PULQUE.

Figure 12.2. **a.** A black slave or domestic servant preparing chocolate in the kitchen of a Spanish household. Detail of José de Páez, De español y negra, mulato, 6, ca. 1770–80, Oil on copper, 50.2 x 63.8 cm. Private collection (José Ignacio González Manterola). **b.** Credit: Extracting Pulque, from 'The Ancient Cities of the New World', by Claude-Joseph-Desire Charney, engraved by Manini, pub. 1887 (engraving) by Riou, Edouard (1833–1900) (after) Private Collection/ The Bridgeman Art Library [Image # BAL 126943]

THE ELEVEN-O'-CLOCK SHOT

As with foods, the variety and quantity of alcoholic beverages steadily increased in the Americas during the colonial period. New drinks (e.g., wine, brandy, rum) became popular alongside, not instead of, traditional native beverages. These included Mexico's maguey-based *pulque* (being made in one of the images here) and the Andean corn beer called *chicha*. Wine was being produced in Peru in the sixteenth century and in Argentina, Bolivia, and Chile not long after that. Wine was soon distilled into brandy, which was more potent and kept longer. Rum – and its cheaper, stronger sibling, *aguardiente de caña* – was made wherever sugarcane grew and was popular throughout the colonies. A Spaniard was more likely to drink brandy, an Afro-Brazilian aguardiente (popularly called *cachaça*, or "booze," by the eighteenth century), and a Nahua *pulque*, but such divisions of consumption were by no means absolute. For example, during a party on an hacienda in Ecuador in 1768, one that led to a murder trial, Spaniards drank large amounts of wine, aguardiente, and a local intoxicant called *punche*.

The following is from a 1758 English edition of *A Voyage to South-America*, the published account of the travels through the colonies of two Spaniards, Antonio de Ulloa and Jorge Juan. The passage refers to what they witnessed in Cartagena, but it reflects patterns of consumption that were widespread throughout Latin America.

"The use of brandy is so common, that the most regular and sober persons, never omit drinking a glass of it every morning about eleven o'clock; alledging that this spirit strengthens the stomach,

IN FOCUS 12.2

THE ELEVEN-O'-CLOCK SHOT, *continued*

weakened by copious, and constant perspiration, and sharpens the appetite. *Hacer las once*, that is to drink a glass of brandy, is the common invitation. This custom, not esteemed pernicious by these people when used with moderation, has degenerated into vice; many being so fond of it, that during the whole day, they do nothing but hacer las once. Persons of distinction use Spanish brandy, but the lower class and Negroes, very contentedly take up with that of the country, extracted from the juice of the sugar cane, and thence called cane brandy, of which sort the consumption is much the greatest.

CHOCOLATE, here known only by the name of cacao, is so common, that there is not a Negro slave but constantly allows himself a regale of it after breakfast; and the Negro women sell it ready made about the streets, at the rate of a quarter of a real (about five farthings sterling) for a dish. This is however so far from being all cacao, that the principal ingredient is maize; but that used by the better sort is neat, and worked as in Spain. This they constantly repeat an hour after dinner, but never use it fasting, or without eating something with it."

In precolonial times, chocolate had been a luxury drink of the Mesoamerican elite, who mixed the ground cacao beans with water, hot chili pepper, and maize flour. During the sixteenth century, the popularity of the drink spread first to all natives, as well as Spaniards and Africans, in Mesoamerica and then into South America. The spicy recipe was also gradually supplanted by a sweet one, using vanilla, cinnamon, and sugar. In the colonial middle, cacao production spread to Ecuador and Venezuela while the market for chocolate drinks began to develop in Europe. In the detail above from a painting of the 1770s by the Mexican artist José de Páez, an enslaved black woman or domestic servant is frothing a hot chocolate drink in the kitchen of a Spanish household in Mexico.

Nevertheless, no native medicines could meet the challenge of the new epidemic diseases that arrived with Europeans and Africans. The Columbian Exchange killed tens of millions of indigenous people who lacked acquired immunity to Old World pathogens. Dealing with disease, deadly and otherwise, was more art than science in the middle-colonial period, and in many cases, alleged cures only exacerbated illness. For those suffering from viral infections such as smallpox, influenza, or measles, there was little to be done in the era before vaccinations beyond keeping the patient sheltered, fed, and hydrated.

Such diseases were often treated with the traditional therapies of bloodletting and purging, both of which probably worsened the patient's condition. Bloodletting was considered a vile but necessary step on the road to recovery by all European colonists. By the middle period it had become a Native American specialty, and indigenous blood-letters, or phlebotomists, were always in high demand. They treated elites, fellow natives, and slaves alike. Even horses and other animals thought to be ill were bled. Purges were mostly made from bitter herbs and powdered tree bark, including a local

Caribbean one called *cañafístola*. Purgative ointments made from mercury were used to treat syphilis, one of the few diseases thought to originate in the Americas. Like modern chemotherapy, the selective application of such toxins could work to staunch disease, but often with unpleasant side effects.

Of the various diseases that afflicted Europeans in the Americas, the most deadly were the mosquito-borne ills of yellow fever and malaria. No treatment was developed for yellow fever before modern times, but malaria was fought fairly successfully with an infusion derived from the bark of a South American bush called *quina quina* (hence the word *quinine*). Its use was first noted by Europeans in early-seventeenth-century southern Ecuador, where natives had adapted a local fever-reducing remedy to a new disease. By the early eighteenth century, in the jungle mining zones of coastal Colombia, African snakebite curers were highly valued by their white masters. As in the case of quinine bark, these curers – usually elder men – had adapted known curative techniques to a new environment. Common wounds were treated with a variety of astringents, or mineral salts, but infections such as tetanus still killed many colonial field and mine workers.

Pirate Life and Imperial Defense

The 1620s was a disastrous decade for the Spanish at sea. Early in the hurricane season of 1622, the silver fleet, or *flota*, set sail out of Havana in good weather, only to run into a furious storm the next day. In the words of an English account of the event (translated from the official Spanish report and published the following year), "tempests will have their courses, and are inexorable." The storm blew up as if "it were covenanting to perpetuate some outrageousness, [and] all the Galleons were dissipated and dissevered." The fleet battled the storm for nine days, after which nine ships were lost, along with thousands of men and a considerable treasure in gold and silver, and the remaining ships limped back into various Spanish Caribbean ports.

The Spanish suffered a much more punishing loss in 1628, when Dutch corsairs led by Piet Heyn captured and looted an entire silver fleet in Cuba's Matanzas Bay, east of Havana. As if to add insult to injury, the Dutch not only made off with nearly ten million silver pesos, but also deeply wounded Spanish pride. Astonishingly, the Spanish, whose fleet was huge, well armed, and manned with hundreds of soldiers, gave up without a fight. How could this have happened? Observers at the time were similarly astounded, and although they understood that a bad decision to enter Matanzas Bay with a tailwind had stranded most of the Spanish ships and left their main guns pointing the wrong way for defense, the case was open for investigation.

Furious, Spanish royal officials arrested the fleet's general and the admiral and charged them with dereliction of duty and desertion. The famous Lima-born jurist Juan de Solórzano Pereira (mentioned at the start of Chapter 2)

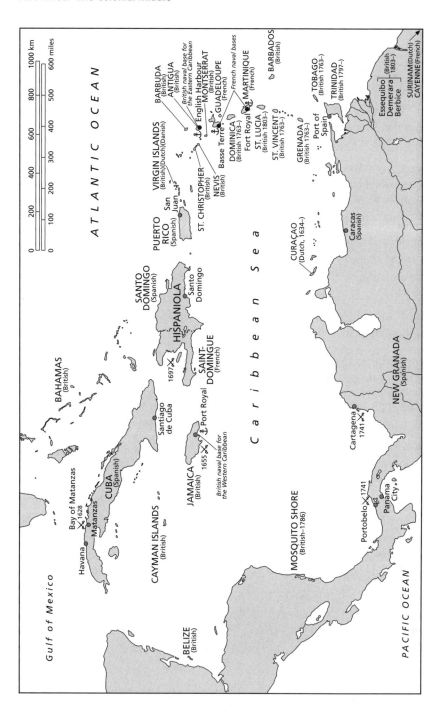

Map 12.3
Competition for the Caribbean

produced an exhaustive, 540-page indictment of the officers, arguing that their cowardice warranted death by hanging, the most ignominious punishment a Spaniard could receive. Unlike the disaster of 1622, Spanish lives were not lost, but among Solórzano's five hundred points of argument were the claims that "kingdoms and states have nothing more important than their reputations" and that "honor and good reputation are worth more than life and property." Fighting high-seas pirates was not only about defending Spanish American wealth, it was a fundamental matter of national honor.

Even so, the Dutch "pirates" in this case represented state interests as much as the Spanish general and admiral represented those of the Spanish crown; their captain, Piet Heyn, was commissioned by the state-backed Dutch West India Company, founded in 1621 with the aim of plundering Spanish and Portuguese wealth in the Americas and establishing a permanent colonial presence. Heyn, who grew up near Rotterdam, became a national hero and is still cheered today by Dutch soccer fans. Thanks to him, Company shareholders received 50 percent dividends, and a portion of the silver fleet treasure was used to finance a much larger enterprise: the capture of northeast Brazil. After seizing, then losing, Salvador da Bahia in 1624 (the Spanish sent the largest fleet ever to save what was then Habsburg Brazil), the Dutch managed to take Recife and gain control of the region's most lucrative sugar plantations. They rapidly extended their dominion to the Amazon and all the way to South America's Wild Coast, near the mouth of the Orinoco River. Exultant West India Company board members named their vast tropical colony New Holland. Under the brief but enlightened administration of Count Maurice of Nassau, Dutch Brazil enjoyed a rare degree of religious tolerance, and Dutch artists and naturalists created a substantial scientific and painterly legacy. For some, at least, Brazil was a kind of paradise. In 1654, a mostly Brazilian force – made up of Native Americans, Africans, and creole Portuguese – drove out the foreigners for good.

Brazil ceased to be a problem after the Portuguese won back their independence in 1640, but unfortunately for Spain, defense against pirates and other foreign interlopers was a longstanding problem that would only grow in the late-seventeenth and eighteenth centuries. Spanish fleets were rarely attacked, but straggling ships and small port towns were almost constantly threatened by marauding English, Dutch, and French sea raiders. Some were sponsored by companies or colonial governors, but increasingly they sailed "on their own account," as true free-lance pirates. The Dutch ultimately lost Brazil, but other pirate or corsair raids yielded lasting colonies. Francophone buccaneers occupied the western half of Hispaniola in the early seventeenth century, giving rise to the lucrative French sugar colony of Saint-Domingue. Saint-Domingue was ceded by the Spanish in 1697 after French naval forces and corsairs sacked the major Caribbean port of Cartagena de Indias. Following a similarly amphibious but failed attack on Santo Domingo in 1655, the English seized Jamaica. Port Royal, its main settlement, became a major base for piratical attacks and contraband trade. In the course of copying the Iberian sugar estate, northern Europeans also made substantial inroads on the Portuguese monopoly on African slaves. Sugar and slavery, after the Brazilian fashion, would characterize the following two centuries of European rule in the Caribbean.

IN FOCUS 12.3

Figure 12.3. a. "The Cruelty of Lolonois." From Alexander Exquemelin's *The Buccaneers of America*, first published in 1678. Image courtesy of the Rare Book division of the Library of Congress. **b.** Portrait of Henry Morgan. From Alexander Exquemelin's *The Buccaneers of America*, first published in 1678. Image courtesy of the Rare Book division of the Library of Congress.

PIRATES OF THE CARIBBEAN

As the Caribbean became home to increasing numbers of Dutch, French, and English settlers after 1650 – most of them young, single, indentured men tied to plantations, merchant ships, or military expeditions – violent pirate attacks grew in frequency and intensity. Former bondservants and soldiers readily joined with experienced sailors to "go on account" and prey on Spanish ships and towns. Bases in Haiti, Jamaica, Belize, Honduras, and Tortuga gave men like Henry Morgan, Laurens de Graaf, and Francois L'Ollonais (a.k.a. Lolonois) room and means to roam. The image at left depicts the Frenchman L'Ollonais (c.1635–c.1668), nicknamed "Bane of the Spaniards" and infamous among them for his cruelty; here he has cut out the heart of one Spanish captive and is feeding it to another. The portrait at right is the Welshman Morgan (c.1635–1688), eventually knighted by the English king.

   In a way reminiscent of the early Spanish conquistadors, the pirates of the Caribbean pooled assets and formed ad hoc companies, sharing out booty according to each individual's contributions when settling accounts. Caribbean buccaneers almost never went after treasure fleets or other large targets. Instead, they preyed mostly on small coastwise traders in hopes of getting word of a big score: a lone, poorly defended galleon carrying a fortune in gold or silver. Such ships remained the stuff of most pirates' dreams, so they turned to invading small coastal towns and holding their inhabitants for ransom. Often they were paid not in coin, but rather in commodities like tobacco or brandy, which they either consumed or attempted to sell elsewhere. Only when they gathered in large numbers in the 1660s and 1670s were the Caribbean buccaneers able to carry out raids on the scale of the earlier Dutch corsairs. Men such as Morgan, de Graaf, and l'Ollonais led massive attacks on Panama City, Veracruz, Campeche, and Maracaibo. Mostly they were ratcheting up their established patterns of kidnapping and extortion, but as English and French colonial authorities began to crack down on their activities many left for the Pacific to raid Spanish America's virtually undefended west coast. Bases were harder to find than in the Caribbean, but some buccaneers camped out on the Galapagos and Juan Fernández Islands between pillaging raids on coastal towns such as Sonsonate, Guayaquil, and Paita. Their numbers remained too small to go after Lima or Acapulco. Although the buccaneers left the Pacific by the early 1690s, terrified Spanish officials ordered many unprotected hamlets abandoned, a policy that had lasting effects on regional development.

Among the corsairs and privateers (state-approved pirates) sponsored by Spain and Portugal's enemies, there were also freelance pirates who sought booty only for themselves. Most claimed to be doing the bidding of some monarch or colonial governor, but usually this was a self-defense ploy. The pirates of the late-seventeenth-century Caribbean were especially legendary (see Window 12.3).

The most obvious and infamous impact of pirates and privateers on Spanish interests in the middle period was their constant pillaging of Spanish port towns. But equally damaging to Spanish commercial and crown interests was pirate involvement in contraband trade. Such men brought cloth and other manufactures from Port Royal, Jamaica, and other bases, but most importantly they brought slaves. On the colonists' side, illegal trade with foreigners was both attractive and dangerous. Contraband trading was punishable by execution, but Spanish colonial coastlines were long and mostly undefended. In the middle period, colonists as far afield as Buenos Aires and Santiago de Cuba engaged in illicit trade with outsiders, usually shielded by corrupt officials who received a share of gains. Foreign contrabandists caught in periodic crackdowns often reacted by engaging in more piratical acts, which then led to the sale of more stolen booty elsewhere. In an era of monopoly trade and in a vast and accessible region rich in precious metals, it seems that both piracy and contraband trade were bound to flourish. In the middle period, legitimate trade, contraband, and piracy were in fact but points along a commercial spectrum.

* * *

The seventeenth century thus saw the northern European empires torment the Iberian powers by sponsoring pirate rampages in the Caribbean, Atlantic, and Pacific – thus leading to the acquisition (sometimes temporary, sometimes permanent) of Spanish and Portuguese colonies by the Dutch, French, and British. In contrast, in the eighteenth century, the northern European empires focused on consolidating, expanding, and profiting by their American possessions. This brought the golden age of piracy to an end, but it hardly brought peace – as we shall see in the next chapter.

Latin America in the middle period was overwhelmingly rural. As such, it was also overwhelmingly black and indigenous. These majority populations, whose colonial cultures we only barely know, blended, split, and regrouped in myriad ways, giving rise to a number of new, colonial traditions of music, art, storytelling, and cuisine. Meanwhile, the city, about which we know much more, was in fact less a European space than its imperialist founders planned. The orderly plazas and massive churches belied a more chaotic underworld, in which peoples of all classes and colors eked out an existence. They also worked for respect and honor, and very shortly left their mark on the colonial city in the form of countless chapels to patron saints. Most important, it was the popular sector that most effectively tied together city, town, and country. In the remaining chapters, we shall see how that popular sector became increasingly restive as the eighteenth century wore on.

SUGGESTIONS FOR FURTHER READING

The Muguburu diary, quoted at the start of this chapter, is available as Robert Ryal Miller, trans. and ed., *Chronicle of Colonial Lima: The Diary of Josephe and Francisco Mugaburu, 1640–1697* (1975). Witness testimony on the Ecuadorian drinking party mentioned in In Focus 12.2 is in chapter 15 of *Colonial Lives: Documents on Latin American History, 1550–1850*, edited by Richard Boyer and Geoffrey Spurling (2000) (chapter 14 is also relevant). Two classic studies for term-paper writers linking city and countryside in Mexico are Eric Van Young, *Hacienda and Market in Eighteenth-Century Mexico: The Rural Economy of the Guadalajara Region, 1675–1820* (1981), and William B. Taylor, *Drinking, Homicide, and Rebellion in Colonial Mexican Villages* (1979).

Suitable as assigned course books are Susan Migden Socolow and Louisa Schell Hoberman's *Cities and Society in Colonial Latin America* (1986) and *The Countryside in Colonial Latin America* (1996), as well as Socolow's *Women of Colonial Latin America* (1999). Also accessible is R. Douglas Cope, *The Limits of Racial Domination: Plebeian Society in Colonial Mexico City, 1660–1720* (1994). An excellent overview is Jay Kinsbruner, *The Colonial Spanish American City* (2005).

For further reading on the topic of piracy and imperial defense in the Caribbean, we suggest Kris Lane, *Pillaging the Empire: Piracy in the Americas, 1500–1750* (1998). Also of use for students doing research papers is Carla Rahn Phillips, *Six Galleons for the King of Spain: Imperial Defense in the Early Seventeenth Century* (1986), and John Lynch, *The Hispanic World in Crisis and Change, 1598–1700* (1992). On medicine, see John Tate Lanning's classic *Royal Protomedicato: The Regulation of the Medical Profession in the Spanish Empire* (1985), and on the book trade, see Irving Leonard's *Books of the Brave*, 2d ed. (1994).

GLOSSARY

Traza [TRAH-sah]: central grid of city blocks, where important buildings and elite homes were located

Villa [VEE-yah]: Spanish town (**Vila** [VEE-lah] in Portuguese)

Trunk line: main economic arteries or trade routes that linked colonial mines, ports, towns, and cities

Creole: someone born in the American colonies, usually of Iberian descent but sometimes including Afro-Americans

Charro [CHA-roh], **Chagra** [CHAG-rah], **Llanero** [yan-EH-roh], **Gaucho** [GOW-cho], and **Vaqueiro** [va-KAY-roo]: the cowboy in Mexico, the Andes, Venezuela, Argentina, and Brazil, respectively

Hacienda [ahs-YEN-dah]: great agricultural estate in Spanish America (*fazenda* in Portuguese)

Engenho [en-ZHEN-you]: sugar mill, or estate, in Brazil

Finca [FEEN-kah], **Chacara** [CHAK-ah-rah], and **Estancia** [ess-TANS-yah]: small agricultural estates, or farms

Flota [FLOH-tah]: fleet, usually a reference to the Spanish silver fleet

PART FOUR

THE AGE OF CHANGE

The final three chapters take the story of colonial Latin America to its conclusion. Our focus is on the long eighteenth century, from about 1700 through to the 1820s – the age of change, as we have called it.

We begin by describing the global wars between imperial Spain, France, and Britain, and Spain's efforts to better defend its empire. Those efforts became part of a larger political and economic reform campaign by the Spanish and Portuguese crowns, outlined in Chapter 13 ("War and Reform"). Chapter 14 ("Late-Colonial Life") looks at three late-colonial trends: demographic and social changes; the recovery of mining, with Brazilian gold and Spanish American silver producing enormous profits and crown revenues; and increasing levels of unrest and rebellion after 1750 (we explore in detail the Great Andean Rebellion of the 1780s).

The closing chapter of Part Four, and of the book, explores the transition to independence, arguing that the conflicts of 1808–1824 were the meeting of four phenomena: a palace-coup style power grab by the local elite; local and regional civil war; social unrest blooming into revolutionary movements; and external events, primarily in Europe. The independence of the Iberian colonies in the Americas was bound to happen eventually, but its occurrence in the 1820s was not inevitable.

13

■ ■ ■ ■ ■ ■ ■ ■ ■ ■ ■ ■ ■ ■ ■ ■ ■ ■ ■

War and Reform

TIMELINE

1700–1815: series of global, imperial wars among the Spanish, French, and British

1701–1713: War of the Spanish Succession

1739–1748: War of Jenkins' Ear and War of Austrian Succession, including 1740–1741 British siege of Cartagena

1739 and 1776: new viceroyalties of New Granada and Río de la Plata created

1750s: Pombal begins reforms in Brazil and the rest of the Portuguese Empire

1756–1763: Seven Years' War

1759 and 1767: Jesuits expelled from Brazil and Spanish America

1775–1783: War of the American Revolution

1789 and 1791: beginning of the French and Haitian revolutions

Concubinage is so general in those countries that the practice of it is esteemed a point of honor, particularly in the small towns; and when a stranger arrives and continues his residence there for some time without having adopted the customs of the country, his continence is attributed not to a principle of virtue, but to the passion of avarice, as it is generally supposed that he lives so in order to save money.

(Juan and Ulloa's *Secret Report*, 1749)

THUS DID THE SPANISH SAVANTS Jorge Juan and Antonio de Ulloa, fresh out of university, expose what they regarded as public immorality during a 1736–1744 journey through South America. Juan and Ulloa had been sent by Spain's first Bourbon king, Philip V, to accompany a French expedition to measure the curvature of the Earth at the equator. Despite their training and participation in scientific experiments, Juan and Ulloa were sent to spy on colonial Spanish Americans. Their book-length *Secret Report*, quoted here, is a scathing catalog of abuses of power by priests, officials, and creole landowners, plus a detailed exposé on contraband trade and weak coastal defenses.

Corruption, contraband, concubinage – all were symptoms of an empire that appeared to be sick and decrepit. Inspired by their French cousins after Louis XIV, and threatened by the rising power of Great Britain, Spain's Bourbon kings would spend most of the eighteenth century attempting to rehabilitate their overseas holdings in hopes of making Spain rich and powerful again. Portugal would embark on a similar reform program in Brazil after 1755, led by the Marquês de Pombal. The success of these reforms has been debated ever since, but the fact remains that, while Britain and France lost American colonies, Spain and Portugal held on to – and even expanded – their vast New World empires into the nineteenth century.

What had caused the breakdown identified by Juan and Ulloa? Were abusive officials, priests, and colonists really to blame for imperial decline, or was it more a matter of events – and of misperceptions – in Europe? The answer is, as might be expected, a mix of both. On the colonial side, as we saw in Part Three, Iberia's subsidiary "kingdoms" (New Spain, New Granada, the captaincies of Brazil, and so on) had grown increasingly independent during the colonial middle; creole elites had become highly adept at sidestepping rules intended to benefit the metropolis. Meanwhile, Europe's balance of power underwent radical changes. The rise of three new seaborne empires – those of the English, Dutch, and French – helped push the Iberian empires into crisis, one that culminated in 1700, when the Spanish king died without an heir and the British and French fought a war to determine who would sit on the Spanish throne. In the end it was Philip V, the French candidate, despite Britain's having won the war. By way of compromise, the Spanish agreed to allow Britain to take over the slave-trade monopoly and begin importing manufactured goods. A 1703 treaty with Portugal against France and Spain, meanwhile, allowed British merchants almost unlimited access to the newfound gold and diamonds of Brazil.

Spain suffered considerable losses during its many battles with the British, yet at the end of the eighteenth century, Spain retained far more of its American possessions than the British did, and silver production and tax revenues were higher than ever. Portugal likewise suffered humiliation and loss for seeking British protection against the Spanish and French, yet by the late eighteenth century, both Portugal and Brazil emerged revitalized, made hugely rich and relatively powerful by the rapid expansion of slave-based plantation agriculture and livestock ranching. In this chapter, we outline the global wars of the late-colonial period before discussing the ambitious and wide-ranging efforts by the Spanish and Portuguese crowns to improve the defense, efficiency, central control, and profitability of their empires. How colonial subjects responded is the subject of the two chapters that then follow.

Imperial Struggles

Some saw Spain's declining fortunes in the seventeenth century as a broad reflection of the Habsburg royal family's declining health. Kings Philip III and IV had suffered humiliating setbacks, but the so-called "bewitched" king, Charles II (1665–1700), seemed almost to embody imperial decline; he was chronically ill, almost mentally incompetent, and unable to produce an heir. Even so, Charles II's reign lasted thirty-five years, and at his death in 1700 Spain's American colonies were still regarded as the most valuable and populous of any held by Europeans overseas. The colonial population had begun to grow again, Spanish American silver was still supplying the world with hard money, and Spanish American consumers were purchasing increasing quantities of luxury imports.

Since Charles II died without an heir, his succession became an instant matter of international concern. Worried by the growing power and ambition of France's King Louis XIV, the English and Portuguese opposed Charles's designation of one of Louis's grandsons, Prince Philippe of Anjou, to succeed him. These and other enemies of Spain and France rightly feared a joint empire ruled by the French house of Bourbon, and war soon broke out. The War of the Spanish Succession carried on until 1713, and although the English, Portuguese, and other allies won, they did not manage to put their Habsburg candidate on the throne.

Under the terms of the Treaty of Utrecht, the Bourbon Philippe acceded and ruled as Philip V of Spain until 1746. In exchange, King Philip renounced any claim to the throne of France, yet the real cost of Bourbon succession was commercial, as English merchants, whose control of crown and parliament was becoming increasingly evident, won control of the coveted Spanish American slave trade contract (or asiento), along with a concession to supply some dry goods to colonists. The English exploited their new access to Spanish America's formerly closed markets to the hilt, introducing heaps of contraband merchandise as well as legally registered slaves. In the Río de la Plata estuary, Portuguese merchants won their own commercial concession: the Colônia do Sacramento, opposite Buenos Aires in present-day Uruguay. Colônia became a major gateway for contraband British goods and Brazilian ranch products, many of which made their way to Potosí and other interior regions of Spanish South America.

Yet the struggles were far from over. Portuguese and Dutch imperial power waned in the Atlantic before 1700, but Britain and France emerged stronger, both anxious to take advantage of the third great power in the region, Spain. The Spanish empire was rich, yet it was overstretched and badly managed, vulnerable on many fronts. It would remain at the center of struggles between Britain and France, usually with Portugal a British ally and Spain a French one, until 1815, when British forces defeated Napoléon. Amid what became increasingly global Anglo-French wars, revolts and revolutions also grew more common and more severe, challenging all of the major European empires from within. The most serious revolts occurred between the mid-1770s and early 1820s. Key among them were the American War of Independence from Great Britain, the French Revolution, the slave rebellion of Saint-Domingue that resulted in Haitian independence, and finally the Latin American independence wars on the mainland. Some historians characterize this period as the "age of Atlantic revolutions."

Continued British contraband trading to Spanish America after the War of the Spanish Succession erupted into open conflict in 1739. The resulting War of Jenkins' Ear (named for smuggler Robert Jenkins, who fell afoul of Spanish patrols and lost an ear) lasted until 1748, translating into the War of Austrian Succession. Less than a decade later, British and French hostilities

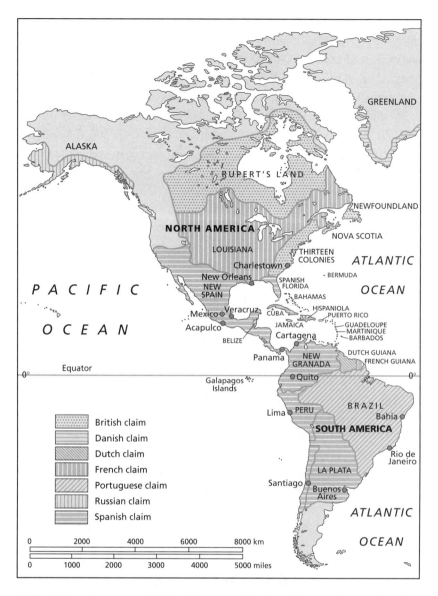

Map 13.1
Competition for
the Americas in the
Eighteenth Century

in North America expanded into the most global and destructive war thus far, the Seven Years' War (1756–1763). The war ended in victory for the British, who won major concessions from the French in the Caribbean, India, and Canada. Spain, which had only decided to enter the war on the side of France in 1762, bore much of its cost as well. Although later returned, the vital Spanish ports of Havana and Manila fell quickly to British naval forces, which also controlled Puerto Rico and the greater part of the Caribbean basin.

Having learned to patrol the Atlantic by fighting pirates in the decades after the Treaty of Utrecht, the British Royal Navy posed a major threat to the Spanish American empire by the 1740s. As illustrated in In Focus 13.1, Admiral Vernon's Siege of Cartagena during the War of Jenkins' Ear anticipated the much more successful seizure of Havana, then all of Cuba, during

DELENDA EST CARTHAGO

The following excerpt is the final two paragraphs of a report written by a British naval officer on board the fleet that sailed to the Caribbean in 1740. The following spring the British fleet laid siege to the Spanish port city of Cartagena, on the Caribbean coast of what is now Colombia (shown on the next page in this contemporary British illustration). As the report remarks, the British deemed the campaign a failure because they were forced to withdraw after two months of fighting; the excerpt illustrates how disease continued to play a role in military encounters in the Americas throughout the colonial period:

The Rains now coming on apace, & the sickness among the Forces increasing dayly, it was thought adviseable to get out to sea again, as fast as we could; therefore after having demolished all the Castles and Forts in the Harbour, upon the 6th of May the Admiral came out, being follow'd the next day by the Rear Admiral & the Commodore, who immediately sail'd for Jamaica, with about 5 or 6 Men of War, (the Transports together with the rest of the Fleet being sent away some time before,) where they arrived & came to an anchor in Port Royal Harbour upon the 19th of May 1741.

And thus ended this unlucky expedition, which in all probability would have succeeded much better, if we had either push'd our Fortune immediately upon our first landing under Madra la Papa, at which time the Enemy was not so well prepar'd for us; or else had not grounded our Hopes of Success so much upon the Behaviour of the Spaniards, as to think they would retire upon our first approach, as they had done before; who were now too well fortified and entrench'd; to be any ways intimidated with either the number or even the uncommon Resolution and Bravery of the Troops, that went upon this Fatal Attack. However, notwithstanding we have been so unfortunate as not to succeed agreeably to our Wishes, which (I believe verily) was more owing to that unavoidable sickness, that reign'd equally amongst the Sea as well as the Land Forces, than to any misconduct in our Commanders; (for the Place would not have been left so, had our Forces continued in Health;) yet we have this satisfaction, to consider, that what with the Forts and Castles that we demolish'd, & the ships & other smaller vessels, which they themselves destroy'd, the Spaniards have sustained more damages than they will be able to repair these Twenty Years; their loss being computed at above a Million of money.

Despite the unfortunate end to the siege (from the British viewpoint), the report ends on a cautiously triumphant note, one that – with the benefit of hindsight – resonates prophetically. The report's subtitle is *Delenda Est Carthago*; this Latin phrase, more properly *Delenda Cartago Est*, "Carthage is no more," is a reference to the decisive Roman destruction of the North African city of Carthage, for which Cartagena was named. The British naval officer's prediction that the Spaniards would not recover from the siege for two decades is supported by two appendices to the report. In the first appendix, the officer lists the total numbers of ships and their guns held by the British and Spanish in the Caribbean as of the spring of 1741. Having sunk twelve enemy ships and having lost none themselves, the British outnumbered the Spanish so comfortably, by thirty-five ships to sixteen, that they were able to send ten vessels back to European waters. Their subsequent advantage of twenty-five to sixteen gave them a parallel advantage of 1,580 onboard guns to the 1,090 on Spanish ships.

DELENDA EST CARTHAGO, *continued*

The second appendix to the British account of the 1740–1741 siege is a translation of an intelligence report taken from a Spanish officer during the Cartagena siege; it details the defensive capacity of the Cuban port city of Santiago, revealing precisely how and where the British might take the city and seize the island. In the end, it was not Santiago but Havana that the British would take – a more decisive means of capturing the Spanish colony. That event would take place twenty-one years later.

Figure 13.1. Credit: A Prospect of the Town and Harbour of Carthagena, taken by the English under the brave Admiral Vernon, 1741 (engraving) (b&w photo) by English School (18th century). Private Collection/ The Bridgeman Art Library [Image # XJF 105408]

the Seven Years War. The worst Dutch corsair attacks in the seventeenth century, including Piet Heyn's taking of the silver fleet in 1628, seemed insignificant when compared to the taking of Havana. A humiliated Spain gave up Florida to the British in 1763 in order to win Cuba back. What followed was something of a surprise. As if invigorated by the loss, Cuba roared into the next century, becoming the Caribbean's most important sugar producer. During their brief occupation, the British had introduced economic reforms and thousands of enslaved Africans, giving Cuban planters incentives to follow the British model established in Jamaica. Ironically, the British would condemn the very system they helped create after 1808, when the Royal Navy took up the task of suppressing the transatlantic slave trade.

Britain's string of successes was rudely interrupted by the war for U.S. Independence. This struggle, lasting from 1775 to 1783, resulted in part from colonist discontent over having to help pay debts accrued during the hugely costly Seven Years' War. British officials responded to a string of anti-tax revolts in the thirteen colonies with increasing intransigence and excessive force, which in turn helped give birth to a full-blown independence movement. Happy to see Great Britain rejected by many of its own colonists, the French stepped in to help out the struggling Anglo-Americans in 1778. They were joined by Spain in 1779, and together these old foes of the British helped guarantee U.S. Independence. A jubilant Spain regained Florida.

The meaning of the American Revolution was just beginning to sink in when a new revolution in Europe broke out. Beginning in 1789, Bourbon rule collapsed in France amid widespread popular protests, violent power struggles, and ultimately regicide. It was when the Revolutionary government executed King Louis XVI and his wife Marie Antoinette in 1793 that traditional foes Britain and Spain declared war on France. Conflicts in the late 1790s propelled the able military leader Napoléon Bonaparte to power in France, and soon he embarked on the largest imperial project Europe had experienced since the early Spanish Habsburgs. For Spanish Americans, Napoléon's 1808 seizure of Spain was a game-changing event. Napoléon's brother Joseph occupied the Spanish throne until 1814, and in the interim many Spanish American colonists began to fight for independence. Thanks largely to British military efforts, Ferdinand VII regained the Spanish throne in 1814, and Napoléon was defeated and neutralized in 1815, but the die had been cast: Spain's American colonies, having had a taste of self-rule, would not return to the imperial fold. The French Revolution's effect on the hugely profitable sugar colony of Saint-Domingue, meanwhile, was even more profound. At first promised freedom, then denied it, Haiti's many thousands of slaves rose up and drove out their French masters beginning in 1791 (we return to this story, and that of independence among the Iberian colonies, in Chapter 15).

The Problem of Defense

International conflicts grew in scale and global reach after 1700, creating new problems of defense for Spain and Portugal and their overseas colonies. The colonies, already vast and now growing in population, had to be defended on many fronts. The middle-colonial scourge of pirates gave way to more organized naval attacks on ships and ports, increasingly led by the British Royal Navy. Traditional internal enemies, mostly unconquered indigenous groups and a few maroon communities, became worrisome as potential allies with European competitors, especially in frontier regions such as Texas. A third threat, internal rebellion in core areas, manifested itself in the form of urban riots, slave revolts, and finally mass indigenous and mixed-race peasant uprisings in the countryside. The Spanish and Portuguese crowns developed a range of new defense policies to meet these shifting challenges, but all were costly, and all relied on raising taxes, which inevitably bred new discontent.

Defensive weaknesses in both the Spanish and Portuguese colonies were revealed by the War of the Spanish Succession. The French and British were more powerful and organized than ever before, and protection now required massive upgrades in fortifications, ships, and armaments, along with the creation of salaried standing armies and navies. The Spanish were most vulnerable, now that they had a Bourbon monarch, but the Portuguese, who increasingly cast their lot with Great Britain, learned of their own weaknesses after French forces seized Rio de Janeiro in 1710–1711. Still, the Spanish had many more fronts to cover, including the vast Pacific coast from Tierra del Fuego to Alta California, plus the annual treasure ships plying between Acapulco and Manila. The so-called South Sea (the Pacific) was not easily penetrated at first, but Spanish vulnerability was made clear by the 1709–1711 voyage of English privateer Woodes Rogers, who managed to seize a silver-laden Manila galleon off the coast of Mexico. Rogers had also taken and ransomed Guayaquil, the main port of the Audiencia of Quito. Such humiliating losses prompted Spanish officials to demand that local citizens supply garrisons and pay for new fortresses. By far the most expensive projects, paid for by colonial subjects living mostly in the highland interior, were the stone ramparts protecting Caribbean ports such as Veracruz, Havana, and Cartagena. Cartagena's enormous fortresses, one of which approached the scale of a pre-Columbian pyramid, proved their worth when the forces of "ye Brave Admiral Vernon" (see In Focus 13.1) attacked in 1741. Fortifications were re-designed by military engineers for dozens of Spanish ports, including Lima, Portobello, Manila, Cádiz, and La Coruña. Most fortresses located in the tropics were built by enslaved Africans and defended by militiamen of color.

Defense sucked up revenues in other ways. The Spanish moved quickly to modernize shipbuilding, weapons manufacture, and officer training. Established shipyards in Manila, Guayaquil, and Havana, along with the older ones of San Sebastián, in the Spanish Basque country, were revamped and expanded. New sources of timber were sought elsewhere. Portuguese demand for worm-resistant Brazilian hardwoods grew so high in the eighteenth century that colonial officials had to step in to slow deforestation. Portuguese and Spanish naval architects mostly copied French and English designs rather than innovating, and the Iberians were forced to play catch-up in almost every other technological realm, from cartography to navigational instrument manufacture. Spanish cannons, used to defend ports and ships of the line, were mostly founded in Seville's expanded and improved bronze works. Colonial artisans, meanwhile, were called upon to produce ever larger quantities of small arms, including muskets, shotguns, and pistols. Since many such artisans were not up to date on the latest designs and lacked access to the best materials, handgun quality was inconsistent and a source of frequent complaint. Gunpowder, a royal monopoly, was produced in expanded factories all over the colonies. The Latacunga factory, in present-day Ecuador, was typical in that it still relied on indigenous draft labor despite updates in plant and other investments. Finally, the Spanish and Portuguese established new French- or British-style military academies to train professional officers.

Spanish and Portuguese defense ministers sent newly trained officers to organize and oversee what were formerly motley groups of local, self-taught militias. In the Spanish colonies there were no standing armies prior to 1767, but the new officer corps managed to assemble near-permanent defense forces made up largely of black and free-colored soldiers who found a new means of social advancement through military service (see In Focus 13.2). Creole Spanish companies were also recognized, but most remained in the highlands or interior and rarely saw action except during urban riots and other internal tumults. Some paid troops were sent to pacify Brazil's mining districts in the first decades of the eighteenth century, but the much larger problem of coastal defense generally relied on incentives to locals. Militiamen, most of them black, defended thousands of miles of Atlantic coastline from the mouth of the Amazon to the far southern outpost of Colônia do Sacramento.

One Spanish innovation was the use of Catholic missions as bases for frontier defense. This was most notable in North America, although some missions in the Amazon and Paraná basins functioned similarly. In Texas, the Spanish built San Antonio in 1718 as a mission hub and base for defense against French encroachments from the Lower Mississippi. The Franciscan missions of Alta California, from San Diego to San Francisco, were also linked to presidios, or defensive outposts manned by small garrisons. The Jesuits ran missions and forts in Arizona and Baja California, but these were taken over by the Franciscans after the 1767 expulsion of the Jesuit Order. The northern Spanish missions and presidios rarely faced foreign attackers. Instead, they largely served to protect native converts against their nonsedentary neighbors. Of particular concern in Texas and northern Mexico were the Commanches, who some historians argue were building an empire of their own based on horse raiding and captive-taking. Frontier life remained precarious, and the threat of indigenous raids and geographical isolation made it difficult for missionaries and colonial officials to entice settlers to migrate north from more central, if economically moribund regions of Mexico.

IN FOCUS 13.2

Figure 13.2. AGI, MP-Uniformes, 83 – Campeche. Pardos Tiradores. © Spain. Ministry of culture. Archivo General de Indias.

COLONIAL LATIN AMERICA'S BUFFALO SOLDIERS

In the late-nineteenth-century United States, "Buffalo Soldiers" was the name given to all-black army units. Centuries earlier, similar units had been formed in Brazil and much of Spanish America, where black and free-colored men served as volunteers or conscripts in the colonial militias. Some were cooks, messengers, or coastal lookouts, but most served as soldiers. The heyday of the black and mulatto militias was the period from the early seventeenth to the late eighteenth century, when such units received privileges such as tax exemption and were led by their own officers – for whom service was an avenue of upward mobility. From Spanish New Orleans to Guatemala and Buenos Aires, thousands of free blacks and free coloreds found militia service to be an avenue of social betterment. The importance of these units to colonial defense allowed colored soldiers to turn militia service into a catalyst for change and a basis for community identity.

The reforms that followed the British capture of Havana in 1762 and other Spanish losses in the Seven Years' War led to an expansion and professionalization of colonial forces. Soldiers of many colors learned to march in step, wear uniforms, and fire on demand. For example, in 1767, don Cristóbal de Zayas, the governor of Yucatán, formed a new regiment of free-colored militia infantry and fusiliers; their uniforms and equipment are depicted here. They received the same modest salary as white soldiers did.

Beginning in the 1760s, colored companies also started to be taken over by white officers, and many were disbanded completely in the 1790s. Yet when revolt and civil war came to the Spanish colonies in the 1810s, men of African descent fought on both sides. In 1813, the Yucatec intellectual and politician José Matías Quintana applauded "the fidelity, patriotism, and notorious virtue of the esteemed *pardos* [free-colored men]," who in fighting against the rebels sought "no salary or remuneration other than the honor and pleasure that great souls enjoy in serving their beloved country with fidelity."

The Crisis of Corruption

The Spanish and Portuguese crowns, weakened by numerous challenges during the colonial middle, had inadvertently encouraged corruption. Mostly this was a result of farming out authority and even auctioning public offices to raise emergency funds, but corruption took many forms, including tax evasion, contraband trade, nepotism, and embezzlement. As Juan and Ulloa described in scathing detail, by the early eighteenth century, royal officials at the highest levels routinely abused their power and enriched themselves at the king's expense. The fact is, the colonies were still viewed as something of an El Dorado for aspiring courtiers and men of letters. Although not entirely modern, the Spanish bureaucratic system as designed by the Habsburgs did employ checks and balances, including investigative mechanisms such as the *residencia* (an investigation into a viceroy or governor's term of office, conducted by a judge appointed by the crown) and the *visita* (a bishop's or inspector's tour of the parishes – and priests – of an episcopate).

In truth, the seemingly stone-clad system was riddled with points of entry for ambitious and avaricious individuals bent on self-enrichment. The largest of these holes in the system was in fact built in – a result of the crown's chronic dependence on tax-collecting subcontractors, the sale of bureaucratic posts, and the auctioning of monopolies on everything from playing-card sales to administration of the cockfight. As is true today, subcontracting of core government duties entailed a general decentralizing of authority and thus carried few incentives for professional, disinterested conduct among bidders. A cash-strapped crown thus all but encouraged malfeasance, even as it denounced corruption with harsh decrees and occasional, exemplary punishments.

The sale of bureaucratic posts and crown monopolies soon augmented the power of locally born elites, people who had since the days of the conquistadors been banned from high office. By the late seventeenth century, creoles (American-born Spaniards) could be found in the highest ranks of church and state bureaucracy – and the interests they protected were more often local ones than those of the distant king. Merchants and mine owners found myriad ways to avoid the many taxes and duties the crown demanded. Mafia-like family networks emerged in many places, with contacts or "plants" in government, the commercial sector, landholding, and key church organizations. A sister in a convent or a brother in the priesthood could provide emergency access to credit, just as an uncle in royal government might provide a convenient pardon for some wayward son's "excess" or peccadillo. In similarly clever ways, merchants found numerous means to avoid official ports of entry – and thus avoid customs offices – trading openly or secretly with the Dutch, French, English, and others in the Río de la Plata estuary and along various points of the Caribbean coasts of New Granada and Central America. The Spanish imperial system was something one learned to work around as much as within.

The Portuguese in Brazil had long dealt with similar problems, but they were greatly exacerbated by the discovery of gold and diamonds after 1695. Contraband trade and corruption exploded, and the crown responded with a host of stop-gap control measures, many of them unpopular or impossible to enforce. All trade to the mines was supposed to go through specified towns and along official roads outfitted with inspection stations. Mining taxes were to be collected at royal smelters, and mine owners, merchants, and even slaves were encouraged to denounce neighbors thought to be defrauding the crown of its revenues. Individual peddlers and, most drastically, the monastic religious orders were entirely banned from the gold and diamond districts. New mints and treasury houses were established, and royal authority shifted to Rio de Janeiro in hopes of keeping tabs on overall production. Rather than improve governance and reduce corruption, however, all these measures simply made the new administrative offices of Minas Gerais and Rio the most valuable plums in the empire for corrupt Portuguese officials. The diamond mines were particularly lucrative, as they fell to a single royal contractor who agreed to pay the king a set fee in exchange for virtually unlimited control of the flow of gems.

The Pombaline and Bourbon Reforms

It was precisely in the age of change that the Spanish and Portuguese crowns set out to address problems of corruption and contraband trade, along with the issues of defense discussed already. These changes were part of a larger reform effort affecting both the home countries of Spain and Portugal and their overseas colonies. In the Spanish world, these efforts were known as the Bourbon reforms (after the dynasty that ruled the Spanish Empire after 1700). The early Bourbon reforms focused mostly on the related problems of coastal defense and contraband trade, but after the Seven Years War ended in 1763 the Bourbons enacted a much more ambitious program encompassing curbs on church power, appointment of Spanish-born officials to new colonial offices, the raising of tributes and a host of other taxes, and the improving of mining output. The Portuguese were already engaged in similar projects of centralization and revenue raising, most of them put forth after the 1755 Lisbon Earthquake by the Marquês de Pombal, the Portuguese minister under King José I (1750–1777). Historians thus refer to Portuguese efforts as the Pombaline Reforms.

Despite the weaknesses made apparent during the War of the Spanish Succession, the empires of Spain and Portugal proved remarkably resilient – and loyal. Colonial conservatism was on the side of the crown. Yet new fracture lines soon appeared. Why? In part because of a widening identity gap between Peninsulars and Creoles. Most Iberian reformers were educated men inspired by the Enlightenment, an intellectual movement that embraced scientific principles of rationality and practicality but distrusted the Catholic

Church, which was seen as overly powerful and an obstacle to change. Reformers also believed in mercantilism, a kind of economic nationalism that treated colonies as mere milk cows for the mother country, not semi-autonomous "kingdoms" as under the Habsburgs. By the later eighteenth century it was clear that many reforms were working as planned, yet few colonial subjects felt they had benefited. Native peoples were more heavily taxed in the Spanish colonies than ever before, and black slavery was vastly expanded in Brazil. Small-scale alcohol and tobacco producers were largely driven out of business, and hundreds of beloved Jesuit priests were exiled from cities, farms, and missions. Some local elites benefited from mining reforms, but many more lost offices and commercial autonomy after the creation of monopoly companies. To boot, European intellectuals began to claim that there was scientific proof that living in the American tropics caused mental and moral degeneration.

Sebastião Carvalho e Melo, better known as the Marquês de Pombal (1699–1782), became Portugal's prime minister in 1750. Intelligent, charismatic, and often ruthless, he would leave a deep imprint in both Portugal and Brazil. The city of Lisbon, whose layout and architectural style Pombal thoroughly altered after a devastating 1755 earthquake, survives as a testament to his reformist will. Portugal in 1750 was a marginal European country with an incredibly extensive but relatively weak and unprofitable overseas empire. Brazil was an exception, but the Braganza royal family used its gold and diamond revenues for palace construction and other luxuries. The trade deficit with Great Britain, a close ally since 1703, was gaping. With Brazilian income diminishing, Pombal set out to revamp the entire imperial system with the aim of lifting Portugal out of economic decadence and dependence on Britain. The plan was to modernize Portugal in a way resembling British industrial policy while making certain that Brazil supplied Portuguese merchants with as many raw materials as possible and also consumed home-country manufactures. Brazil was to be utterly dependent on Portugal.

Partly on the advice of his brother, who served in the Brazilian colonial administration, Pombal moved quickly and decisively to fix what he saw as a range of problems. First, he eliminated remaining vestiges of the donatary captaincy system and carved up portions of Brazil into manageable administrative units resembling French departments. Each was headed by an official who reported directly to Pombal. Second, in 1763, he moved the capital from Salvador to Rio de Janeiro, a reflection of the colony's southern shift after the gold rush but also a means of breaking down local colonial power structures. The colonial economy fell under the purview of the new Junta do Comércio (Board of Trade), created in Lisbon in 1755. Tax collection was further centralized in 1767 with the creation of the Junta da Fazenda (Board of Treasury), which monitored state revenues down to the provincial level. The head of each junta was responsible for producing an assessed amount of revenue for the crown and had to report back to the central Board of Trade. Monopoly trading companies, a fashion among Europe's imperial powers at the time, were formed to extract resources and plant new slave-produced crops in the Amazon basin and Pernambuco, and also to render whale oil along Brazil's huge coast. Inspired by French economic thinkers, Pombal sought to seize upon Brazil's full potential for tropical agriculture. He encouraged production of new export crops such as cotton, rice, and indigo, and also called for experimentation with new strains of tobacco and sugar, Brazil's traditional export crops. Monitoring was in the hands of new inspection boards in the Amazon, northeast, and in Rio. The slave trade from both Upper Guinea and West Central Africa was greatly expanded, and slavery was even abolished in Portugal itself to ensure that no slave might be spared the rigors of plantation or mine work in Brazil. By the time he fell from power in 1777, Pombal had succeeded in tightening Portugal's control over its most important colony, and in sucking as much revenue as possible from it. He had also succeeded in enriching a number of favorite families in Portugal, which looked a lot like the old corruption, and helped bring about his ouster.

Brazilian society was affected by the Pombaline reforms in several ways, not all of them negative. In the realm of defense, Pombal's creation of civic militias led to new avenues of status gain, sometimes for men of color, but also for Portuguese creoles and recent immigrants. Some bandeirante units took on a more formal military character as they attacked indigenous rebels and maroons in the backcountry. In terms of the Catholic Church, Pombal saw problems at many levels, but he focused his anger on the Jesuits, whom he regarded as particularly arrogant challengers to crown authority. He resented Jesuit control over indigenous populations in both Amazonia and the far south, and after suspending missions near the Paraguayan border he exiled the entire Jesuit order from Brazil – and the whole Portuguese empire – in 1759. Jesuit schools and universities were placed under state control, and an overall curriculum shift away from theology toward science and practical concerns was soon evident. Pombal also stripped the church of legal authority, instituting a more secular code of justice and diminishing the power of the Inquisition. Some of Pombal's reforms were undone after his fall, and increasingly powerful Brazilians managed to challenge centralized authority, yet overall the Pombaline project revealed how vital Brazil was to Portugal's revival. By the end of the eighteenth century, thanks to slave-based tropical agriculture, Portugal could boast a trade surplus with Great Britain.

Beginning with Philip V, Spain's Bourbon kings enacted a similar range of reforms aimed at improving defenses, raising revenues, and centralizing authority. Since Spain's American colonies were far more scattered and extensive than Brazil, some early Bourbon reforms focused on more efficient administration. This entailed creating new jurisdictions and staffing colonial posts with trained professionals rather than favorites or those who could afford to

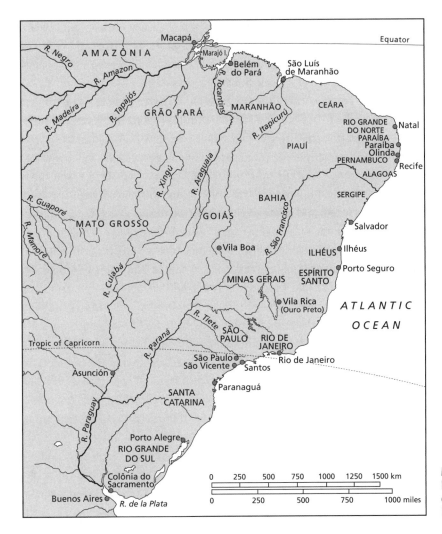

Map 13.2
Brazil in the Age of the Pombaline Reforms

purchase them. The huge viceroyalty of Peru was successively carved up, first with the 1739 creation of the viceroyalty of New Granada, with its capital in Bogotá, and then in 1776, with the creation of the viceroyalty of the Río de la Plata, with its capital in Buenos Aires. Officials and merchants in Lima were particularly upset by this second split, which gave Buenos Aires control over the great silver mines and mint of Potosí. Also in 1776, the Bourbons created a *comandancia general* (high command) for New Spain's northern frontier, a vast territory called the Provincias Internas (Interior Provinces) that included the Californias, New Mexico, Texas, and what are today's Mexican border states. Regions of growing economic importance, but traditionally distant from viceregal authority, such as Guatemala and Caracas, became somewhat autonomous captaincies general. Last was the so-called intendancy system. First tried in Cuba after the Seven Years War, the Bourbons began to apply this French bureaucratic model in the 1780s to the mainland viceroyalties. Old, often-corrupt corregidores and their jurisdictions were replaced with crown-appointed intendants (*intendentes*) and their newly mapped intendancies. Intendants collected revenues, reported on the problems and potential of their jurisdictions, and oversaw defense. Increasingly, defense was against unhappy colonial subjects made to pay more taxes.

Intendants and corregidores (where these latter remained before the transition to the new system) became lightning rods for indigenous discontent, partly because they were visible, but also because they made ever-greater demands on struggling communities. Indigenous caciques and governors clashed with these officials over tribute collection, labor drafts, and other old but now ramped-up impositions. A few intendants and corregidores were physically attacked, and many were vilified and driven from office. Colonial elites resented them because most were Spanish-born, and not only did they have no desire to protect local interests, they blocked creoles from entering the colonial administration. Some creoles benefited from increased Bourbon spending on defense, but most felt only the burdens of higher taxation and increased labor costs driven in part by the demands of fortress-building and other public works projects. Some resentful creoles began to question Bourbon authority more generally, especially when they seemed to be giving up more and more in the name of defense and receiving nothing but scorn in return. Their increased military training also fostered confidence, and ultimately helped staff the independence struggle. Well before that, the creole militia of Buenos Aires proved its mettle in 1806, driving the British out of the city after it was allowed to fall by a cowardly viceroy.

The Spanish Bourbons also sought to increase their empire's economic output, but their task was far bigger and more complex than that faced by Pombal in the case of Portugal and Brazil. Spanish America had inherited a far more cumbersome bureaucracy and an ossified commercial system, both of which encouraged corruption, tax evasion, and smuggling. The challenge as the Bourbons saw it was to encourage economic growth in every possible colonial sector without sacrificing control over either colonial products or markets, all for the good of Spain. The old monopoly system, by which all trade was required to pass through the central Casa de Contratación (House of Trade) in Spain, was slowly widened, but not dismantled. This was still highly protective mercantilism by modern standards, but a 1765 free-trade act opened nine Spanish ports to direct trade with the colonies. Goods no longer had to pass through the Seville clearinghouse, but all trade had to be licensed and carefully recorded. In another small gesture, colonists were allowed to trade with one another after 1774. The free-trade act of 1778 opened even more possibilities, allowing twenty-four American ports to receive Spanish goods as long as they maintained a customs house and submitted thorough records along with revenues. Last, Spain's labyrinthine commercial tax structure was simplified by a shift to a flat 6 percent tax on the appraised value of all goods. Bourbon commercial reforms represented a move toward liberalization, but

Map 13.3
Spanish America in the Age of the Bourbon Reforms

they remained well behind the actions of enterprising Spanish and colonial merchants who sought to take advantage of new trading opportunities.

Despite rapid growth in both Atlantic and global trade, particularly in the last quarter of the eighteenth century, Spanish colonists could not trade directly with foreigners without facing prosecution. By law, Spanish trade with the Americas was to be carried out only in vessels built in Spanish yards and sailed by Spanish (or mostly Spanish) crews. All official documents, including bills of sale, had to use stamped paper monopolized by the crown. Other royal monopolies included tobacco, alcohol, olive oil, salt, and playing cards, plus all gaming venues, including bull-fighting rings and cockpits. Bourbon trading companies were even older than those established in Brazil by Pombal. First was the Caracas Company, formed in 1728 to give Basque merchants control over the sale of Venezuelan chocolate. Later came the Havana Company (1740) and the Barcelona Company (1755), both similarly aimed at privileging Peninsular merchant interests. This preferential treatment of Spanish investors at the expense of colonial producers and merchants created a reservoir of resentment that later helped propel calls for independence. It was no accident that Simón Bolívar came from a family of Caracas cacao producers.

Although the Spanish Bourbons were never as rabidly anticlerical as Portugal's Pombal, they did follow his and Bourbon France's lead in trying to curb the enormous power and tap into the tremendous wealth of the Catholic Church. Most of the reforms came toward the end of the eighteenth century, and they included attempts to limit the number of men entering the priesthood through minimum-age requirements. The church, it was believed, was absorbing too many able young men. The most controversial interventions came in the first years of the nineteenth century, when the Napoleonic crisis in Spain led the Bourbons to confiscate church real estate and call in millions of pesos' worth of church-funded private mortgages. Even colonists who resented church power howled in protest.

An earlier shock came in 1767, when the Bourbons followed Pombal's lead by expelling the Jesuits. Whereas the Jesuits in Brazil had long provoked mixed feelings among colonists, those of Spanish America were deeply enmeshed in colonial society and a considerable number of them came from creole families. Jesuit colleges and universities were numerous and venerable in Spanish America as well, and most creoles educated by them retained a certain respect for if not blind loyalty to the order. Indigenous groups living on fast-growing and sometimes profitable Jesuit missions, abundant in greater Paraguay and parts of frontier North America, also resented the expulsion, which left them vulnerable to land- and labor-hungry settlers and other foes. The only thing that calmed creole tempers after the expulsion was the cheap auctioning of confiscated Jesuit properties, which included thousands of enslaved Africans and their descendants, plus huge cattle ranches, textile works, and sugar estates.

* * *

Although Pombal and the Bourbons succeeded in achieving many of their goals, from improved defenses to more efficient revenue collection, they did so at the expense of nearly all of their colonial American subjects. Creole elites, especially in Spanish America, were shocked to see themselves excluded wholesale from government, military, and even religious posts, many of which they had gradually gained access to under Habsburg rule. Creole elites in Brazil were generally less perturbed only because they had rarely enjoyed such positions, but they shared the discontent of Spanish Americans when it came to taxes and monopoly trade privileges. Anger and alienation festered in numerous ports, mining towns, and capital cities. Added to this powder keg of colonial resentment was the effect of the new philosophical ideas of liberty, fraternity, equality, democracy, republicanism, and self-government that emerged from the American, Haitian, and French revolutions.

In the next chapter, we examine other aspects of late-colonial times – from the new gold boom to societal changes to rebellion in the Andes – before turning to independence.

SUGGESTIONS FOR FURTHER READING

For students doing research on the period of the reforms, a fine biography is *Pombal: Paradox of the Enlightenment*, by Kenneth Maxwell (1995). See also Dauril Alden's masterful *Royal Government in Late-Colonial Brazil* (1968). For the Spanish world, see Henry Kamen, *Philip V of Spain* (2001), and John Lynch, *Bourbon Spain, 1700–1808* (1989). On Caribbean smuggling, see Lance Grahn, *Smuggling in Eighteenth-Century New Granada* (1994), and Wim Klooster's extensive essay in Bernard Bailyn, ed., *Soundings in Atlantic History* (2009). For attempts to control smuggling in Brazil, see C. R. Boxer's classic *Golden Age of Brazil, 1695–1750* (1962); Kenneth Maxwell, *Conflicts and Conspiracies: Brazil and Portugal, 1750–1808*, 2d ed. (2005); and A. J. R. Russell-Wood, "The Gold-Cycle in Brazil," in *Colonial Brazil* (1987), edited by Leslie Bethell.

On mining reforms, see Enrique Tandeter, *Coercion and Market* (1993); John R. Fisher, *Silver Mines and Silver Miners in Colonial Peru* (1977); Anthony McFarlane, *Colombia before Independence* (1993); and David Brading, *Miners and Merchants in Bourbon Mexico* (1970).

On the scientific missions of the eighteenth century, including the one in which Juan and Ulloa participated, see Neil Safier, *Measuring the New World* (2008).

On Mexico's reformed eighteenth-century militias, see Christon Archer's classic, *The Army in Bourbon Mexico* (1977), and Ben Vinson, *Bearing Arms for His Majesty* (2001), and on Brazilian militias in the period leading up to independence, see Hendrik Kraay, *Race, State, and Armed Forces in Independence-Era Brazil* (2004).

GLOSSARY

Residencia and visita: official investigations into a viceroy or governor's term of office, or into the parishes of a bishop's episcopate or diocese

Intendente: a new office created under the Bourbon reforms; the intendant was responsible for military and financial affairs in a designated colonial region

Asiento: monopoly contract, granted by the crown, to sell African slaves in Spanish America

14

![decorative bar]

Late-Colonial Life

TIMELINE

1693: discovery of gold in south-central Brazil

1780–1784: Inca revivalists Túpac Amaru and Túpac Katari lead the Great Andean Rebellion

1781–1782: Comunero Revolt in New Granada (Colombia)

Long live the king! Down with bad government!

(Rebels' refrain, eighteenth century)

I N 1780, a crowd of female gold panners, most of them free women of color, attacked a Spanish tax collector in a small town not far from modern Medellín, Colombia. The official, stunned first by coarse insults and then a shower of rocks, wisely fled; and although he complained to his superiors about the "insolence," he recommended a temporary suspension of the new policy to collect head taxes in gold dust from independent miners. Before long, a huge portion of northern New Granada was swept up in a massive rebellion that became known as the Comunero Revolt, a wholesale rejection of Bourbon tax policy as it related to small-scale miners; weavers; tobacco farmers; and producers of sugarcane spirits, or aguardiente. The rebels' cry, quoted in the epigraph to this chapter, echoed throughout the Andes in these years. By 1781, after a failed march on Bogotá, several of the Comunero Revolt's alleged ringleaders were captured, tried, and executed. But Spanish officials knew that resentment of new policies ran deep and had not been simply stirred up by a few bad apples. The crown backed off.

As we saw in the previous chapter, in much of the Atlantic world, the eighteenth century came on with a bang, and change seemed to gather pace only as the century advanced. A new royal family, the House of Bourbon, came to the Spanish throne in the first decade of the century, and the discovery of major gold deposits in the Brazilian interior beginning in the 1690s promised to revive the long-embattled fortunes of Portugal. As a result of these changes, both of which coincided with the eclipse of the Netherlands and the rise of French-British rivalry, the Spanish and Portuguese hoped to return to their past glory. More than ever, Iberian monarchs turned to their American colonies to finance imperial recovery. Comeback was not easy. Recovery entailed at the very least profound administrative and jurisdictional reforms, coupled with and intended to finance expansion and professionalization of the military; as we saw in the previous chapter, the efforts we call the Bourbon and Pombaline reforms were ambitious, far-reaching, and often successful from the metropolitan perspective. All crown officials understood that imperial recovery in the face of British and French challenges depended on improved collection of taxes, tributes, and other colonial duties, preferably in gold or silver. As in the age of the Habsburgs, American treasure would once again constitute the sinews of war.

In the colonies, meanwhile, a number of profound changes were also under way. Populations were growing in both city and countryside, spurring the expansion of agricultural and livestock-raising enterprises and enabling the revival of the mining sector. Deadly epidemics of smallpox, influenza, and other diseases still cut through the colonies from time to time, and many lowland tropical areas remained permanently deadly. Yet the general trend was toward growth and adaptation. Most indigenous peoples had by this time acquired the same immunities as European immigrants, whereas most Africans and their descendants still possessed a unique acquired immunity to certain types of malaria.

In Spanish America, powerful hacienda and ranch owners increasingly bumped against and fought with indigenous subsistence farmers, who in turn increasingly struggled to meet the basic needs of their growing communities. In the language of Thomas Malthus (the effective founder of modern population studies in 1798), land pressures pushed and labor demands pulled; many rural folk who found subsistence farming difficult or impossible migrated to cities, mining camps, and, more often, haciendas and ranches, in search of a living. Migration in such hard times often entailed indebtedness, and it always entailed the search for a patron, someone who would protect you in exchange for your labor. Population growth in eighteenth-century Brazil, meanwhile, was mostly the result of (male) migration – in the form of enslaved Africans forcibly brought to mine gold and to revive the plantation sector, plus a wave of fortune-seeking immigrants from Portugal and the eastern Atlantic islands.

This chapter explores three late-colonial phenomena: the revival in gold and silver production; the changes in late-colonial society – including the evolution of regional American or "creole" identities; and the increase in levels of unrest, with the Great Andean Rebellion of the 1780s as a dramatic example.

Silver and Gold Return

In the seventeenth century, a combination of disease epidemics, overwork, malnutrition, and even administrative corruption had drastically reduced the number of natives available to pay tribute, mine for gold and silver, build roads and bridges, buy manufactured goods, and otherwise support

Figure 14.1. Virgin of the Mountain of Potosí, 1720. National Art Museum Collection – La Paz, Bolivia. Reproduced from "El Barroco Peruano, Volume 2" by Ramón Mujica Pinilla (Banco de Crédito, 2003), page 311, fig. 40.

THE VIRGIN OF POTOSÍ

In a painting from 1720 (preserved in the National Art Museum in La Paz, Bolivia), the Virgin Mary of the Mountain of Potosí is seen emblazoned on the hillside. By this date, however, her protection could not bring back Potosí's glory days of silver production; those had faded by the end of middle-colonial times, and in the eighteenth century, it was the Mexican silver mines that made Spaniards millionaires.

the Spanish imperial system and its lumbering mercantile economy. Population decline coincided with a profound crisis in the vast majority of Spanish America's famed mines – some flooded and collapsed; others played out; and in all but a few places, gold and silver yields dropped.

In the northern Andes, the turnaround began in the late seventeenth century with the conquest of Pacific lowlands, or Greater Chocó. As we have seen, beginning as early as the 1610s, a small cluster of wealthy families based in and around the towns of Popayán, Cali, and Pasto began to invest gains from the encomienda era in African slaves, whom they moved into increasingly remote, jungle mining frontiers all along the Pacific coast from modern Ecuador to Panama. Gold began to flow and stimulate commerce, much of it illegal and in the hands of foreigners based in Jamaica and Curaçao, but in any case, the forced colonization of the Pacific lowlands spearheaded a revival in Spanish America's mining fortunes more generally. Gold mining was soon revived in Chile, as well, but it was silver, Spanish America's most famous metal, that drew most attention and before long restored Spain's hope for the future.

The fabled Cerro Rico of Potosí and surrounding silver mines fell into decline in the later seventeenth century, but they were slowly replaced by the many and scattered silver districts of New Spain, among them the namesake San Luis Potosí. Mexican investors used crown-subsidized mercury from Spain to increase output, and also took advantage of the rebounding rural population to employ mostly free wageworkers, most of them mestizos and mulattos. As had become customary in Potosí, Mexican wageworkers demanded a share of production as compensation. When mine owners such as the Spanish-born Count of Regla attempted to reduce wages and cut mine workers out of their share of rich ores, violent strikes ensued. Regla responded by replacing many free workers with enslaved Africans, but few mine owners were wealthy enough to do likewise. The silver boom and the reformist mentality of the late eighteenth century encouraged attempts to build a paved road – a true *camino real*, or royal highway – from Mexico City to Veracruz, although the half-century-long project was still not finished when the Independence wars of the 1810s stopped all construction (see In Focus 14.2).

In desperate need of silver to finance their many projects, the Bourbons did everything they could to stimulate new discoveries and revive moribund mining districts in New Spain, Peru, and elsewhere. The crown lowered mercury prices, reduced taxes on gross production, established miners' credit unions, sent European metallurgists and mining engineers, and expanded or rebuilt mint facilities. Potosí's new mint, completed in 1773, was a shining example of Bourbon belief in this legendary district's revival. In the Andes, as in Mexico, labor was the main hurdle. Wageworkers were simply too free and costly for most investors' tastes. The crown responded to mine owners' demands by reviving the detested Potosí *mita*, which would eventually help spark the rebellions discussed later in this chapter.

Spanish America's gold mines, most of them alluvial, or riverbed diggings, presented different challenges. New Granada's many lowland tropical mines were staffed by enslaved Africans, and those of the dry regions of northern Chile by free mestizos and native men. Labor was expensive in both places, and draftees unavailable, so the crown responded by lowering gross production taxes to 3 percent by 1777. The crown was willing to do this in part because gold kept gaining in value against silver, and it tended to be taxed in commercial exchanges sooner or later anyway. Mints were built in Popayán and Santiago de Chile to turn gold dust into doubloons and other coins in hopes of stimulating investment and reducing contraband trade. The results of all these measures led to a steep rise in registered gold production, spiking just before 1800. The basic lesson the Bourbons learned, one that would be followed much more haphazardly in the Portuguese gold diggings of Brazil, was that taxing the trade generated by mining was wiser than taxing gross production. Mining was risky, labor was expensive, and important technical innovations were rare.

IN FOCUS 14.2

Figure 14.2. Vista De Jalapa, Carlos Nebel

THE PERILS OF THE HIGHWAY

Descriptions of travel within and between the Latin American colonies abound in expressions of fear and frustration. Thomas Gage, an Englishman who lived in Guatemala in the 1630s, wrote that the highway into the provincial capital of Santiago was full of perils. Escaped slaves and other bandits, complained Gage, "often come out to the roadway and set upon" the mule trains or carriages of unsuspecting travelers. Remarked another English visitor of his journeys by road in Mexico: "none but those who have traveled in a country like this, hungry and fatigued, having been constantly disappointed in the estimate of distance, and with expectation about to give way to a species of despair, can have a true conception of the nervous irritability which it produced." The comment was penned in 1825, when the journey from Mexico City to Valladolid in Michoacán – today a three-hour bus ride – took six to nine days. In the seventeenth and eighteenth centuries, journeys between major colonial settlements could take weeks. Before the late eighteenth century, the *camino real*, or royal road system, was more of an ideal than a reality, with many such highways "frequently nothing but a narrow and crooked path." Conditions were exacerbated by congestion, especially along the trunk lines or major trade routes; by 1700, thousands of mules were entering Mexico City every day. A protracted effort to build a fully paved highway from Mexico City to Veracruz was begun in 1757, but financing and labor problems dragged the project out until the 1810s, when it was cut short by war just shy of completion.

It was no better in the southern colonies, where llamas jostled with mule trains. For example, when the Andean rains came, the busy track from the port of Guayaquil up to the provincial capital of Quito

IN FOCUS 14.2

THE PERILS OF THE HIGHWAY, *continued*

notoriously turned into "the worst road in the world." Brazil was also plagued with poor roads, where they existed at all, but the "Caminho do Ouro," or "Golden Road," which climbed from the Atlantic coast over the Serra do Mar and into the highlands of Minas Gerais boasted many stone-paved sections by the mid-eighteenth century. Portions of this road can still be traveled by foot or horseback today.

This lithograph by Carlos Nebel from the end of the colonial period of the approach to the colonial Mexican city of Xalapa illustrates in the foreground the nature of most roads in colonial times. Even flatter, straighter roads (like the one leading into Xalapa in the lithograph) were often sandy, rocky, and potholed – and targeted by bandits like those that Gage had encountered.

Spanish America's eighteenth-century gold mining revival might have garnered more attention were it not for the much larger gold rush taking place in Brazil. Around 1693, an enslaved mulatto traveling with *bandeirantes* from São Paulo encountered dark metal flakes while panning a stream in the rugged highlands of south-central Brazil. The flakes – once smelted to remove the thin, dark outer layer – turned out to be gold. Almost overnight, a massive gold rush hit Brazil. It centered on a new town, the Vila Rica do Ouro Prêto, or the "Rich Town of Black Gold," named in 1720 as seat of the new captaincy of Minas Gerais, or "General Mines." Governing Minas Gerais in the early boom years was difficult. The district already counted thirty thousand slaves by 1720, and nearly as many young Portuguese men. Crime was rampant, and the tiny number of women combined with easy money promoted prostitution. Fights between Paulista discoverers and Portuguese "greenhorns" erupted into near civil war, prompting the crown to send in troops to keep order.

Following the example of Spanish mining law, the Portuguese crown set a flat 20 percent tax on all gold production, the so-called *quinto real*. A fifth was a huge cut, so most Brazilian mine owners and merchants practiced every possible subterfuge to avoid paying it. Whereas the Spanish had steadily reduced gold mining taxes as a means of encouraging production and discouraging fraud since the late Habsburg era, the Portuguese – less experienced in these matters – refused to drop the higher tax. Before long, however, declining revenues forced them to try other measures, including head taxes on slaves and yearly quotas for whole mining districts. Nothing seemed to work.

Like the Bourbons in Spanish America, the Portuguese also tried to halt losses by banning exchanges in gold dust. Legal tender consisted of gold bars inspected by royal officials and stamped with the crown seal, showing that taxes had been paid. Ouro Prêto's mint began to produce gold coins in the early 1720s, yet these were mostly exported and the problem persisted. In a nutshell, gold, even in the form of unrefined dust, worked reasonably well as money. Many exchanges in Minas Gerais thus remained outside crown control. To make matters worse, at least from the crown's perspective, corruption of incoming officials was rampant.

Where the Portuguese differed most from their Spanish American counterparts was in trying to control church involvement in the goldfields. The regular religious orders, including the powerful Jesuits, were entirely banned from Minas Gerais. There would thus be no similar abundance of monasteries, convents, and such like as found in Potosí or Zacatecas. Instead, Brazil's miners founded religious brotherhoods, or *irmandades*, which served as burial societies but also sponsored a kind of church-building and religious artistic tradition unique to Minas Gerais.

Gold mining on such a large and unprecedented scale also had a profound effect on Brazil's natural environment. Miners disturbed thousands of square miles of topsoil, permanently redirected streams and rivers, and cut extensive stands of timber. The subsistence needs of the miners led to even greater deforestation in order to run cattle and expand farms. There was little of the mercury or other heavy metal contamination typical of Spanish America's silver districts, but erosion was severe enough within a hundred miles or so of Ouro Prêto to make the core mining districts dependent on food produced as far away as São Paulo. A similar pattern, though on a smaller scale, followed the discovery of diamonds on the northern fringe of Minas Gerais around 1725. Although Brazil's mines began to play out in the mid-eighteenth century, the colony had already been radically transformed. The discovery of mineral riches in the interior stimulated mass migration, the slave trade, and numerous subsidiary colonial industries, from mule breeding to cloth manufacture. Brazil's famous coastal plantations would also be revived, but the colony's overall center of gravity had shifted south, made permanent in 1763 when Rio de Janeiro replaced Salvador as the viceregal capital.

Late-Colonial Social Change

A set of social transformations accompanied the political and economic changes that swept through Latin America in the eighteenth century, particularly after 1750. Demographic changes were among the most important.

For the first time since the Conquest era, the total population grew. Spanish and Portuguese migrants came in larger numbers than ever in the eighteenth century, but all other sectors of the population also expanded. More and more slaves were brought from Africa, and the free-colored population exploded as a result of increased miscegenation with Iberians,

mestizos, and natives. Indigenous numbers began to rise, too, at first tenta-
tively and haltingly in the seventeenth century but then steadily during the
eighteenth. Finally, the *casta*, or mixed-race, population of all kinds grew
dramatically. In short, Latin Americans were rapidly becoming greater in
number and variety.

How did these demographic trends specifically alter the colonies? For
one, the colonies looked more multiracial. As Brazil's population doubled
to 2 million during the eighteenth century, the greatest increases were
among free people of African descent (by 1800, Brazil comprised well
over a third African slaves, slightly less than a third free coloreds, slightly
less than a third Portuguese and other whites, and a small indigenous
minority). In the century before 1750, the population of New Spain grew by
more than 50 percent, a result more of *casta* than of native Mesoamerican
growth. By the turn of the nineteenth century, there were some 6 million
people in New Spain, about 140,000 of them in Mexico City (the largest
city in the Americas and larger than any Iberian city). The multiracial shift
was especially visible in the cities, big and small. Caracas, for example,
had grown to some thirty thousand inhabitants by 1750; Yucatan's capital
of Mérida was about half that size but getting bigger every year; so was
Buenos Aires, which grew so rapidly in the eighteenth century that it was
as populous as Caracas by the 1780s. In all cases, the mixed-race sector of
mestizos and free coloreds grew proportionately far faster than all other
sectors.

Another impact of the demographic transformation was the late-colonial
boom of areas that had earlier been marginal or peripheral, as reflected in
the growth of the provincial cities. Increasing demand in Europe for hides,
dyes, tropical beverages and medicines, and other American products
stimulated growth in these old peripheries, as did the opening of new ports
for official trade. Frontiers became more settled, and new frontiers were
created farther from the centers. Towns became small cities. Increases in the
variety and quantity of trade goods attracted more people, whose increasing
access to wealth in turn stimulated more commerce. Settlers from Mexico
migrated north into Texas, New Mexico, and California. In Brazil, in the
wake of the gold boom, the once sparsely settled southern coast became as
populous as the old sugar-oriented northern coast. Chile became a virtually
independent state.

Demographic changes also had a profound impact on social relations. The gap between rich and poor widened, especially in the cities and
towns. The wealthy were richer than ever, particularly in Mexico, where
the late-colonial silver boom accounted in part for the presence of more
than a hundred millionaire families (families whose assets came to more
than a million silver pesos, an astronomical sum). By contrast, the poor
underclasses grew larger in number and more underprivileged than

ever, especially in Mexico City, where thousands lived in destitution. The middle sectors in between the elite and the poor were increasingly varied and included less privileged Spaniards as well as Hispanized natives and free coloreds. Spaniards could be found among the poor, and people of quite dark complexion could be found among the rich. In other words, increasing socioracial complexity had slowly eliminated the original binary division of Spanish elite and indigenous subjects. Identity was most hotly contested, as happened frequently in late-colonial Quito, in cases where young men claiming to be mestizos had been identified by crown authorities, and even indigenous caciques, as "Indians." At stake for the crown was tribute income and free labor, and for the individuals claiming to be misidentified mestizos, lifelong freedom from those onerous obligations. In Quito, the courts tended to err on the side of granting "official" mestizo identity, as, according to one public defender, "color, Your Mercies, is but an accident of nature; who among us might not be taken for an Indian if dressed in their clothes?"

Concerned by pervasive miscegenation and what some "enlightened" Europeans claimed to be its debilitating effects, Spanish elites sought to distance themselves more and more from the rest of the colonial population. Efforts were made to stem the tide of social change and interaction by imposing new sumptuary (dress-code) restrictions and by mandating segregated neighborhoods in cities – all with little success (see In Focus 14.3). Although also motivated by snobbish curiosity, the late-colonial vogue for so-called *casta* paintings reflected elite anxiety over race mixing and a preoccupation with racial classifications (see In Focus 14.4). In the last decades of the eighteenth century, many took advantage of an edict called the Royal Pragmatic, which banned marriage between Spaniards and people of African descent. The ability of parents to control the marriage choices of their children had declined since the early colonial period – with couples claiming, and the church supporting, the right to free choice based on romantic affection. The Royal Pragmatic thus allowed a father, for example, to prevent his daughter from marrying an unsuitable suitor by accusing the young man of being a mulatto. In many (perhaps most) lawsuits involving this edict, the real issue at stake was money; for example, two women who stopped their sister from marrying a man in a small town in Yucatán in the 1790s, on the grounds that he was a mulatto, admitted that they objected to his lack of means and feared he would spend the modest fortune the three sisters had inherited from their father. The irony of this, like many such cases, was that the ancestry of the sisters themselves was probably not entirely Spanish. The more mixed the colonies became, the more the elite protested too much; by the late eighteenth century, trying to prevent mixed marriages was like closing the barn door after the horse had bolted.

LA TAPADA
(Seja y Manto)

Figure 14.3. a. Portrait of Manso de Velasco from Basílica Catedral de Lima. Photograph by Daniel Giannoni. Used with permission. **b.** Tapada image. From *Recuerdos de Lima* (1856). Image provided by Charles F. Walker.

COLONIAL FAULT LINES: THE AFTERSHOCKS OF THE LIMA EARTHQUAKE

In 1746, Lima was the largest and most important city in South America – a busy, wealthy metropolis and the viceregal capital of the Kingdom of Peru. On the night of October 28 of that year, it was all but destroyed by a massive earthquake. As terrified Limeños ran in the dark to the coast, a fifty-foot tidal wave completely wiped out the port town of Callao.

The earthquake-tsunami, its numerous aftershocks, and the subsequent outbreaks of disease, killed thousands and left tens of thousands homeless. The efforts by Viceroy Manso de Velasco (portrayed on the left) to rebuild the city exposed the fault lines in colonial society. The church and city elite fought to prevent the widening of city streets and banning of two-story houses, both of which would have reduced the scale of their properties. The disaster was widely believed to be a manifestation of divine wrath over Lima's "depraved customs" and excesses of baroque public life. Women in particular were scapegoated and their dress condemned – especially the *tapada*, which managed to be both revealing and dangerously disguising (see the image on the right). Meanwhile, a crime wave of looting, and native revolts both in the city and in the nearby countryside, underscored the limits of governmental authority at a time when the crown was hoping to increase its control over the colonies.

IN FOCUS 14.4

Figure 14.4. **a.** Casta painting containing complete set of 16 casta combinations (racial classifications in Spanish colonies in the Americas). Oil on canvas, 148 cm x 104 cm (58 1/4 inches x 40 15/16 inches). / Anonymous, Las Castas, 18th century. Oil on Canvas, 58 1/4″ x 40 15/16″. Museo Nacional del Virreinato, Tepotzotlán, Mexico. Reproducción Autorizada por el Instituto Nacional de Antropología e Historia. **b.** Credit: From a Spaniard and a Negress you a get a Half-Caste, from a Series on Mixed Marriages by Spanish School (18th century) Museo de America, Madrid, Spain/ The Bridgeman Art Library (Image # XJL 62185).

THE WISHFUL THINKING OF CASTA PAINTINGS

A genre of painting today called *casta* paintings (they had no genre name at the time) appeared in the 1720s in Mexico and remained popular through to the turn of the nineteenth century. They consisted of sets of twelve to sixteen panels, sometimes combined (as in the left-hand example from 1750) but usually separate, depicting mixed-race couples and their offspring, as well as local flora and fauna. Later mistakenly viewed as depicting a rigid caste system, the paintings in fact did almost the opposite. No such system existed; the paintings were an expression of wishful thinking on the part of the elite, who were disturbed by the pace of miscegenation and the lack of segregation. More than just phenotypical portraits, the paintings also sought to present social contexts – including cautionary messages on the supposed dangers of race mixing, such as the domestic violence between a Spanish man and black woman in the 1785 example (shown on the right).

The Inca Strikes Back

Theorists of revolution suggest that the gravest threats to colonial order come not during periods of neglect but rather when central authorities try to reassert their control and become more active in their overseas affairs. During the last decades of the eighteenth century – as the urban professional classes expanded in numbers, confidence, and economic power, and as indigenous villagers and enslaved Africans labored under increasing demands and brutal treatment – both the Portuguese and the Spanish crowns embarked on a most ambitious overhaul of their colonial system. "The road to hell," as the saying goes, "is paved with good intentions."

For all their good intentions, Iberia's newly energized central administrations tore apart the delicate balance that had existed between Europeans and their American subjects, and they worsened the already-tenuous socioracial balance in the colonies themselves. The pattern was repeated throughout Latin America. Imperial arrogance alienated urban creoles, who then made common cause with people of lower classes and different racial groups to oppose the one thing that together they grew to despise: foreign domination. Meanwhile, the lower classes tenaciously resisted the imposition of higher taxes, military conscription, and monopolies on tobacco and cane alcohol that destroyed their livelihoods. In the early eighteenth century, there were about fifty village riots in greater Mexico; between 1760 and 1820, there were more than a hundred such incidents of unrest, many of them organized and violent.

Throughout the colonial period, an excessive reliance on silver production in Mexico and Upper Peru (today's Bolivia) meant that other potential sources of wealth were left underdeveloped. There was little investment in agricultural or manufacturing sectors and entrepreneurial dynamism among the general population was not encouraged; in fact, the colonial administration's economic policies were restrictive and often outright destructive.

For example, when the Bourbon reformers created the viceroyalty of Río de la Plata in 1776, they reassigned the labor-rich region of Upper Peru to Buenos Aires's control. The Lima authorities were furious; in retaliation, they banned the importation of any goods that passed through Buenos Aires's port, thereby hurting their own local traders as well. The Lima elite had vast fortunes based in silver mines and ferociously protected their privileged status by trying to hold any change at bay. In the words of historian Timothy Anna, colonial Lima was characterized by "suspicion, name-calling, deep-seated personal feuds and rapacious ambition" (see In Focus 14.3). In more dynamic, less conservative places like Buenos Aires and Caracas, Enlightenment ideals of personal liberty and freer trade had a tremendous practical appeal; in Lima they were viewed with suspicion or indifference. Any pressure for change that was felt in colonial Peru was generated by the real poverty of its indigenous population and the creole Americans' growing resentment of bad local governance.

Although there had been intermittent revolts in rural areas throughout the colonial period, the first serious indication that the Spanish Empire in America was facing a mortal crisis came through a series of loosely connected events known as the Great Andean Rebellion. The uprising lasted from 1780 until 1784 and spanned half a continent, stretching from the northern part of what is today Argentina through Bolivia and Peru. Numerous uprisings erupted throughout the Andes and in New Spain in the late eighteenth century, most notably the 1780–1781 Comunero Revolt of New Granada

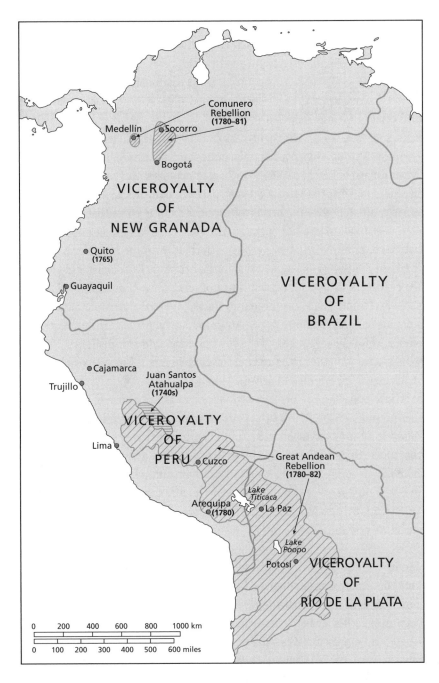

Map 14.1
Rebellion in the Andes

discussed at the start of this chapter. But the Great Andean Rebellion was fundamentally different from these other revolts because its leaders represented a nominally "Inca" but in reality multiracial, multiethnic, and cross-class agenda. The movement thus amounted to a broader rejection of the imperial order than anything that had come before.

The rebellion's most famous leader was José Gabriel Condorcanqui Túpac Amaru. Although rejected by the established and conservative Inca elites of Cuzco as an upstart, Condorcanqui claimed to be a descendant of pre-Hispanic Inca royalty. Whatever the truth of his ancestry, he held the prominent position of *curaca* (cacique, or dynastic ruler) of Tinta, a small town in the hinterland of Cuzco. Túpac Amaru (whose name means "resplendent serpent") married a petite, feisty woman named Micaela Bastidas who became his passionate love and a shrewd political collaborator; together they had three sons and amassed a significant personal fortune through their mule-train business. Through his official public duties and his private business ventures, Túpac Amaru built up a vast network of connections that later he used to mobilize forces against the corrupt Spanish government in Peru. As cacique, Túpac Amaru initiated several complaints on behalf of his constituents, including a request to eliminate use of the *mita* to work the mines, an imposition on native communities that was explicitly forbidden in the king's own Laws of the Indies (although long practiced in the breach). He also protested against the ever-increasing taxes (which hurt not just native Andeans but all Americans) and against bad government in the person of the venal new corregidor (regional colonial administrator), Antonio Juan de Arriaga. His petitions met with stony silence. Enraged by the corruption and gross injustice that he had witnessed among the crown's representatives in Lima, Túpac Amaru returned to his people determined to organize them in rebellion.

While Túpac Amaru began plotting against the presence of Spanish colonial administrators in his ancestors' domain, two other indigenous men raised the banner of revolt in separate but similar movements elsewhere in the Andes. One was Tomás Katari, the *kuraka* of Chayanta (in Upper Peru or Bolivia). The other, an Aymara commoner named Julián Apaza, who assumed the nom de guerre of Túpac Katari, emerged as a leader in the environs of La Paz. Like Túpac Amaru, both men protested both the burdensome tax structure and the arbitrary and cruel actions of their regions' corregidors.

When the corregidor Joaquín de Alos ordered Tomás Katari's arrest, despite a royal order that had expressly forbidden it, Katari's two brothers held Alos captive until their rebel sibling was released. Túpac Amaru and Tomás Katari theoretically remained loyal to the Spanish crown in the beginning, but they began their movements by criticizing the actions of its hated local representatives – the classic causes and strategies of late-colonial revolts. Túpac Katari, however, was more radical from the start. Just as in New Granada, "Long live the king! Down with bad government!" was a popular cry that could rally supporters from many ethnic groups, regions, and economic classes without seeming unduly radical.

Meanwhile, Túpac Amaru set his rebellion for November 4, 1780, a highly symbolic choice because that date also was King Charles III's birthday. On that Saturday, after sharing a sumptuous breakfast, the cacique Túpac Amaru suddenly stood up and arrested the corregidor Antonio Juan de Arriaga, symbolically reversing 250 years of colonial domination. Less than a week later, the unfortunate Spanish official was executed at Tungasuca in a spot the rebels called "the plaza of social justice." Acutely aware of the power of visual symbols, Túpac Amaru and Micaela Bastidas began to dress in clothing styled after pre-Hispanic royalty and demanded that the Inca Empire be restored to its legitimate leaders. On November 16, Túpac Amaru issued his famous Proclamation of Liberty, which freed the country's slaves. What had begun as an individual protest against localized political abuses quickly took on greater social, racial, and economic implications. A revolt, in other words, turned into a revolution.

Because of his enormous personal popularity and the responsive chord that his demands struck in the countryside, Túpac Amaru's movement spread quickly in all directions. It was as though a huge rural underclass had suddenly awakened to its power after more than two centuries of more or less quiet acquiescence. All racial groups in Peru could be found fighting under Túpac Amaru's standard – white creoles, native Andeans, mestizos, Afro-Andeans, and escaped slaves. He may, in fact, have had as many as ten thousand natives and up to a thousand creoles under his command within a few days. Colonial officials were initially caught off guard by the magnitude of the Great Andean Rebellion, but they recovered quickly and sent out a hastily assembled "Army of Pacification" to deal with the problem. Inca-descended nobles based in Cuzco who considered Túpac Amaru an upstart and a threat to their interests joined in the suppression. The military defeat of the rebels was swift. Tomás Katari was captured and executed on January 9, 1781. Túpac Amaru, Micaela Bastidas, one of their sons, and several friends and family members were executed soon after, on May 18, 1781 (see In Focus 14.5).

However, the reputation of the Andean rebels as freedom fighters, anti-imperialists, and redeemers of oppressed races has survived to the present day. In the highly charged political climate of the 1960s, Marxist urban guerrillas in Uruguay called themselves *Tupamaros* (and a future rap star was given the name Tupac Amaru Shakur by his African American activist mother). In late-twentieth-century Peru, the Movimiento Revolucionario Túpac Amaru (Tupac Amaru Revolutionary Movement) mounted a guerrilla insurgency in an effort to topple the central government and set up a socialist state.

Meanwhile, the execution of the revolt's main leaders failed to suppress resentments festering in the Andes of the 1780s. Far to the north in New Granada, crown officials faced off against the similarly mixed-race and multiclass rebels. More than sixty cabildos lodged protests over recently raised taxes, the imposition of new crown monopolies on tobacco and alcohol, and other intrusive aspects of the centralizing Bourbon reforms. Furthermore, in an effort to disgorge more funds from its overseas colonies, Spanish royal officials increased the tribute requirements levied on native communities;

IN FOCUS 14.5

A BAROQUE POSTSCRIPT: THE DISTRIBUTION OF BODY PARTS

The rebels	José Gabriel Túpac Amaru
	Micaela Bastidas, his wife
	Hipólito Túpac Amaru, his son
	Francisco Túpac Amaru, his uncle
	Antonio Bastidas, his brother-in-law
	The *cacica* de Acos
	Diego Verdejo, commander
	Andrés Castelo, colonel
	Antonio Oblitas, criminal follower
Tinta	José Gabriel Túpac Amaru's head
	José Gabriel Túpac Amaru's arm goes to Tungasuca
	The same for Micaela Bastidas
	Antonio Bastidas's arm to Pampamarca
	Hipólito Túpac Amaru's head to Tungasuca
	One of Castelo's arms to Surinama
	The other to Pampamarca
	The arm of Verdejo to Coporaque
	The other to Yauri
	The rest of his body to Tinta
	One arm to Tungasuca
	Francisco Túpac Amaru's head to Pilpinto
Quispicanchis	Antonio Bastidas's arm to Urcos
	Hipólito Túpac Amaru's leg to Quiquijana
	Antonio Bastidas's leg to Sangarara
	The *cacica* of Acos's body to Sangarara
	Castelo's head to Acomayo
Cuzco	José Gabriel Túpac Amaru's body to Picchu
	His wife's body and head to Picchu as well
	Antonio Oblitas' arm on the road to San Sebastián
Carabaya	José Gabriel Túpac Amaru's arm
	His wife's leg
	Francisco Túpac Amaru's arm
Azangaro	Hipólito Túpac Amaru's leg
Lampa	José Gabriel Túpac Amaru's leg to Santa Rosa
	His son's arm to Ayaviri
Arequipa	Micaela Bastidas' arm
Chumbivilcas	José Gabriel Túpac Amaru's leg to Livitaca
	His son's arm to Santo Tomás
Paucartambo	Castelo's body to the capital
	Antonio Bastidas' head too
Chilques and Masquez	Francisco Túpac Amaru's arm to Paruro
Condesuyos de Arequipa	Antonio Verdejo's head, to Chuquibamba
Puno	Francisco Túpac Amaru's leg, to the capital

After the execution of Túpac Amaru, his family members, and fellow rebel leaders, their corpses were dismembered and the parts dispatched to be put on display in the Peruvian provinces. The order was titled: "Distribution of the Bodies, or parts thereof, of the Nine Offenders of the Rebellion, Brought to Justice in the Plaza of Cuzco, on the 18th of May 1781." The order listed the executed rebels and then detailed which body parts were to go to which provinces.

This woven belt depicts Túpac Amaru's execution; four horses can be seen "quartering" him, or pulling his body in four directions until his arms and legs were separated from his torso.

Figure 14.5. Gregoria Pumayalli Awkakusi Belt. 2002 Quechua Camelid fibers, 2 13/16 x 45 1/2 in. (7.1 x 115.6 cm) Place Collected: Chinchero, Peru © Brooklyn Museum Collections Photograph by Barbara E. Mundy, Ph.D. Used with permission of Brooklyn Museum Collections and Barbara E. Mundy.

added free people of color to tribute lists, including women gold miners; and demanded that the colonists pay for their own coastal protection. In this way, royal policies alienated all social and racial groups and their imperial policies had a detrimental effect on all economic classes. Creoles realized that this imperial arrogance revealed that Americans' true interests lay with other Americans; there could be no hope of fair treatment from Europeans.

On June 6, 1781, a group of creoles in Socorro (in today's Colombia) who called themselves the Comuneros (literally, "commoners") compiled a list of thirty-five grievances. Their local economy had been ravaged by crown monopolies on tobacco, white rum, and aniseed. Like Túpac Amaru and Túpac Katari, they stressed their loyalty to the king and the Catholic religion but demanded to have some input into their own governance. Led by Juan Francisco de Berbeo, José Antonio Galán, and Manuela Beltrán, the Comuneros asked the crown to repeal the unpopular taxes and monopolies that they found excessively burdensome and to reduce the unfair demand placed on indigenous labor. They also insisted that crown ministers end their preferential treatment of European Spaniards when making government appointments in the New World.

The Comuneros successfully expelled the Spanish authorities from Socorro and began to discuss further reforms as part of their broader agenda. There was significant pressure from Afro-Andeans who wished to abolish slavery, while indigenous villagers wanted an end to tribute requirements and the restitution of their communal lands. As these issues started to divide the Comuneros, crown officials regrouped and moved against them.

Authorities in New Granada initially acceded to the Comuneros' requests to buy some time, but then reneged on their promises once military reinforcements arrived from Spain. Again, showing little creativity and proving that they had little perspective or foresight, colonial officials rounded up suspected conspirators and executed many of them, including the alleged ringleader, Galán, on January 30, 1782.

* * *

Imperial reorganization was expensive. Where would the money come from? As we have seen, the Spanish and Portuguese crowns improved income through a variety of ingenious and predatory means, and most especially through more rigorous tax collection. Natives were hounded for tributes, merchants for customs duties and sales taxes, and tobacco growers and distillers for their valuable, monopoly products. But the overall colonial money supply was itself a critical issue, and both the Spanish and Portuguese spent an overwhelming amount of their efforts in the eighteenth century trying to increase the output of their American colonies' many gold and silver mines. To an extent, they succeeded.

But there was also a price to pay. The Great Andean Rebellion and Comunero Revolt showed that the negotiated arrangements that made colonial rule across centuries possible in the sixteenth and seventeenth centuries were being sorely challenged in the late eighteenth century, and with momentous consequences. Furthermore, whether or not the Spanish and Portuguese elite liked it, Latin America's future was multiracial. It was not long before the colonies would break free and become proudly mestizo and mulatto nations. As the next chapter shows, that transition would not be an easy one.

SUGGESTIONS FOR FURTHER READING

On the Comunero Revolt, see John L. Phelan's classic *People and the King* (1978). On Venezuela through the age of the cacao monopoly, see Robert J. Ferry, *The Colonial Elite of Early Caracas* (1987). For Ecuador, see Kenneth Andrien, *The Kingdom of Quito, 1690–1830* (1995).

Three books on late-colonial Peru that are relevant here and to Chapter 15 are Sarah Chambers, *From Subjects to Citizens: Honor, Gender and Politics in Arequipa, Peru, 1780–1854* (1999); Charles Walker, *Smoldering Ashes: Cuzco and the Creation of Republican Peru, 1780–1840* (1999); and David Garrett, *Shadows of Empire: the Indian Nobility of Cusco* (2005). For Bolivia, see Sinclair Thomson, *We Alone Will Rule* (2003), and Sergio Serulnikov, *Tupac Katari* (2003). Charles Walker's *Shaky Colonialism: The 1746 Earthquake-Tsunami in Lima, Peru, and Its Long Aftermath* (Durham, NC: Duke University Press, 2008) is the definitive study on that disaster and its era. Robert Patch's *Maya and Spaniard in Yucatan, 1648–1812* (1993) explores some of the larger economic and social issues of this chapter in the regional context of one province. On the *camino real*, see Bruce Castleman, *Building the King's Highway* (2005), and on everyday priestly violence and its consequences in Mexico, see William B. Taylor, *Magistrates of the Sacred* (1996).

For primary documents, see Ward Stavig and Ella Schmidt, eds., *The Tupac Amaru and Catarista Rebellions: An Anthology of Sources* (2008). A wonderful primary source is Alexander Von Humboldt's 1812 *Political Essay on the Kingdom of New Spain* (1973 edition).

GLOSSARY

Peso: (literally, "weight") basic silver monetary unit in Spanish America, consisting of eight reales, or approximately one ounce

Quinto real [KEEN-toh ray-AL]: the "royal fifth," or 20 percent tax, claimed by the Spanish and Portuguese crowns on gold and silver mined in the colonies

Camino real: royal road, highway

15

Independence

[S]upposing that it were legitimate for a Christian King to despoil of his dominions a gentile King so that his vassals embrace the Catholic religion, since Moctezuma was as much natural lord of these kingdoms as Charles V was of his (Solórzano treats of this at length – James the Apostle [i.e., Santiago] brought religion to Spain, but did not because of that despoil its Kings of their Crown); and supposing that this were not the time determined by God for the Europeans to pay for the iniquities, robberies, cruelties, and deaths that with such impiety they committed in the Conquest of these Kingdoms, as noted in the representations of Bishop Las Casas . . . and many other authors . . . I ask you, according to what has been said, upon what basis rest the censures fulminated against Señor Hidalgo and those who follow his party?

(Chito Villagrán, 1812)

I
N JUNE 1812, the famous Mexican bandit Chito Villagrán signed a letter to a royalist priest defending his violent actions and those of other followers of Padre Miguel Hidalgo, Mexico's first independence leader. Hidalgo's uprising, which broke out in the tiny town of Dolores on September 16, 1810, led to massive bloodshed and looting throughout Mexico's core ranching and mining district – until Hidalgo was caught, tried by the Inquisition, and executed in 1811. The Hidalgo revolt, with its legendary cries of "*¡Viva México! ¡Viva la Virgen de Guadalupe!* Death to the Gachupines!" shook New Spain to its foundations. After Hidalgo's death, the struggle was taken up by regional headmen, many of them bandits like Villagrán, along with a few radical priests and thousands of indigenous and mixed-race peasants. In his rhetorically sophisticated letter, quoted in the epigraph to this chapter, Villagrán justifies the Hidalgo revolt and its aftermath as a kind of payback for the Conquest.

TIMELINE

1788–1789: Tiradentes plot in Minas Gerais (Brazil)

1791–1804: slave revolt and independence wars in Haiti

1797: two Spaniards, Gual and España, lead a revolt against royal government in Venezuela

1798: Conspiracy of the Tailors in Bahia (Brazil)

1810–1811 and 1813–1815: Hidalgo and Morelos revolts in Mexico

1815: Napoléon defeated in Europe

1821: independence declared in Mexico and Peru

1822: Pedro, prince regent of Brazil, declares the colony an independent empire

1822–1825: independence movement spreads to the rest of Latin America, leaving only Cuba and Puerto Rico as Spanish colonies (until 1898)

As the historian Eric Van Young has shown, Chito Villagrán's letter was probably composed by a rebel priest in his entourage, but his signature and other evidence suggest that he heartily agreed with its contents. Like the Mexican-born Hidalgo, Villagrán resented the hypocrisy of Spanish authorities who argued that they had in mind the best interests of Mexico's people (whom Villagrán refers to as his fellow "Americans"), when all they seemed intent on doing was raising taxes, attacking the church, hoarding emergency grain supplies, and forbidding political self-expression. Surrounded by royalist forces in his fortified hometown of Huichápan, in the modern Mexican state named for Hidalgo, Chito Villagrán was captured and executed by firing squad in May 1813. Another eight years of armed conflict would pass before Mexican independence from Spain was finally won.

Radical as their words and actions may seem today, the struggles of Hidalgo and Villagrán were not intentionally revolutionary. Their rebellions were in fact very much in the mold of colonial uprisings – aimed not at independence or the overturning of the colonial regime but at righting local wrongs, replacing abusive local officials, and reducing taxes and other unpopular government demands. Like the tumults of the 1780s, they sought restoration of an imaginary golden age of mutual respect and reciprocity. It ended up the other way around: a revolution took place that turned the great viceregal kingdoms of the Spanish American empire into a quarreling network of independent republics by the early 1820s. As if to complicate the picture further, Brazil followed a completely different path, winning independence from Portugal in 1822, but with an heir to the Portuguese throne serving as emperor. In any event, it is certain that neither Brazil's nor Spanish America's twisted paths to independence could have been predicted by the previous generation.

In this chapter, we argue that independence in Latin America came about not as a result of careful planning or able leadership, although there were notable instances of both, but rather as a result of a "perfect storm" combining four major factors. The four factors were the following: (1) an increase in largely rural social unrest, driven in part by population growth and land pressure; (2) external, international events, primarily in Europe, most notably Napoléon's invasion of the Iberian Peninsula in 1807–1808; (3) the snowballing of local and regional civil wars driven by micropatriotic loyalties; and finally (4), the decision of both liberal and conservative creole elites to seize power from the crown and hold it for themselves. Despite the emergence of capable and truly revolutionary visionaries like "the Liberator" Simón Bolívar, there was no simple formula to Latin American independence. Indeed, rebels like the bandit Villagrán complicate our understanding of the struggle in part because they freely deployed their global awareness and sense of Conquest legacies to seek redress for highly local grievances.

Yet neither should Latin American independence be regarded as purely local, accidental, or entirely manipulated by cynical elites. People of all classes began to think differently around the turn of the nineteenth century and to have new aspirations for both their and their children's futures. Their testimonies tell us this. Watershed events like the execution of Hidalgo opened new spaces for thought and action, driving many passive doubters to become active players on the stage of history. The casting call was wide, as Hidalgo, Bolívar, and other leaders of Spanish American independence – and later, royalists as well – appealed directly to oppressed Native Americans and enslaved people of color. Many thousands took up the challenge. In the end, far more people of color than white or even mestizo elites paid with their lives.

Brazilian conspiracies in 1789 and 1798 suggest that similar discontent was brewing in the key mining and sugar districts, but both movements were harshly suppressed before they even got going. Brazilian independence would be engineered by conservative planters, who, unlike Spanish America's mostly liberal leaders, sought desperately to maintain the slave regime that supported them. Even so, they faced massive slave uprisings soon after independence.

The pace of change in Latin America and the greater Atlantic world around the turn of the nineteenth century was so quick that history seemed to march to double-time. One series of unpredictable events seemed only to spawn another, and another after that. The period may be broken into three phases: (1) escalating unrest in the wake of the French Revolution (1789–1808); (2) colonial self-assertion in the absence of a monarch and early wars against Spanish royalists (1808–1816); and (3) the later wars (1817–1824), which saw the steady crumbling of colonial authority, major victories by Bolívar and other South American leaders, and initial consolidation of independent republics.

Europe and Haiti

Although U.S. independence in 1783 served as an inspiration to some, it was the start of the French Revolution in 1789 that set in motion the chain of events leading to Latin American independence. First, the French Revolution drew Spain and Britain into yet another costly war. Spain's new king, Charles IV (1788–1808), was not up to the challenge of governing in such difficult times. After suffering punishing losses on land and at sea, first as an ally of Britain, then of France, a previously solvent Spain – thanks to Charles III's reforms – was again driven to the brink of bankruptcy. Only the continually rising production of Mexican silver, at the workers' expense, kept the empire afloat. By the time the Peace of Amiens was signed in 1802, Spain's fleet was in tatters and Spanish Americans were left to cope with the humiliating losses of Louisiana (ceded to France) and the island of Trinidad (ceded to Britain).

Napoléon Bonaparte had come to power in France, and he soon sold Louisiana to the fledgling United States to help finance his ambitions to create a European empire. These ambitions led to the invasion of both Portugal and Spain in 1807–1808. Madrid was occupied; Charles IV and his son and heir Ferdinand exiled; and Napoléon's brother, Joseph, was made king of Spain. Meanwhile, Portugal's prince regent (soon to be King John VI) fled to Brazil under British escort. Brazilian ambitions for independence, previously regarded as anarchic sedition, were suddenly stoked by the prospect of being the seat of a world empire.

For Spanish subjects at home and abroad, Napoléon's actions had the effect of undermining the legitimacy of the old regime. Although Charles IV's heir regained the Spanish throne as Ferdinand VII in 1814, six years of rule by a republican resistance in Spain and virtual self-rule by the colonial elite convinced many that the colonies were better off not answering – and sending tax revenue – to Spain. A new constitution, written in 1812 in Cádiz and applied across the empire, broke the back of absolutist rule and permitted greater participation in government from local elites. Spanish Americans were reluctant to give up these gains when Ferdinand sought to overturn them when he came to power. Colonists had lost the "habit of obedience" (in the words of Simón Bolívar).

There was another link in the chain of Atlantic upheavals that proved deeply influential in much of Latin America. This was the astonishing 1791–1804 Haitian Revolution, the world's only successful takeover by African slaves and their descendants of a major European possession. Within a year or two of the outbreak of the French Revolution, radical ideas had spread to Saint-Domingue, as the colony was known. Thanks to the work of nearly half a million slaves, Saint-Domingue was the most lucrative French possession in the Americas; indeed, acre for acre, it was the most profitable colony in the world. French Revolutionaries were slow to deliver on early promises of abolition once they recognized the island's value, and in 1791, Haitians took matters into their own hands. An uprising by free coloreds triggered a full-scale revolt by the slaves, who made up 90 percent of the colony's population. War then consumed almost the whole island of Hispaniola until 1804; both Spain and Britain sent armies to suppress the uprising, but they were defeated by the main leader of the former slaves, Toussaint Louverture, who had acquired the neighboring Spanish colony of Santo Domingo. Napoléon also sent a large force to reconquer Haiti, but, despite the capture of Louverture, the French could not prevent Haiti's birth as an independent nation in 1804. The "habit of obedience," long since overcome, would never be regained.

For enslaved Latin Americans as far away as Brazil and Buenos Aires, Haiti was a major inspiration, and Louverture a hero. By contrast, colonial elites, even those who owned no slaves, were terrified by the prospect of such a "revolt of the masses," a complete overturning of the social and economic order (for some in the Andes, Haiti reminded them of the Native American–led Great Rebellion of 1780–1783). Fear was most palpable in nearby Cuba and Puerto Rico, where some of Haiti's plantation owners fled to reestablish themselves. Before long, the islands' massive, slave-based plantations outstripped Saint-Domingue's legendary production of sugar and coffee. Haiti's revolution, in short, encouraged Cuban and Puerto Rican planters (like their distant cohort in Brazil) to remain loyal to the crown, which they trusted to defend them in the event of a similar uprising.

Bolívar was inspired by the Haitian Revolution, and even sought assistance from one of Louverture's successors, Alexandre Pétion. But for most mainland elites finally convinced of the need to break colonial ties, U.S. independence provided a somewhat more attractive model – the colonial elite retained control of the independence movement, with their political prerogatives and property rights (including slavery) firmly intact. Even so, most elite Latin Americans feared U.S.-style federal politics, which they considered too open and unpredictable. In lands where even primary education was rare and illiteracy the norm outside a few urban enclaves, a U.S.-style republican system struck many rich creoles as a recipe for disaster. As staunch Catholics, furthermore, they disliked the U.S. rejection of monarchy and embrace of religious freedom. Some hoped to create modified, Catholic versions of Britain's constitutional monarchy. With those models in mind, plus the cautionary tale of France's wild swing from popular revolution to Napoleonic dictatorship, Latin American elites moved cautiously and sought to prevent social upheaval even more zealously than they fought for self-rule. Following are three examples of popular movements that provoked conservative elite reaction.

A Venezuelan Uprising Foiled

While parts of Europe and the Caribbean became engulfed in war and revolutionary upheaval in the 1790s, so, too, was discontent brewing on the Latin American mainland. The middle sectors of society in places as far afield as Caracas, Minas Gerais, Bahia, and highland Mexico started to resent imperial demands on their lives and increasingly used the revolutionary rhetoric of freedom, liberty, and independence to give voice to their frustrations. Furthermore, indigenous people and enslaved Africans did not need Enlightenment philosophers to explain to them what justice meant; like Chito Villagrán, they knew instinctively that a different social order was possible, even desirable.

For our first example of this discontent, we turn to Venezuela. There, the local elite, primarily the merchant and cacao-producing classes, opposed the Caracas Company's monopolistic control and actively sought freer trade.

Venezuela's elites were supported by a large, enslaved African population, but the colony also boasted an unusually high proportion of freed blacks and mixed-race residents who enjoyed greater social and economic mobility than in many parts of the empire. Furthermore, Venezuela's strategic location as the gateway to the Caribbean and Spanish Main (and possibly even the Amazon via the Orinoco) made it of great interest to both crown authorities and foreign smugglers.

Conspiracy first brewed in La Guaira, the Caribbean port town serving nearby Caracas, in December 1796. The plan was to drive the Spanish out of Venezuela and create an egalitarian, democratic republic. The plot's leaders were a local lawyer, José María España, and Manuel Gual, a retired military captain, but they were joined by a number of middle- and lower-class professionals, including soldiers, priests, and artisans, some of them *pardos* (free men of mixed African descent). Spreading their ideas to Caracas by secret code and employing safe houses, Gual and España quickly expanded the number of recruits by appealing to creole Venezuelans' sense of outrage and micropatriotism. They promised that members of all races would be considered brothers in the new society, a promise embodied in their flag, which used the four colors of white, blue, yellow, and red to symbolize racial unity.

The rebels' first decisive act came on June 4, 1797, when they attacked La Guaira's jail and freed three political prisoners held by Spanish authorities. Conspirator Juan Bautista Picornell then printed and distributed two thousand broadsides with the French-inspired title "The Rights of Man and Citizen." He also composed a song with the lyrics "Long live the People / the Sovereign People / Death to the oppressors / Death to their cronies." The tone was set for a general uprising, and Gual and España chose July 16, the feast day of the Virgin of Carmen, as the birthday for the new revolution.

The plan was for *pardo* militiamen to rise up in arms amid the religious festivities, to be followed by middle- and lower-class members of the broader society. Keeping secrets in such heady times was difficult, however, and word got out before the uprising could occur. Royal authorities moved quickly to arrest the movement's lower-level leaders, but Gual and España proved hard to find. Despite a five-thousand peso bounty on his head, España remained at large for almost eighteen months, after which he was executed in Caracas's central plaza. Gual, whose bounty was set at ten thousand pesos, fled to Trinidad, a British colony since 1797, but he appears to have been killed by poisoning, probably by a Spanish royalist agent, in 1800. Although it failed, the Gual and España revolt was among the most revolutionary of any proposed in the late colonial period in Spanish America. Rebel documents outlined plans for an independent Venezuela free of slavery and without racial distinctions. Only Spanish-born residents were to face some exclusions as a kind of payback for years of prejudice against creoles. The documents also called for free trade, a free press, and a republican government headed by elected representatives.

It may be tempting to think that these ideas were rare, perhaps isolated to Atlantic export enclaves like coastal Venezuela, but the fact that they bounced back in full force by 1810, in places as distant as highland Mexico and Buenos Aires, suggests only that the crown was lucky to have nipped the Gual and España revolt in the bud, aided by the threat of massive retaliatory force. Successors such as Simón Bolívar would ably tap Gual and España's cross-race sentiment for equality, but a powerful counterweight would come from many of Caracas's elite families. Although they, too, resented the Caracas Company and other aspects of Spanish rule, none wanted to hand over power to the likes of these "plebeian" men. Independence on their terms would be a far more conservative enterprise.

Brazilian Conspiracies

Meanwhile, similar events were unfolding in Brazil. The first great conspiracy against Portuguese rule appeared in the capital of Minas Gerais in 1789. The elites of Vila Rica (today Ouro Prêto) had long resented royal tax demands and other impositions, but few sought radical solutions. Thus, it was something of a surprise when twelve prominent citizens, inspired by the Enlightenment and the American Revolution, hatched a plot to rebel and call for home rule. The basic plan was to assassinate the royal governor of Minas Gerais and proclaim the region an independent, U.S.-style republic. Ambitious and violent as this sounds, the plot was not coherent and only barely developed when it was betrayed to authorities. The Miners', or Tooth Pullers', Conspiracy, as it came to be known, appears to have been a small and isolated event, yet the very fact of its existence, growing from deep within the colonial interior, implies a shift in the range of imagined possibilities. That some were willing to die for such an unlikely cause was shocking at the time, and the drama of the moment has persisted; Brazilians today commemorate the "Inconfidência Mineira" as the first true cry for independence.

The conspirators of Vila Rica were in some ways more connected to the outside world than they were to average Brazilians. Rebel leader José Joaquim Maia e Barbalho was a former mathematics student who had made contact with Thomas Jefferson in Paris and used the code name Vendek. Though inspired by Enlightenment ideals, Vendek was – like Jefferson – a proud member of the colonial elite, not a born champion of the common folk. He and his fellow conspirators spoke of freeing slaves born in Brazil, but did not call for an end to the transatlantic slave trade. Mostly, they called for an independent Minas Gerais that would harness its broad economic potential beyond gold mining and become a regional powerhouse, more or less in the model of Britain's former 13 colonies. Vendek and his friends chose a red-and-white flag for their new nation, emblazoned with the half-committed motto "Liberty, even if delayed." Since the twelve conspirators were mostly

white, upper-class youths, some historians have described them as naive dab-
blers who had little idea of the fear and retribution their ideas and actions
would provoke among royal authorities.

The Inconfidência Mineira did include one nonelite member, Joaquim
José da Silva Xavier, a petty officer better known as Tiradentes, the "Tooth
Puller," because he had practiced this unofficial and much-loathed trade
during his military service. Tiradentes' mixed-race and common origins
made him a perfect scapegoat once the conspiracy was betrayed. He alone
was sentenced to death by hanging, whereas most of the white youths were
fined and exiled. Tiradentes' stoic behavior on the gallows on April 21, 1792,
helped feed a later belief that he was the first true martyr for the Brazilian
nation. At the time, however, crown authorities hoped to use his death as
a negative example. On the orders of Portugal's Queen Maria, Tiradentes'
corpse was dismembered and its bloody pieces were displayed throughout
Brazil as a warning to anyone wishing to challenge royal authority. April 21
is now celebrated as a national holiday, and all Brazilian schoolchildren learn
of the sacrifice of Tiradentes.

The spirit of rebellion did not die with Tiradentes. In 1798, a number
of artisans, most of them mulattos, along with a few whites and blacks,
came together to form a radical conspiracy in Salvador da Bahia, the old
colonial capital on Brazil's northeast coast. Known as the Conjuração dos
Alfaiates (Conspiracy of the Tailors), the movement appealed mostly to
young working-class men of mixed race who were literate and very much
aware of political trends sweeping the Atlantic. Far more radical than the
earlier *inconfidenceiros*, and much more like the Gual and España rebels of
contemporary Venezuela, the tailors drew from the "rights of man" rhetoric
of the Enlightenment to call for a full-blown social revolution. Along with
political independence from Portugal and typical liberal demands for free
trade and freedom of religion, the Bahian rebels demanded an end to racial
and aristocratic designations and total abolition of slavery. One fiery broad-
side declared that "each soldier is a citizen, particularly the brown and black
men who are abused and abandoned. All are equal. There is no difference.
There will be only liberty, equality, and fraternity." Lucas Dantas do Amorim
Tôrres, a twenty-three-year-old soldier, exclaimed, "We want a republic in
order to breathe freely because we live subjugated and we cannot advance; if
there was a republic there would be equality for everyone."

Forty-eight people were arrested as conspirators, but only eleven of them
were in fact tailors. Forty-six were male, thirty-three were mulatto, eleven
were white, and four were black. Most were artisans, including carpenters,
masons, shoemakers, and goldsmiths, plus a few soldiers and a folk healer.
Despite their working-class origins, nearly all were literate. Four were
somewhat higher-ranking professionals, including a Latin professor, a sur-
geon, and two military officers. Aside from the number of people involved,

the Conspiracy of the Tailors far exceeded the scope and sophistication of the Miners' Conspiracy in that it included members from many sectors of Bahian society and exhibited a profound class and race consciousness. Like the seemingly naive *inconfidenceiros*, however, the survivors of the Tailors' Conspiracy would see their dreams of independence and abolition not only delayed but also crushed by the arrival of the Portuguese prince-regent in 1808.

Revolution in Mexico

For our third example of popular discontent anticipating the independence movement and final wars of 1817–1824, we turn to Mexico. As we saw at the start of the chapter, on September 16, 1810, a Mexican parish priest named Miguel Hidalgo y Costilla (1753–1811) called upon his followers in the town of Dolores, in the northern interior, to take direct action against Spanish tyranny. No text of Hidalgo's speech survives, but according to tradition his so-called Grito de Dolores (Cry of Dolores) included the rousing phrases "Long live Mexico! Long live the Virgin of Guadalupe! Death to the Gachupines!" (Only the first of these "cries" is repeated by Mexico's president every September 16). Nationalist as these phrases sounded, Hidalgo was a colonial rebel who did not yet imagine an independent Mexico. It is highly likely that he also yelled "Long live Ferdinand VII! Death to bad government!" Although he was something of a social revolutionary, Hidalgo's core sentiments were not uncommon among creoles at this time. He called not for total independence, but rather for greater political autonomy, more access to foreign markets, and fewer restrictions on creole office holding. Hidalgo was socially revolutionary in that he believed Mexicans of all races should be treated as legal equals to European-born Spaniards. This sentiment struck a chord among central Mexico's disaffected masses, and Hidalgo's followers, mainly natives and the rural poor, men like Chito Villagrán, heard the Grito de Dolores as a long-awaited call to arms against European Spaniards and their property.

Hidalgo was a charismatic, Jesuit-educated figure who saw his religious duties as including bettering the social and economic lives of his flock rather than merely attending to their spiritual needs. He was posted to the thriving parish of Dolores, near the important silver mining town of Guanajuato, in 1803. Hidalgo enjoyed a fairly generous salary, and much like the priests denounced by Jorge Juan and Antonio de Ulloa in the mid-eighteenth-century Andes, he embraced such earthly delights as dancing and gambling, and he openly kept a mistress. His parishioners seemed not to mind. Hidalgo was also an avid reader of Enlightenment literature, and at some point he organized a *tertulia* (discussion group) that was called Chiquita Francia (Little France). Chiquita Francia was not restricted to educated white creoles like

Hidalgo, but also included members of poor and mixed background. Hidalgo's radical social ideas extended into the economic sphere. He saw Bourbon economic policy for what it was, a bold-faced attempt to reduce colonies like New Spain to utterly dependent status, supplying silver money and raw materials and consuming dictated imports. One "rebellious" response was to encourage petty industry, for Hidalgo the first step in a longer march back to self-sufficiency and autonomous economic growth. Hidalgo urged his parishioners to keep bees, make pottery, weave textiles, and even attempt to plant olive trees and grapevines in hopes of ending dependency on expensive Spanish imports. From the crown's perspective, this was economic sedition.

As Hidalgo came under increasing suspicion in 1810, he began plotting direct action. The plan was to use mostly rudimentary weapons, including spears, machetes, and slingshots, to take over the important city of Querétaro. The attack, which would link Hidalgo's rural parishioners to Querétaro's urban poor, was to take place on October 2, 1810. When this audacious plan was betrayed, Hidalgo moved the date up to September 16, when he issued his famous cry. The embittered masses were more ready for revolution than even Hidalgo realized, and within a week he was followed by twenty-five thousand indigenous rural folk. Querétaro was spared, but the rebels descended on Guanajuato on September 28, where they seized and killed a number of alleged gachupines, or European-born Spaniards, holed up in the town granary. The rebel priest's following continued to grow, and the decision was made to march on Mexico City at the end of October. Once on the outskirts of the capital, Hidalgo's eighty thousand followers met a much smaller force of twenty-five hundred royalist troops. What the royalists lacked in numbers, they made up for in training, discipline, and arms. Wounded but not defeated, Hidalgo's disorganized rebels backed off.

After a retreat to Guadalajara and the looting of many haciendas, Hidalgo abandoned the struggle and fled northward. He was captured in Chihuahua and sent in chains back to Mexico City, where he was first tried and excommunicated by the Inquisition, then handed over to a military court. Furious at his seditious and destructive acts, both as a priest and as a subject of the crown, Spanish authorities charged Hidalgo with every crime they could think of; he was found guilty of being "a libertine, a heretic, a partisan of the French Revolution, a Judaizer, a Lutheran, a Calvinist, and a rebel schismatic suspected atheist." Defrocked and dejected, Hidalgo was executed by hanging on July 30, 1811. His corpse was dismembered and its parts dispersed for display. His head was taken to Guanajuato and left hanging from the wall of the town granary for the next ten years.

Although Hidalgo's forces dispersed, and some even went over to the royalist side, the problems that had caused many rural folk to risk their lives in the name of revolution had not disappeared. Festering anger was fueled by royalist reprisals that left thousands of poor, rural Mexicans of indigenous and mixed-race heritage dead. Chito Villagrán was but one of many who fought back and took up Hidalgo's cause. Most notable, however, was another parish priest, José María Morelos y Pavón. Morelos was far more organized and more politically revolutionary than Hidalgo, and he quickly assembled a trained and disciplined rebel army to demand Mexican independence. According to an 1813 document, Morelos and his followers sought to create a Mexican nation-state headed by a representative government, one that abolished slavery, indigenous tribute requirements, and all racial distinctions. Morelos was perhaps less revolutionary in arguing for the restoration of the Catholic Church to a central role in society, but he was after all a priest, and Bourbon anticlericalism was hugely unpopular. The Morelos movement was short-lived. He and his followers were on the run by late 1813, and although the guerrilla game of cat-and-mouse continued for a time, Morelos was captured and executed in 1815.

The Chain of Independence

The executions of Hidalgo and Morelos in 1811 and 1815, respectively, might have marked the end of that chapter of unrest in Mexico. And indeed, in 1816, it looked as though Spain and its empire might return to the tenuous stability and expansionism they had enjoyed under Charles III. But the events of the previous decade, plus the seemingly unstoppable momentum of ideas and events throughout the Atlantic, were too strong for the old regime to withstand. A guerrilla war persisted in Mexico's backlands following Morelos's execution, and it was ended only by an alliance between the rebels and a creole royalist officer, Agustín de Iturbide. Their alliance, called the Plan de Ayala, sealed Mexican independence in 1821. An empire was declared, and Iturbide took the audacious, Napoleonic step of having himself crowned Agustín I in lieu of a legitimate European monarch.

Iturbide threatened to annex the Central American provinces to his Mexican Empire, but leaders in Guatemala City chose to join voluntarily in January 1822. Guatemala and its neighbors had barely felt the independence movement, and conservative elites warily joined Iturbide in hopes that little would change. Central Americans had, however, long resented rule from Mexico City, and when Iturbide's empire fell in 1824, they quickly broke away. Like Mexico, Central America declared itself a federal republic, but it soon split up into the nations of Guatemala, El Salvador, Honduras, Nicaragua, and Costa Rica.

In Chapter 6, we described how the events of the Spanish conquest proceeded in a chain, beginning in the Caribbean and then progressing to the centers of what became the viceroyalties of Mexico and Peru – before stretching out over the centuries into the near and then distant peripheries. Three centuries later, Independence followed the same chain, only in the reverse direction. In South America, the regions that had been conquered

Map 15.1
The Chain of
Independence in
South America

and settled the latest, such as Argentina and Venezuela, were the first to
declare Independence (in 1811). As Map 15.1 shows, the chain then proceeded
toward the Andean center, where the more conservative, older core colonies
of central and Upper Peru (today's Bolivia) were more or less forced into
accepting independence in the mid-1820s.

The first genuine push for independence in Spanish South America emerged in the Río de la Plata region, when local Spanish leaders – rather than the crown-appointed viceroy who had forgotten that his first duty was to defend the colony – defeated a rogue British force under Hope Popham that had captured Buenos Aires in 1806 and Montevideo in 1807. The divide between crown officials and local elites grew, leading to angry showdowns in Upper Peru in 1809 and in 1810. Creoles consolidated their power in Buenos Aires, but thanks to infighting among the city's elites and intense micropatriotism among many of the viceroyalty of La Plata's subdistricts, the struggle for independence in the Spanish Southern Cone remained disjointed. Nevertheless, Spain remained crippled and imperial authority absent until Ferdinand VII's restoration in 1814, helping the movement spread quickly into the viceroyalty of La Plata's many subdistricts as well as into Chile.

A more carefully planned but similarly halting creole takeover was under way in Venezuela at almost the same time, led first by Francisco de Miranda, then by Simón Bolívar. After living in Europe and visiting the United States, Miranda launched a failed assault on Venezuela from New York in 1806. He survived to become leader of Caracas's rebel government from 1810 to 1812, but he was captured by royalists and imprisoned, where he died as a kind of martyr (later called "the Precursor"). Bolívar, whose dreams far exceeded those of Miranda, fled to Colombia, then Haiti and Jamaica. When he finally organized a powerful rebel army in eastern Venezuela in 1819, Bolívar was an experienced guerrilla leader whose vision now extended to freeing all of Spanish South America. His first success, after a number of grueling marches, was to seize highland New Granada in 1819. When his able lieutenant, Antonio José de Sucre, led rebels to defeat royalist forces near Quito in 1822, Bolívar's Republic of Gran Colombia, encompassing Ecuador, Venezuela, Colombia, and Panama, officially came into being (see In Focus 15.1).

For a brief time, Spanish South American unity seemed possible. After receiving the blessing of General José de San Martín in Guayaquil in 1822, Bolívar extended his own authority into Peru, where he and Sucre won key battles in the highlands and forced independence on the Lima elites in 1824. Upper Peru, home of the great silver mines of Potosí, fell to the rebels the next year. The new nation was named Bolivia in Bolívar's honor. Its capital was called Sucre, seat of the former Audiencia of Charcas, and Sucre served as Bolivia's first president. Bolívar believed that not only Spanish South America but all the former American colonies could hold together and emerge as a major world power. Delegates from Gran Colombia, Mexico, Central America, and Peru signed a unification declaration in Panama in 1826, but micropatriotism soon negated their efforts and dashed Bolívar's dream. By 1830, the year of Bolívar's death, even Gran Colombia had split apart, with Ecuador and Venezuela declaring their independence from Bogotá.

Figure 15.1 Constancio Franco Vargas, *Jose Prudencio Padilla*, ca. 1880. Painting (Oil/fabric). 63.4 x 50 cm. Reg. 380. Courtesy of The National Museum of Colombia Collection.

FROM CABIN BOY TO ADMIRAL TO THE EXECUTIONER'S BLOCK

José Prudencio Padilla was born on the coast of Colombia in 1778. He was of mixed Spanish African descent, a *pardo*. At the age of fourteen, he joined the Spanish Royal Navy. Over the following thirteen years, he rose from being a cabin boy to a boatswain, seeing action against the British in the Battle of Trafalgar – where he was captured. Released by the British in 1808, he returned to Colombia, where he fought for the revolutionaries against the Spaniards through to the rebel victory at Maracaibo (Venezuela) in 1823. His military and leadership skills allowed him to rise rapidly through the ranks; in 1822, he was elected a senator of Colombia, and in 1824, he became commander of the republic's navy.

Not surprisingly, Padilla made enemies in the course of his ascent to admiral. Many of the attacks on him had heavy racial overtones; *pardos* had played a central role in the creation of independence in Colombia and Venezuela, but the initial enthusiasm for racial harmony by the ruling elite of the new republics soon turned to suspicion, fear, and resentment. In 1828, Padilla became a victim of the violent turmoil that accompanied personal rivalries, racial tensions, and the larger division between the supporters of the two prominent Independence leaders, President Bolívar and Vice President Santander. Accused of sedition and promoting race war – of "fomenting the most implacable hatred among compatriots" – the admiral was executed in the main plaza of Bogotá on October 2 of that year. Bolívar himself witnessed the death of the man who had helped him create the independent Gran Colombia.

Although the chain pattern was not paralleled quite so tidily in New Spain (e.g., Yucatán, Guatemala, and the rest of Central America were conquered and accepted independence after Mexico), it does fit in terms of the regions of Mexico itself; the revolts of Hidalgo and Morelos had been based well outside the capital, and the same was true of the final phase of revolt in 1817–1821, with Iturbide and the Mexico City elite finally embracing independence to secure their own positions and end the costly war.

Independence in Central America and Bolivia had come about largely as a reaction to events in Europe rather than as a result of internal power struggles or popular revolts. Brazil followed a similar trajectory, only it was even more conservative. Local elites did not seek to sever all ties with Portugal by the early 1820s, but rather to create an autonomous nation with an heir to the Braganza throne as emperor. They simply felt that Portugal had become too weak to protect their interests, and they had ample evidence to support this claim. When Napoléon's forces invaded Portugal in 1807, the Portuguese prince-regent, as we have seen, crossed to Brazil and made Rio de Janeiro the capital of the Portuguese Empire. Brazil became a kingdom in its own right, and Brazilian elites found it easy to adjust to having the king himself in their midst. King John, or João, assuaged them further by remaining in Brazil until 1821. Even so, he did face one great challenge from the disgruntled elites of Bahia. When in 1817 rebels in the northeast declared a republic, João quickly crushed the uprising, had twenty leaders executed, and brought additional troops over from Portugal. A coup in Portugal obliged the king to sail home to Lisbon in 1821, but his son Pedro remained as regent in Brazil. Within a year, young Pedro was persuaded by local elites – and by the British, who backed their words with naval force – to proclaim Brazil an independent empire. He would rule as Emperor Pedro I (see In Focus 15.2).

* * *

Latin America's indigenous and enslaved majorities, its free and mixed people of color, and even its creole elites appear from a distance to have had much in common with one another, and sometimes they saw themselves as similarly oppressed colonists with shared interests. Yet independence remained a hard sell throughout the region, and political unity except in Brazil proved impossible. Why? For one thing, identities in the Americas had been micropatriotic before the Iberian invasions, and they remained largely so during the colonial period. The Habsburg system, in particular, had fostered competing regional identities from the start as a means of preventing unified rebellion. Guatemalans were raised to resent the authority of Mexico City, Chileans, the authority of Lima, and so on. As we have seen, even the revolts that eventually led to the independence movement grew out of local grievances and many who fought in the fields and trenches remained blinkered by local concerns.

The cost of more than a decade of warfare was astronomical. Hundreds of thousands had died, entire regions and industries lay in ruin, the infrastructure that Bourbon administrators and native and colored workers had labored to build over the previous century was wrecked. The factors that had

IN FOCUS 15.2

Figure 15.2. a. Credit: The Coronation of Dom Pedro I (1798–1834) as Emperor of Brazil, 1st December 1822, engraved by Thierry Freres (engraving) by Jean Baptiste Debret (1768–1848) (after) Biblioteca Nacional, Rio de Janeiro, Brazil/ Index/ The Bridgeman Art Library [Image # IND 146585] **b.** Credit: The Acclamation of Pedro I (1798–1834) Emperor of Brazil, Rio de Janeiro, 7th April 1831, illustration from 'Voyage Pittoresque et Historique au Bresil', Paris, 1835 (litho) (b/w photo) by Jean Baptiste Debret (1768–1848) Bibliotheque Nationale, Paris, France/ Archives Charmet/ The Bridgeman Art Library [Image # CHT207841].

BRAZIL BECOMES AN EMPIRE

These French versions of contemporary illustrations depict (top) the coronation of Dom Pedro I as "constitutional emperor and perpetual defender" of Brazil in 1822. Pedro ruled until 1831, when he abdicated in favor of his son, who is shown here (bottom) being acclaimed Emperor Pedro II in Rio de Janeiro that year. Whereas the Spanish colonies broke up into numerous republics (with slavery abolished), Brazil remained united, as a monarchy (with slavery still legal); Pedro II ruled until 1889, when Brazil became a republic at last (slavery was abolished only the previous year).

combined to bring about independence remained unfortunately relevant: (1) external events affected the continent as foreign powers continued to interfere in – and even invade – Latin American nations; (2) civil wars persisted, as political elites fought one another for control of the new nations, and larger republics splintered or ravaged one another over border disputes; and (3), the issue of whether independence was a conservative power grab by the elite or a revolutionary movement that would free the masses from exploitation, poverty, and political disenfranchisement has continued to be disputed to this day.

SUGGESTIONS FOR FURTHER READING

The most accessible, succinct book on independence movements (excluding Brazil) is Jay Kinsbruner's *Independence in Spanish America*, 4th ed. (2004). See also Jaime Rodríguez, *The Independence of Spanish America* (1998). A useful collection of essays on Brazilian independence is A. J. R. Russell-Wood, ed., *From Colony to Nation: Essays on the Independence of Brazil* (1975). Another essay collection for Spanish America is Christon Archer, ed., *The Wars of Independence in Spanish America* (2001). For an inside-out look at independence in Mexico, see Eric Van Young, *The Other Rebellion: Popular Violence, Ideology, and the Mexican Struggle for Independence, 1810–1821* (2001) (which discusses the Villagrán letter quoted earlier in this chapter).

One of the best biographies of independence leaders is Karen Racine, *Francisco de Miranda: A Transatlantic Life in the Age of Revolution* (2002); we also recommend John Lynch's biographies of *Simón Bolívar* (2007) and *José de San Martín* (2009), along with the biographical novel, *The General in His Labyrinth*, by Gabriel García Márquez (2003).

On the Haitian Revolution, see Laurent Dubois, *Avengers of the New World* (2004), and David Geggus, *Haitian Revolutionary Studies* (2004).

GLOSSARY

Kuraka [koo-RAH-kah]: native Andean lord of a town or province, usually from an old ruling dynasty (called a cacique by the Spaniards)

Corregidor: regional colonial Spanish administrator and frequent target of local grievances and revolts

The Latin American Puzzle

THIS BOOK HAS TOLD THE STORY of what happened when, after being apart and unaware of one another's existence for millennia, the native peoples of the Americas and the peoples of Iberia and Western Africa were brought together. In the volume's introduction, we suggested that the oldest question surrounding this encounter is how: how were small numbers of Spanish and Portuguese settlers able to build, maintain, and defend such vast colonies across three hundred years? Without resorting to the explanations promoted by the colonists themselves – that it was all God's will, for example, or the result of civilization meeting barbarism – the question seems to be something of a puzzle.

The preceding pages set out to solve and explain that puzzle, offering solutions both simple and complex. The simple solution is that Iberians did not build, maintain, and defend their colonies alone. Most of the blood and sweat that went into such efforts was expended by Africans and Native Americans. In the crucible of the colonies in the Americas, European settlers were deeply dependent on the local native population, and/or on African slaves and their free-colored descendants, who typically outnumbered European settlers many times over. It was therefore not only Spaniards and Portuguese conquerors and settlers who forged colonial Latin American societies and gave birth to Latin American civilization but also Mixtecs and Muiscas, Nahuas and Guaranís, Mandingas and Wolofs, and many others.

The more complex explanations can be found in the details of the fifteen chapters here. There we have explored how the roles played by all inhabitants of the Iberian colonies were developed through a combination of coercion and collaboration. Recent scholarship reveals how colonial subjects of all sorts had their own views of history and of their ability to shape the future, whether peacefully or violently. Colonialism was not only the inequity and exploitation that stemmed from military conquest; it was also an arrangement that was consistently subject to renegotiation. From the protracted conflicts and accommodations of the Long Conquest, through the cultural interactions and social developments of the colonial middle and into the vicissitudes of the age of change, colonial Latin America remained a compelling example of how humans insist on making history complicated. For in the end, there are always (at least) two sides to every story.

INDEX